DATE DUE

Demco, Inc. 38-293

THE GERMAN EDUCATION OF CHRISTIAN SCHOLAR PHILIP SCHAFF

THE GERMAN EDUCATION OF CHRISTIAN SCHOLAR PHILIP SCHAFF
The Formative Years, 1819-1844

Klaus Penzel

Toronto Studies in Theology
Volume 95

The Edwin Mellen Press
Lewiston•Queenston•Lampeter

Library of Congress Cataloging-in-Publication Data

Penzel, Klaus.
   The German education of Christian scholar Philip Schaff : the formative years,
1819-1844 / Klaus Penzel.
      p. cm. -- (Toronto studies in theology ; v. 95)
   Includes bibliographical references and index.
   ISBN 0-7734-6428-X (hard)
      1. Schaff, Philip, 1819-1893. 2. Church historians--United States--Biography. 3.
Theologians--United States--Biography. I. Title. II. Series.

BR139.S4P45 2004
230'.044'092--dc22
[B]
                                                                      2004042658

This is volume 95 in the continuing series
Toronto Studies in Theology
Volume 95 ISBN 0-7734-6428-X
TST Series ISBN 0-88946-975-X

A CIP catalog record for this book is available from the British Library

The Edwin Mellen Press   The Edwin Mellen Press
          Box 450   Box 67
   Lewiston, New York   Queenston, Ontario
   USA 14092-0450   CANADA L0S 1L0

            The Edwin Mellen Press, Ltd.
            Lampeter, Ceredigion, Wales
            UNITED KINGDOM SA48 8LT

         Printed in the United States of America

For Pat

Table of Contents

[Copyright Permissions]

Foreword

When Klaus Penzel brought out his splendid volume of extracts from Schaff's entire literary production, all laced together with masterly editorial introductions, one reader commented—with good reason—that it would be "the final word on Philip Schaff for many years to come." *Philip Schaff, Historian and Ambassador of the Universal Church: Selected Writings* (Mercer University Press, 1991) was a worthy tribute to the breadth and depth of a great theological mind: it amounted to an intellectual biography of Schaff, firmly grounded in generous citations from his own writings. But it was not the *last* word! In the present volume, Professor Penzel draws attention to a gap that remains in the literature on Schaff: very little notice has been taken of his early years in Germany, before he embarked for the New World. Penzel completes his previous work by closing the gap, tracing the formation of Schaff's indomitable Christian faith and his immersion in the intellectual world of one of the most creative periods in western religious thought. Pietism, the Prussian high-church movement, and the romantic-idealistic philosophy of history had decisively shaped the immigrant's mind before he began his distinguished American career as church historian and theologian. Among the rival theological schools in Germany, Penzel identifies Schaff as a mediating theologian in the tradition of Schleiermacher. He was "a transplanted mediating theologian," a liberal evangelical.

Historical research since Schaff's time has in large part superseded the ambitious historical studies that the theological convictions he brought with him were to inspire. But the convictions themselves retain their fascination, perhaps even an abiding worth, although they, too, had their roots in another time and place. Especially interesting is the very first major writing of his years at

Mercersburg, based on the inaugural address (1844) that introduced his ideas to the German Reformed Church in America and plunged him into immediate controversy. In *The Principle of Protestantism as Related to the Present State of the Church* (1845), as he himself later said, he poured everything his German professors had taught him. There he dutifully reaffirmed what by then had come to be called the formal and material principles of the Reformation, the supreme scriptural norm and the message of justification by grace alone. But he showed no inclination to celebrate the Reformation as a *revolution* in the history of the church: it was rather the legitimate offspring of the medieval church, an *advance* insofar as the Reformers learned from Scripture a more profound insight into human depravity and the creative grace of God. And if Schaff exhibited a rare Protestant appreciation for the medieval church, he was also ruthless in exposing the destructive elements in Protestantism, especially when the affirmation of freedom and subjectivity led to the glorification of private judgment, to the "sect plague," and to unbelieving rationalism. The remedy was by no means to return to the inflexible authoritarianism of the Roman Church, but it was certainly to learn respect for the "power of the objective" in history and the life of the church.

The key to this reappraisal of Protestantism and its place in church history was the idea of historical development, which, as Schaff remarked elsewhere, "underlies all the more important German historical works of modern times." Applied to the history of the church, the idea of *organic* development enabled Schaff to represent church history as the continuation of the "theanthropic" life of Christ in the church, which is his body. "[A]s the life of the parents flows forward in the child, so the Church also is the depository and continuation of the earthly life of the Redeemer, in his threefold office of prophet, priest, and king." Schaff also liked the dialectical language of *logical* development so beloved by the Hegelians, according to which history progresses by way of negation—that is, through sharp contradictions that must be unified in a higher stage of the movement of the whole. Hence he could do justice to Protestant subjectivity as the negation of one-sided medieval objectivism, while insisting that both needed to be taken up into a higher synthesis. Indeed, "Protestantism," as a critical principle, runs through the entire history of the church: the Reformation was but "the most grand and widely influential exhibition" of it.

Clearly, the idea of development had a quitedifferent function for Schaff than it had for John Henry Newman, whose *Essay on the Development of Christian Doctrine* appeared coincidentally the same year. In Newman's scheme, "development" served to legitimize the obvious contrast between the simple apostolic gospel, the dogmatic edifice of the undivided early church, and the Roman Catholicism of his day, Protestantism being repudiated as a rupture in dogmatic progress, not a further moment of it. A German Protestant theologian, at the very zenith of the historical consciousness and historical productivity in Germany, must have read with astonishment, or perhaps amusement, Newman's *bon mot* that "to be deep in history is to cease being a Protestant." But Schaff did believe that the true idea of development, though it required immersion in the past, must finally drive us forward, not backward. "The signs of the time, then, and the teachings of history, point us, not backward, but forward to a new era of the Church...enriched with the entire positive gain of Protestantism." In a sense (not Newman's!), perhaps this does mean ceasing to be Protestant, if being Protestant entails the paralysis that cannot see beyond the Reformation—or the new Protestantism of the modern world. To Schaff, *any* theological standpoint that remained fixated on some favored portion of the past--whether Protestant primitivist, Roman Catholic, Anglo-Catholic, or Lutheran confessionalist--lacked the true idea of development. He thought it likely that the next stage of progress would come about in the New World. He was thin on the details but liked to call the future that beckoned the church "evangelical catholicism." "May we hope to see our Protestant Zion conducted safely out of the Babylonish captivity of sectarism and faction, without being carried to old Rome or young Oxford?" He would certainly not mind our adding, And not to old Wittenberg or old Geneva either?

No one is better qualified than Professor Penzel to lead us through the details of the theological principles Schaff brought with him from Germany. Himself an immigrant from Germany, for half a century Penzel has made a special study of Philip Schaff. The present volume does not merely fill a gap in the literature but brings together a lifetime of research. Moreover, many readers will be grateful for the clarity and skill with which he sketches the complexities of German historical, theological, and philosophical thought in its most creative period, adorned with such illustrious names as Herder, Schelling, Hegel, Schleiermacher, and Neander. Perhaps, too, this little book may spark further interest in the relationship between Anglo-American and German religious thought, a theme that is still insufficiently researched and often obscured by bias and lack of information.

B. A. Gerrish
John Nuveen Professor Emeritus
University of Chicago Divinity School

Preface

The focus of this present study is Philip Schaff (1819-1893), whose life spans two continents and nearly a whole century. Schaff liked to say of himself that he was "a Swiss by birth, a German by education, and an American by choice." When he arrived in this country in 1844, he embarked on a unique and truly distinguished American career which over almost five decades unfolded first at the Mercersburg Seminary of the German Reformed Church in Pennsylvania and then at Union Theological Seminary in New York. Incredibly productive throughout his long career, his scholarly and practical contributions were monumental, touching on almost every aspect of religious scholarship and interest in the United States in the second half of the nineteenth century. As a matter of fact, his life is an open window into nearly a whole century of religious developments in the United States and western Europe, Germany in particular.

Book-length publications--not to mention important published articles and unpublished doctoral dissertations--show that in the last decades interest in Schaff's life and career has been widespread: partly because of renewed interest in the high-church and ecumenical views of the Mercersburg Theology which Schaff and his colleague John Williamson Nevin (1803-86) developed at that isolated Seminary in the western foothills of the Appalachian mountains; partly in connection with the Centennial of the American Society of Church History (1988), of which Schaff was the founder and first president. These numerous studies of Schaff have understandably focussed on his outstanding American career, but they have so far failed to offer a scholarly and detailed exploration of his German years of education. This gap in Schaff studies my own study attempts to fill. It is a significant gap since I am convinced that Schaff's life to a remarkable extent bears out the truth of Arthur Schopenhauer's (1788-1860) observation:

The impression which the world makes on the individual mind, and the ideas with which such a mind, after it has gone through the process of education, reacts to that impression, all this is over and done with by the thirtieth year: what comes later are only the developments and variations of the same theme.[1]

One might say that Schopenhauer's observation as applied to Schaff states the thesis of my study. Only a thorough understanding of Schaff's formative years, the years of his German education, will allow us to do full justice to the distinguished American career of this immigrant scholar who in his long and versatile career excelled above all as church historian, biblical scholar, apologist of Christianity and fervent advocate of the reunion of the Christian churches. As I show, his German education largely shaped his American career.

An intellectual portrayal of Schaff's formative years requires careful attention also to the larger German scene, which in the context of the romantic-idealistic era in German culture was dominated by the *Erweckungsbewegung* (Awakening), Schleiermacher's theology and Hegel's philosophy. After all, Schaff was one of the first to introduce Americans to the new German modes of thought in theology and philosophy and especially to the historical consciousness and historiography of nineteenth-century German culture.

As indicated by the chapter headings of my study, Schaff's German education passed through three stages, each in turn shaping and enriching his intellectual outlook and theology: the Awakening in Württemberg, the mediating theology (*Vermittlungstheologie*) and the Prussian High Orthodoxy, that influential circle of conservative Lutheran aristocrats and theologians gathered in Berlin in the 1840s.

Born in poverty as an illegitimate child and expelled from school in his Swiss hometown because of deviant sexual behavior, (Chapter 1) Schaff was sent to a boarding school at Kornthal, a center of Württemberg pietism, which became his "spiritual birthplace." Indeed, the religious ethos and outlook of the Württemberg Awakening was to adhere to Schaff throughout his life, forming the

2

permanent background of the imposing scholarship and churchmanship of his American career. (Chapter 2) A presentation of the dominant forces in German Protestantism in the 1830s—the *Erweckungsbewegung*, Schleiermacher, Hegel—provides the necessary background for understanding Schaff's university years. For Schaff was first and foremost an *heir* of this brilliantly creative age. When David Friedrich Strauss's sensational *Life of Jesus Critically Examined* (1835) hastened the division of German Protestantism into the "free" and "radical" theology, the mediating theology and the Lutheran confessional theology, Schaff also became a *participant* in the confrontations and discussions of these three schools of theology, against the background of the division of Hegel's school into Left and Right also caused by Strauss's book. (Chapter 3) Schaff's doctoral dissertation *The Sin against the Holy Spirit* confirms that at the universities of Tübingen, Halle and Berlin the dominant influence was the mediating theology, and it was this theology, representing a progressive orthodoxy or liberal evangelicalism, that made the decisive and lasting impact on Schaff. (Chapter 4) But during Schaff's last two years in Berlin he came also under the powerful influence of the Prussian High Orthodoxy as well as the church historian August Neander and the philosopher Schelling, called to Berlin in 1841. Once more Schaff participated in a dramatic change in the theological climate of German Protestantism, a growing "church consciousness," which issued into two antagonistic concepts of the church, the "neo-Protestant" and the "neo-orthodox." By the early 1840s the Berlin Awakening had evolved into the Prussian High Orthodoxy, combining ecumenical and orthodox Lutheran aims and thus becoming a unique representative of the "neo-orthodox" concept of the church. Schaff was in particular influenced by the theological and ecumenical views of the Prussian aristocrat Ludwig von Gerlach. Schaff left Germany as a mediating theologian, whose contribution to the Mercersburg Theology at the beginning of his American career was the provocative and eclectic fusion of an ecumenical high-church pietism and a romantic-idealistic philosophy of history. (Chapter 5) The missionary and ecumenical impulses of the Awakening most of

3

all motivated Schaff's decision to emigrate to the New World and, after an important six-week sojourn in England, to begin his teaching career at the Mercersburg Seminary in Pennsylvania as a self-styled "missionary of [German] science." (Chapter 6) A review and appraisal of Schaff's American career, which is about two-thirds (slightly revised) of an article I published in *Church History* (1990), seems an appropriate way of completing my study, for the formative years of Schaff's German education, after all, turned out to be nothing but a preparation for his distinguished American career. (Epilogue)

Within its broad compass and with its focus on outstanding personalities and theological positions in nineteenth-century German Protestantism, my study is intended to contribute to the ongoing scholarly discussion both of a significant figure in nineteenth-century American Christianity and of German Protestantism in the nineteenth century's first half, as it also, I hope, will contribute to the important field of immigration studies. Indeed, Schaff's life offers a good case study for any student interested in exploring "the history of that mysterious process called 'Americanization'."[2] This exploration, I might add, could well include the study of the lives of three contemporary German fellow-immigrants: Julius Mann (1819-92), who remained a Lutheran, William (Wilhelm) Nast (1807-99), who joined the Methodists and became the patriarch of German Methodism in this country and abroad, and August Rauschenbusch (1816-99), who later turned Baptist, though none of these was to equal Schaff in scholarly attainment and influence, and none was to utilize his immigrant experience so impressively in pioneering the internationalization of theology as was to be true of Schaff, who remained rooted in the Reformed/Presbyterian tradition. In the extensive bibliography of relevant German literature that I utilized in my study I want to call particular attention to the magnificent volumes (still in the process of appearing) of the *Theologische Realencyklopädie* (1977ff), for its articles offer up-to-date summaries and comprehensive listings of the literature of all those movements, schools of theology and individuals, who, because they bear on Schaff's German education, are included in my study.

4

While my study will be of primary interest to the historian of religion, I hope that it will also appeal to a wider public of ministers and laity alike, who aim, as did Schaff in his own time, at representing a liberal evangelicalism and at accomplishing ecumenical goals. My study presents issues and raises questions that can help theologically engaged Christians even today to develop an understanding of the Christian faith appropriate to our time and to address in our own time the ever urgent task of the renewal and unity of the Christian churches.

Schaff himself provided important sources on which I could draw. Twice he reviewed for American readers the larger German scene that was the context of the formative years of his life: initially in a series of articles, "Gallerie der bedeutendsten jetzt lebenden Universitätstheologen Deutschlands," in *Der deutsche Kirchenfreund* (April—September 1852), and then again in *Germany: Its Universities, Theology, and Religion. With sketches of Neander, Tholuck, Olshausen, Hengstenberg, Twesten, Müller, Ullmann, Rothe, Dorner, Lange, Ebrard, Wichern, and other distinguished German divines of the age* (1857). Furthermore, in the "General Introduction to Church History," with which he prefaced his *History of the Apostolic Church* (1853), he discussed brilliantly those German church historians who as his teachers, fellow-students or more distant contemporaries helped to shape his own evolving position as a church historian in the years immediately following his emigration. Thus this account also becomes important for understanding the formative influences of contemporary German historical scholarship upon his mind during the first years at Mercersburg. The "Autobiographical Reminiscences," a manuscript he commenced writing on the last day of 1871, was conceived as a review "of my youth till my Arrival in America" but was written for the benefit of his children only. He worked intermittently for almost twenty years on this manuscript, incorporating several lengthy chapters that dealt with events of the years just past, so that he wrote the chapters on Stuttgart and Tübingen as late as 1884. The final three chapters on Halle, Berlin and his arrival in America he even added only three years before his death. It is regrettable that these important chapters about the formative years of his German education turned out to be brief and to show the dimming effect of the distance of time. Still another valuable source is the son's biography of his father: David S. Schaff, *The Life of Philip Schaff, in Part Autobiographical* (1897). It might be appropriate to add that in his "Autobiographical Reminiscences" Schaff asserted that the record of his American career are his books. What satisfaction it must have given him when a month before his death he discovered that no less than 13 of his own books were included in the Model Village Library with its 5,000 volumes, which was one of the many attractions at the World's Columbian Exhibition at Chicago in 1893.[3]

I should finally mention that Schaff has held a fascination for me ever since I myself arrived as an immigrant, like Schaff twenty-five years old, in this country and was assigned by Wilhelm Pauck at New York's Union Theological Seminary, another German immigrant scholar, "Philip Schaff " as the subject of my doctoral dissertation. It was at about the time that I started working on my dissertation that I met my wife, to whom I therefore gratefully dedicate this volume, for she has made it possible in many ways for me to claim Schaff, albeit in the lofty sphere of scholarship, as another companion of my life. Beginning in the 1970s, as the Bibliography will show, I made Schaff's versatile career the subject of several scholarly efforts that now find their conclusion in my study of Schaff's formative years. Given these earlier publications, it was unavoidable that I would occasionally draw upon them in this present study. I gratefully acknowledge permission to reprint this previously published material. I am especially pleased that my two most recent publications are German-language contributions to the study of Schaff. For Schaff is hardly known today in Germany; he had not even been found worthy of an article in the *Theologische Realencyklopädie*. I am therefore glad to say that belatedly, and then readily, the encyclopedia's editors accepted my article on Schaff for inclusion in their vol. 30 (appropriately in close proximity to Schelling and Schleiermacher!). Perhaps my hope is justified that Schaff will now, and once again, be a presence even in German scholarship.

All translations are mine, unless otherwise indicated. German book titles are presented in English translation in the text, the original German title will be found in the corresponding endnote. I thought it best, however, to retain the title of German journals also in the text. I believe that the American context requires an explanation of the German term *evangelisch*, which is always translated as *evangelical*. In order to avoid all confusion it should be stated clearly that in the German context *evangelisch* means generally the opposite of Roman Catholic, that is, Protestant; additionally, especially since the early nineteenth century *evangelisch* also identifies an ecclesiastical and theological position that supersedes the traditional distinctions in German Protestantism of *Lutheran* and *Reformed*, as representing their unity, either as a fact or as an aspiration.

A word also about the spelling of Schaff's name. Prior to 1847, he spelled his name "Philipp Schaf" or "Philipp Schaaf." Only in the New World, a few years after his arrival, did he change the spelling to "Philip Schaff," though in his German publications he continued to retain "Philipp." For simplicity's sake I have used the American spelling in my study from the beginning.

Over these past years I have become indebted to several fellow historians who have offered their own valuable contributions to the study of Schaff. Their names stand out in the Bibliography of this study, especially John Payne and Georg Shriver, who with such warmth and expert knowledge has helped us to understand the human side of Philip Schaff. I also want to acknowledge gratefully the help I received from the staffs of the libraries that contain such rich resources of Schaff papers and related materials and books: the Philip Schaff Library and the Archives of the Evangelical and Reformed Historical Society at Lancaster Theological Seminary, Lancaster, Pennsylvania, and the Burke Library of Union Theological Seminary in New York City. No less indebted am I to the ever helpful staff of the Bridwell Library of Southern Methodist University's Perkins School of Theology in Dallas, Texas. I also deeply appreciate the award of a Faculty Research Grant of Southern Methodist University. For that grant enabled me to spend time and do research first at Lancaster, Pennsylvania (the locality to which Mercersburg Seminary was removed in 1871), and then at the libraries of the University of Tübingen. This grant also made possible memorable visits to Mercersburg on this side of the Atlantic and to Kornthal and Stuttgart in Germany, as a later trip to the Swiss and French Alps allowed me to spend two memorable days in Chur. I am grateful also to the archivist of the Evangelical and Reformed Historical Society for having provided the photo of Schaff in his early manhood for the cover illustration: an engraving by John Sartain, about 1856, of which the original is unknown. Finally I would like to thank my distinguished colleague Brian Gerrish for the "Foreword" he so readily was willing to contribute to this volume. In years past I have learned much from his own publications that span the history of Christian thought from the sixteenth-century Reformers to the present. I am more than ever in his debt.

El Prado, New Mexico
Christmas 2003

A Swiss by Birth

Chapter 1

Childhood at Chur (1819-1834)

Graubünden (the Grisons)--with its glorious snow-covered mountains and with its valleys blooming in the summer, the source of two great rivers, the Rhine and the Inn, where three languages, German, Italian and Romansch, were spoken, and where Catholics and Protestants had learned to live peacefully side by side-- had joined the Swiss Republic late, in 1803, when Chur had become the capital of the new canton.[1] Chur, located in the German-language area, at that time had a population of 3,200. Here, too, Catholics and Protestants practiced peaceful tolerance toward each other. The Catholic cathedral and episcopal palace were situated on a hill; in the center of town, not more than a stone's throw away, stood the Protestant churches, St. Martin's and Regula. The canton school established in 1804 had accordingly both a Protestant and a Catholic section. In this town Philip Schaff was born on January 1, 1819. He was an illegitimate child.[2] His thirty-year old mother, Anna Louis, née Schindler, had left her husband in another Swiss village and come to Chur, where, in October of 1818, she took a poor local carpenter, also thirty-years old, Philip Schaff senior, to court in order to force him to acknowledge the paternity of the child she was about to bear. The court found in her favor. A few days after the child's birth, on January 7, the child was baptized. The father and Magaretha von Salis, a well-known Christian hymn- and song-writer, were the godparents, who expressed in the baptismal certificate the pious hope that God would be the child's guide, refuge and strength and that He, "who sees in the deepest darkness as if it were bright daylight," would always keep the child "intently vigilant" in his "abhorrence of all vices."[3] A few weeks later the mother was expelled from Chur because of her scandalous behavior; she left but without her child. After nine years she married a widower with six children in another Swiss village, and after his death she married a third time. Philip, however, remained her only child. Only many years later, during occasional visits after Schaff's emigration to America, did mother and son develop a firm and intimate relationship. According to the son, the mother was a simple woman of peasant background but of fine appearance, independent will and native wit. She died in 1876 at the age of 86 in her native Switzerland. Schaff certainly owed to his mother his robust nature, without which the astounding scope of his later accomplishments would have been unthinkable. Sadly, the father had died shortly after his son's first birthday. The grandfather, a widower since 1817, who is first mentioned as living in Chur in 1781, did still not enjoy full citizenship; moreover, he was so poor that he belonged to the social underclass. After a few years young Philip moved from the grandfather's house into the care of a foster family in Chur. For five years he attended the lower school. Then he was awarded a scholarship in the respected canton school of his hometown, where already in his second year he stood first in his class.

Yet in the summer of 1834 his life took a dramatic turn. The boy, now aged fifteen, suffered the indignity of being expelled from school, for what his elders then darkly called "the secret sin," that is, masturbation. The school records indicate that "the secret sin" had been a group practice, with young Philip standing out as one of the leaders.[4] But since he had been born in Chur and had no parents, the town magistrate, who from the beginning had supported him financially, was ready even now to continue assisting the gifted boy. Among those who were attracted to him was also the Antistes (chief pastor) at the St. Martin's Church, Paul Kind (1783-1876). This remarkable man had been active in Chur since 1808, at first as the pastor of the Regula Church and for several years also as a professor at the Theological Institute of the cantonal church, and he soon also served his hometown in several positions of honor. He was imbued with the spirit of pietism and hence interested in mission and various charitable enterprises, and he maintained close contact with fellow-pietists especially in Basel and Württemberg. The link was provided by the *Deutsche Christentumsgesellschaft*, a society, with its headquarters in Basel, which had been founded in 1780 as a countermeasure against the rationalistic spirit then rampant in the churches of continental Europe. It aimed at gathering and uniting the devout, regardless of nationality and denominational affiliation, and at rousing them to the defense and propagation of the evangelical faith in word and charitable deed.[5] It was primarily owing to Antistes Kind and his contacts with fellow-pietists elsewhere that the town's Commission for the Poor arranged for Schaff to continue his studies at the boys' school at Kornthal, a quiet village near Stuttgart, which was a center of Württemberg pietism. In the fall of 1834 young Schaff started out alone and on foot, carrying all his possessions in his knapsack, leaving his native Switzerland. Schaff visited Switzerland during his German university years and later during his many European journeys. He retained a deep love for the sublime beauty of its mountains and valleys, but he conceded that he would rather visit the country of his birth occasionally than live there permanently. Like Scotland and New-England, he wrote, it is "a good place to emigrate from and to cleave to in fond recollection."[6]

In his "Autobiographical Reminiscences" written for his children, Schaff recorded, for reasons easily understood, neither his illegitimate birth nor his expulsion from the school. He wrote that he was "born and bred in poverty and obscurity." He lamented the lack of the blessings of a refined Christian home in his youth, but then praised poverty's "redeeming features: it stimulates energy, breeds industry and develops the spirit of self-reliance and manly independence."[7] That the mother soon left Chur without her child, he explained inaccurately by noting her quick remarriage after the father's death with a widower with children. He did mention that in his hometown in his youth he was surrounded by "uncongenial and dangerous influences." When he later claimed that his removal from Chur to Kornthal was "an experimental argument for the mystery of predestination," it is obvious that this statement carries far more meaning than he was ever willing to admit publicly or even privately.[8] How traumatic the events leading to his expulsion from the school were for the adolescent boy is revealed in a short play he wrote while still in Chur (which, incidentally, is the first extant Schaff manuscript). Entitled "Friendship," it is the touching story of the last two hours two young friends are able to spend together--in a dark dungeon, where one of the two, condemned to die, is expecting the arrival of his executioners! Several revised drafts of this play show that young Schaff wrestled for two long years with this story, his own story. The play's last stanza is of additional interest, the condemned boy speaking: "There (in the world beyond) will then no sad hour of separation meet us, there a god will bless our beautiful bond with eternal happiness." Two years later this stanza was revised to read: "There no pain of separation will desecrate the blissful paradise, there the Savior will consecrate our hearts to friendship's eternal happiness."[9] In the meantime Schaff had experienced his "conversion" among the pietists at Kornthal, had in this community been helped to resolve the tension and guilt feeling engendered by his immediate past!

It is not possible to say when Schaff first learned of his illegitimate birth. Since the Reformed Church of Graubünden at that time did not allow an illegitimate child to be ordained to the ministry, one might surmise that Schaff must have discovered the special circumstances of his birth certainly as a student, when he considered service in his home church. Only in 1854 did the Synod of the Reformed Church of Graubünden discontinue the requirement of legitimate parentage for the ministry. Five years later the Synod added Schaff as an honorary member to the clerical rolls of his hometown church. According to Ulrich Gäbler, this "extraordinary distinction" was bestowed upon Schaff as a kind of compensation, for the Synod believed "that his emigration had been prompted by the strictures of the church order." And Gäbler concludes: "By the time he reached the age of forty, the disgrace of Philip Schaff's origins had been definitely redeemed."[10]

Schaff, orphaned and poor, left Switzerland in 1834. Ten years later, at the beginning of a promising academic career in the theological faculty of the University of Berlin, he left for the United States. He had accepted a call to assume the professorship of Biblical Exegesis and Church History at the Seminary of the German Reformed Church at Mercersburg in Pennsylvania. Those years, 1834-1844, constitute the decade in which Schaff grew to manhood and to the imposing stature of a scholar who had learned to combine in his intellectual outlook some of the most important cultural and theological currents of his time. But it was due to the chief pastor at the St. Martin's Church in Chur-- and the *Deutsche Christentumsgesellschaft*--that Württemberg pietism not only determined the beginning of Schaff's development as a Christian and a theologian, but also continued to be one of the decisive strands in the rich and complex fabric of his life and thought.

15

A German by Education

Chapter 2

Kornthal and Stuttgart (1834-1837)

The Württemberg Awakening

Pietism in Germany was a part of the revival of the evangelical spirit that in the late seventeenth and early eighteenth centuries began to sweep across much of continental Europe and of the English-speaking world on both sides of the Atlantic.[1] Under the inspiring leadership of Jacob Spener (1635-1705), the German revival faulted Lutheran Orthodoxy for having stifled the religious life of German Protestantism with its heavy emphasis on doctrinal correctness and theological controversies. Those who were caught up in this revival were soon called pietists. They were Christians who stressed the necessity of biblical devotion, a personal, heartfelt decision for Christ and a morally perfected life. With this emphasis pietism gained a deepened consciousness of the unity of all of God's people wherever they are to be found, but, unlike the Wesleyan movement which in the end separated itself from the Church of England, it remained as a powerful leaven within the established Lutheran church. The work that Spener had initiated was further expanded by August Hermann Francke (1663-1727) at Halle, Count Ludwig von Zinzendorf (1700-60) at Herrnhut in Saxony, and in Württemberg in the eighteenth century by two leading ministers of the established church, Johann Albrecht Bengel (1687-1752) and Friedrich Christoph Ötinger (1702-82).

Bengel was the profound, solid biblicist whose biblically based understanding of the divine plan of salvation prompted him to anticipate Christ's return in the summer of 1836. Ötinger, the learned theosoph, drawing especially on the writings of the mystic Jacob Böhme (1575-1624), developed a grand system of divine and human knowledge that was later also to leave its mark on the philosophical speculations of fellow-Württembergers like Schelling (1775-1854) and Hegel (1770-1831). Under Bengel's and Ötinger's influence two divergent strands developed in Württemberg pietism, one inclining toward theosophical-chiliastic speculations, the other embracing a conciliatory, mildly Lutheran piety. Still others among the devout were influenced by the Moravians gathered at Herrnhut under Zinzendorf's leadership. Hence pious speculations, chiliastic expectations, separatist tendencies and an affective-lively piety that remained attached to the established church were found side by side among these Württemberg pietists. All, however, had in common that they met regularly in independent conventicles for Bible study, mutual spiritual edification and fervent prayer. Only when toward the end of the eighteenth century the cold wind of rationalism was blowing through the churches in Germany, only then did the tendency to separate from the institutional church manifest itself in Württemberg even among those who so far had remained attached to the state church and loyal to the royal family. Two measures in particular--a new hymnal (1791) and a new liturgy (1809), both imbued with the spirit of rationalism and enforced by the state--upset and agitated the pietists. They viewed these measures as a convincing proof of "the un- and half-belief" now prevailing in the established church, and many even saw them as " an omen of the anti-Christ whose coming, according to Bengel, was soon to be expected."[2] The unrest and misery caused by the Napoleonic wars, resistance to the state church and chiliastic expectations combined to foster the desire to be closer to the anticipated events of the end times through emigration, primarily to southern Russia and Palestine, which was the logical direction, since many expected the coming of Christ to occur either near or in Palestine. Only King Wilhelm I, who ascended to the throne in 1816, sought actively to keep his restless pietists at home by granting them certain civil and ecclesiastical privileges, including the royal permission to establish communities that would be self-governing and self-supporting and hence independent of the state church and, to a certain degree, even of the state: first

Kornthal (1819) near Stuttgart and then Wilhelmsdorf (1824). These communities conscientiously modeled themselves after the Moravian church of Zinzendorf's brand of pietism and the apostolic church. In Kornthal in particular Württemberg pietism found perhaps its clearest expression, for the members of that community represented both the theosophical-chiliastic and the conciliatory, mildly Lutheran parties as well as those influenced by Zinzendorf's Moravians. Soon the Kornthal congregation established charitable and educational institutions, among them the boys' school already mentioned. This school was under the direction of Johannes Kullen (1787-1842), a member of a respected Swabian family of educators, and attracted students also from outside Württemberg, especially from Switzerland.[3]

In the 1830s, however, these old pietistic traditions were infused with new life, when they were caught up in the *Erweckungsbewegung*, the great religious Awakening that at the beginning of the nineteenth century spread throughout much of Germany and other parts of western Europe.[4] Württemberg pietism, it should therefore be noted, was undergoing a remarkable transformation during those very years when young Schaff came under its influence. Since in Württemberg the new Awakening won its most ardent advocates among the younger generation of ministers--Ludwig Hofacker (1798-1828) was the first, who through his powerful preaching also exerted the greatest influence, even though he died young--, relations between the old pietism and the established church now gradually improved. In the 1830s, the pietists began again to think of themselves as the "salt" of the Württemberg church; the separatist tendencies of old were forgotten. After the revolution of 1848 this new pietism, in alliance with political conservatism, even came to dominate the government of the Württemberg church. This further development is illustrated by the career of Sixtus Carl Kapff (1805-79), the pastor of the Kornthal congregation for almost a decade,1833-1842, who was to play so important a role in Schaff's youth.[5] His predecessor at Kornthal had been expelled from the state church because of his refusal to use the new liturgy of 1809. Kapff, on the other hand, was called to Kornthal from a pastorate in the established church. Some years later he wrote that the Kornthal congregation now emphasizes "the affinity rather than the differences" in its relation to the Württemberg church.[6] After the revolution of 1848 Kapff even assumed a role of leadership in the Württemberg church and decisively influenced its life for almost 30 years until his death in 1879.

A similar story is told by what happened in Stuttgart, Württemberg's capital, where Schaff arrived in the spring of 1835 to attend the famed *Gymnasium* for the next two years. Here the old pietism had been kept alive especially by a number of reputable merchants and their families, among them Johann Georg Mann (1778-1858), whose son Julius became Schaff's closest boyhood friend and in whose house he found lodging for several months. But precisely at this time the leaders of the younger generation of "awakened" ministers were called to Stuttgart's churches: Wilhelm Hofacker (1805-48) in 1835, Albert Knapp (1798-1864) in 1836, Christoph Friedrich Dettinger (d. 1876) in 1837. They found an ally in Christian Adam Dann (1758-1837), a dignified and forceful representative of the old pietism, serving as Dean (*Amtsdekan*) in Stuttgart from 1824 until his death in 1837, and also presiding over the Stuttgart branch of the *Christentumsgesellschaft*. These men were always welcome in Mann's hospitable home--Mann, for instance, drove Kapff in his carriage to Kornthal in 1833 for Kapff's initial visit--and Schaff regularly attended their church services and devotional meetings. The old Dann even grew so fond of Schaff that after his death the boy was presented with a lock of his hair.

The conditions under which Schaff grew up at Kornthal and Stuttgart could hardly have been more favorable for his religious development and for turning him into a pietist. Indeed, Kornthal became his "spiritual birthplace."[7] This is the more surprising since Schaff spent only six months in that community. Moreover, shortly after his arrival, in the fall of 1834, first an outbreak of dysentery then of typhoid caused havoc especially among the boarders of the boys' school, killing six boys, of whom five were Swiss, and necessitating for a time the removal of the sick students, Schaff among them, to a building of the nearby royal castle Solitude. But here in Kornthal Schaff was "converted," here he was confirmed, and already here he committed himself to the ministry of the church as his vocational goal.

Many years later, in 1869, Schaff participated in the festivities celebrating Kornthal's fiftieth anniversary. On that occasion Schaff, himself now fifty years old, appealingly described his youthful "conversion" in a presentation addressed especially to the students of his old school, among whom was now also his son David. Speaking of himself in the third person, he told his youthful audience how he had one night secretly left his bed at 3 o'clock for a nearby forest, where he was overcome by homesickness. Miserable and wretched, he threw himself to the ground, praying and crying, since he had not yet experienced the forgiveness of sins. But God heard his cries, so that his homesickness became the pain of a new birth from above. In that hour he realized for the first time what it means to have peace with God through the atoning blood of Jesus that cleanses from all sins. When afterwards he was introduced by the faithful instruction of Kullen and Kapff into the mysteries of evangelical truth, the seeds of the Word of God took root in his soul and soon thereafter he dedicated himself at this very altar to the service of God. "Never, never will he forget the day of his Confirmation on Easter Sunday 1835, and the solemn vow he then made."[8]

The religious instruction he had received in Chur had obviously made no impression upon the young boy, though, as Schaff later wrote, in his hometown he was "never irreligious," but he was "somewhat skeptical and lacked that childlike faith without which no one can enter the kingdom of God."[9] Kornthal now gave him that "childlike faith," by immersing him in the religious world of the Württemberg Awakening.

It should be noted, however, that Schaff's "conversion," as far as its force and depth are concerned, was unlike the experience of the Awakening's first generation. Ludwig Hofacker, for instance, had been "awakened" in the year of Schaff's birth after passing through an extended, fearfully severe penitential struggle which several times was at the point of being terminated by illness and physical exhaustion. Schaff's conversion, on the other hand, as he would later maintain, was but the resolution of a crisis to which an acute case of "Swiss" homesickness had led the lonely youth in an environment still strange and alien to him. Out of this crisis the fatherless boy emerged as one who had found in God the beloved heavenly father and in Christ a protective friend and savior. Elsewhere Schaff referred again to what he thought was the heart of his "conversion: "For many terrestial homesickness has been a bridge to the longing for heaven."[10] His pietistic mentors, especially Kapff, then taught him to think of himself not only as a beloved child of the heavenly Father, but also as a sinner who had been washed clean of his sins by the blood of Jesus, his Savior.

In his diary of 1836 there are two characteristic entries. One is the copy of an effusive, moving letter of thanks written in response to the gift of "three big thalers" he had received from the duchess Henrietta, the royal friend of the Württemberg pietists. In this letter the seventeen-year old youth called himself "a wretched worm in the dust," who nevertheless is certain that he lies at the heart of the Lord of heaven and earth. He spoke of "the crucified Savior" as "a companion on the thorny, seductive path of life," as the "light," which "illuminates even the darkest stretches of his life's path," as the "guide.....in whose presence he no longer need to fear the threatening cliffs that the ship of his life may encounter." Having seen God's love, which gives us all things, made manifest in Christ's cross (here he cited Romans 8:32), he was "no longer tormented by worries about food and clothing." For those who support him with their gifts are moved to do so by "my heavenly friend, who bears me as a high priest in his heart." The other entry, written on the same day and again characteristically pietistic in tone and imagery, recorded that a young girl of his acquaintance had been confirmed "with blessings," because she had been "suffused with profound contempt for the sinful world."[11]

One may justifiably claim that the deepest roots of Schaff's mature faith and theology are already recognizable in his conversion experience and the subsequent instruction he received from his Kornthal teachers. Schaff's understanding of the Christian faith was given distinctive shape neither by

Luther's nor Calvin's theology, for it was not determined by the stark contrast and confrontation between the sinful creature and the holy yet merciful God, with Christ being both the victim and the victor in that dramatic confrontation. Rather, faith remained for him always the simple certainty, spontaneously arising from the Bible and his own heart, of God's love and presence, both being guaranteed by the divine savior Christ. Indeed, the relationship of Schaff to his God remained throughout his life that of a humble and grateful child, who in awe and wonder knows of his kinship with the heavenly Father and with Christ and of their continuous presence in his life and in the world at large; and heaven, the supernatural world, was always to him very close at hand and that "higher and better home,"[12] for which the homesick youth in Kornthal had begun to long. Characteristically, Schaff's first sermon in 1838, delivered in the village church of Gomaringen near Tübingen, was based on John 3:16, the love of God as shown in Christ. According to his son, this verse remained his favorite biblical text and the heart of the gospel to the end of his life.[13] By opening the door to the world of the Württemberg Awakening, Kornthal had given Schaff the "childlike faith," without which the mature personality of the great scholar and churchman is unthinkable. Indeed, throughout his entire life he was never tempted to throw away this treasure--the certainty of knowing himself embraced by that divine, heavenly love--or to exchange it for the modern coins of less clearly supernaturalistic and pious beliefs and sentiments.

But the Württemberg Awakening helped to shape Schaff's religious outlook in still other ways as well. We should note, for instance, that Schaff's "conversion" was deepened in the religious instruction he received at Kornthal and especially in the confirmation classes that Kapff taught. Kapff considered these confirmation classes to be particularly important, and with his engaging and compelling personality and his deeply felt religious convictions he had no doubt a profound impact on the receptive hearts and minds of the young people in his charge. It is no wonder, therefore, that Schaff's confirmation on Easter Sunday 1835 should have made an even deeper impression on him than his earlier

25

conversion. It is of special interest to note that Kapff based his instruction on Luther's *Small Catechism* and that Schaff, baptized in the Reformed Church of Chur, was now confirmed as a Lutheran at Kornthal.

Since the Württemberg Awakening and the revivals across the Atlantic Ocean shared the same goal of the heart's conversion to Christ, it might at first come as a surprise that at Mercersburg Schaff was to be a severe critic of the American revivals, especially the "New Measures" propagated by Charles Finney (1792-1875). But in contrast to the American revivals with their contrived and emotional techniques for communicating the gospel to the sinners and doubters the Württemberg Awakening employed the traditional means of the established church: catechetical instruction, the preaching of the Biblical word, the sacraments. Furthermore, Württemberg pietists scorned to induce, much less to force, a conversion by artificially contrived means. Kapff maintained that the rebirth of the individual is "the concern of the Holy Spirit, and the more is said about it, the less power there is."[14] After attending a devotional meeting in Stuttgart, Schaff recorded in his diary that the preacher, Wilhelm Hofacker, in interpreting John 1:13, had declared: "Rebirth is God's concern; it cannot be achieved by a sudden emotional upheaval, by the ordinary efforts of man, nor by the influence of even the most Christian teacher."[15] It should therefore come as no surprise that Schaff already in Kornthal made the vocational decision of entering the ministry of the established church. As he wrote in his "Autobiography:" "As soon as I awoke to the sense of the paramount importance of religion, I chose the ministry of the gospel for my vocation, and adhered to this resolution ever after without a moment's doubt. This was in my sixteenth year."[16]

It needs to be stressed, however, that the "churchly" character of Württemberg's new pietism was of a special kind. It is true that the pietists once again acknowledged the necessary place of the institutional church in the divine plan of salvation. Nevertheless, the individual's relationship to the Savior continued among them to take precedence over the institutional forms of Christian life, especially the denominational particularities and divisions. When American

Methodists started evangelizing in Württemberg around 1850, those older ministers who had once been "awakened" praised their work, calling it "blessed and not exaggerated." And they countered the opposition of some of their younger colleagues, who had again acquired a more strictly Lutheran outlook, with the characteristic words: "First the salvation of the souls, then the church."[17]

This lack of confessional exclusiveness and denominational partisanship was therefore also the very source of the Württemberg Awakening's tolerant ecumenical outlook. Indeed, Kapff asserted for the Kornthal congregation: "The communion of saints is one of the most precious articles of our faith," and he added: "For this reason we feel warm brotherly love toward the members of other denominations, e. g., the Reformed, the English Church, English and American sects, if only they worship God in the spirit and in truth," and he was willing to overlook the difference between them to the extent that this is "required by love and allowed by truth."[18] Württemberg's new pietism, while embracing an irenic, conciliatory Lutheranism, remained ever mindful of the necessity to strive for the unity of all of God's true children. Characteristically, the Kornthal congregation had based itself on the *Augsburg Confession*, but only after excising its damnatory clauses. There can be no doubt that the Württemberg Awakening laid the foundation for Schaff's ecumenical outlook and broadened his ecclesiastical horizon. Already at Kornthal and Stuttgart Schaff caught the inspiring vision of the universal fellowship of all those whose hearts the Savior has won, and this fellowship he saw then rising above all denominational divisions. It was in the spirit of the pietism of his youth, when Schaff later in life time and again asserted that the "hill of Zion" rises far above "all sectarian steeples."[19]

The Württemberg Awakening also helped to determine Schaff's educational and cultural ideal, at the very time when German literature was passing through its two greatest periods, the classical and the romantic, boasting of brilliant writers and poets such as Gotthold Ephraim Lessing (1729-81), Johann Gottfried Herder (1744-1803), Johann Wolfgang von Goethe (1749-1832) and Friedrich Schiller (1759-1805). The liberal arts education at German high

27

schools--at Kornthal and the Stuttgart *Gymnasium*--was still centered in a most thorough study of Greek and Roman antiquity, with students also acquiring a knowledge of the ancient languages of Greek and Latin. By contrast, the physical sciences continued in this pre-industrial era to be sadly neglected. Once again it was Kapff who aptly articulated the educational and cultural aspirations of the Württemberg pietists: "When youth has been lit by the radiance of Christ's sun, the stars of Athens and the lightening flashes of Rome fade....We therefore have our young people read the classics, but make brief comments: Cicero said this, but Jesus said otherwise; the heathens hated, but Jesus loved, etc."[20] This ambiguous, moralizing attitude of the pietists toward ancient and contemporary culture was aptly if acidly described by Friedrich Theodor Vischer (1807-87), one of Schaff's teachers at Tübingen (Schaff took a course in aesthetics with him). The pietists, he claimed, praise Greece and its glory, but regret that Athens had no pastor, Homer did not compose a hymn-book, and Achilles did not attend confirmation classes. When Vischer assumed the chair of aesthetics at the University of Tübingen in 1844, he promised in his inaugural lecture the pietistic opponents of contemporary culture "on principle a fight without restraint, his full, undivided enmity, his open and honest hatred." That night the students honored him with a torchlight parade through the streets of Tübingen.[21] One can be sure that Schaff, had he still been in Tübingen, would not have marched and cheered in that parade. Fortunately, however, Schaff's attitude toward contemporary culture was not poisoned by the arrogance and narrow-mindedness of the average Württemberg pietist. For in the Stuttgart *Gymnasium* he had teachers who bent their effort at bridging the chasm that was opening between pietistic Christianity and the brilliant achievements of the classical and romantic periods in German culture. One of them was Gustav Schwab (1792-1850), himself a poet, who in 1837 returned to the parish ministry and in whose church at Gomaringen near Tübingen Schaff preached his first sermons. Still, Schaff remained one with his pietistic mentors and friends in continuing to assert the superiority of the Christian faith and piety over all the fields of human knowledge and artistic endeavors. So

28

strong were the impressions of his youth that Schaff would later never concede that any sphere of human activity--morality, literature, science and above all the education of the young--should be without the benefit of the Christian faith, preferably as pietists understood it. In 1857 Schaff characteristically still called Goethe "a refined heathen, without even a desire after salvation."[22] It was also significant that Schaff later sent his son David for his pre-college education across the Atlantic Ocean to Kornthal.

The isolation of large segments of Württemberg pietism from the cultural developments of the times was obviously reinforced by Bengel's prediction of Christ's victorious return and of the end of the world in the summer of 1836, when Schaff was still a student at the Stuttgart *Gymnasium*. These vivid chiliastic expectations (which differed from the end time calculations of the Millerites in the United States by only a few years) caused not only considerable excitement among the pietists, doubtlessly affecting Schaff as well, but also deepened their sense of alienation from the social and cultural currents of their time. Once again it was Sixtus Carl Kapff, who found the right word for his fellow-pietists who were sorely disappointed and upset by the error in Bengel's calculations. In his little book, *The Second Advent of the Lord, Instructions from Matthew 24 and 25, Compared with the Signs of the Times*, published in late 1836, he insisted that Bengel is not the Bible, and not the Bible but only Bengel has erred.[23] The signs of the time—he mentioned, among others, Hegel's worship of reason, Goethe ("who is to be considered the most enticing and persuasive preacher of carnal desire" [!]), the increasing demoralization of the young, "steam and iron", the dominance of the urban proletariat, the immorality of the French--clearly point to Christ's return in the near future.[24] Those signs of the approaching end times, however, need to be viewed in the light of the correct interpretation of Matthew 24 and 25: Christ's return is close at hand, but the exact time of his return the Lord has, on purpose, left open. These instructions were especially important for the Kornthal congregation, where chiliastic expectations ran high. At Kornthal the so-called "Jerusalem carriage" stood ever ready to get the faithful to Jerusalem in time for the expected triumphant return of Christ. And some of the farmers were in the habit of putting their coat down at the eastern edge of the field where they were working, since they expected the Lord's return to occur in the East and had taken to heart Mk 13:16 that in the end times "the one in the field must not turn back to get a coat." Schaff certainly also inherited from Württemberg pietism this lively hope for a return of Christ in the not too distant future, that eschatological realism that was to be an important element of his mature faith. However, the obvious failure of calculating correctly the date of Christ's return, together with the biblically grounded advice that mentors like Kapff offered, would serve him well throughout his life as a warning against being too specific in his end-time expectations.

Finally, some additional remarks about Schaff's sexual problem may yield some further insights into his youthful development. And once again we turn to a book authored by the Kornthal pastor and prolific writer, Sixtus Carl Kapff. Published in 1841, by 1902 it had run through 20 editions! An English translation appeared in Philadelphia in 1858 under the intriguing title: *Admonitions of a Friend of Youth, against the most dangerous enemy of youth; or instructions in regard to secret sins, their consequences, cure, and prevention. Commended to the affectionate consideration of the young and their teachers.*[25] Manifesting the narrowly restrictive and misguided sexual attitudes of those times, this book seemed almost to delight in telling the horror stories of young boys who are said to have suffered in later years the devastating physical and mental consequences of masturbation, the "secret sin," hell on earth, their final destination being the eternal hell. Reading this book could have frightened any young person to the point of succumbing, in a kind of self-fulfilling prophecy, to all those dreadful neuroses and their equally dreadful psychosomatic consequences the book so luridly described. And yet, the last chapter made no shrill noises but instead recorded the quiet conversation about masturbation in which the Kornthal pastor engaged each boy and girl in his charge just prior to their confirmation. This caring conversation, which was distinguished by the anxious and loving concern

30

of a gifted Christian pedagogue, occurred in Schaff's life as well, since, as already mentioned, he was confirmed at Kornthal on Easter Sunday 1835. Schaff's later claim that his emotional conversion experience had been nothing but the wrenching resolution of a case of Swiss homesickness should therefore be amended, for we can be sure that his conversion and the young Kornthal pastor's instructions and conversations with him also helped to induce a cleansing and vivifying release from the shame and guilt engendered by the young boy's immediate past. Repressive as the Victorian attitudes were toward sexuality, in particular toward masturbation, the religious influence at Kornthal was such that young Schaff's "premature activation of his sexuality," as Sigmund Freud (1856-1939) put it in one of his case studies,[26] did not remain embedded in the adolescent's maturing personality as a destructive force, poisoning the roots of his sense of selfhood and possibly leading to various adult neuroses. For Schaff had the good fortune of finding himself in the presence of a spiritual mentor who did talk about his sexual drives. And these open, intimate conversations, rather than the horror stories about the consequences of the "secret sin" that the same young pastor later saw fit to include in his book, were bound to have a healing effect upon the young boy.

It might be well at this point to turn to psychoanalytical theory also for an explanation of the remarkable fact that the disturbing experience of his deviant sexual behavior resolved itself in young Schaff's case with such astonishing quickness into a single-minded devotion to the religious ideals of his pietistic mentors, resolved itself, moreover, so firmly and completely, and without leaving behind any psychic disorders, that throughout his long life and career Schaff would never even be tempted to depart from the religious ideals acquired so suddenly and permanently in his youth. Psychoanalytical theory has called attention to defensive stratagems employed instinctively in the face of the whirlpool of aggressive human drives and feelings, and has asserted that these defensive mechanisms take, particularly in the young, the form of obedience, conformity and socialization. This insight should therefore allow us to understand even better why unquestioning obedience and conformity to the world view and ethos of his pietistic mentors, and a total socialization into that same milieu, came to distinguish Schaff's life in his youth no less than in his later years.[27]

But Schaff's pietistic friends and patrons did not only help him to find his spiritual home in the world of their piety but also secured his material well-being. Schaff later observed, with obvious and justified pride, that before his emigration to the United States he returned "with interest" the money his patrons had offered him, with the exception of a larger gift--for reasons left unmentioned--that he had received from the Rev. Theophil Passavant (1787-1864) in Basel. Passavant was known to encourage with his advice and to support financially promising pietistic candidates for the ministry, especially from Graubünden, and there is evidence that he repeatedly sent Schaff money and corresponded with him at least until 1842.[28]

Of the friendships that Schaff formed during his school years in Württemberg three in particular stand out. Two of his Stuttgart friends, Julius Mann (1819-92) and Gustav Schwab (d. 1888), the younger son of the poet of the same name, remained closely associated with him throughout his life, for they too left Württemberg for America. Gustav Schwab, emigrating like Schaff in 1844, settled in New York City, where he later represented the North German Lloyd and became one of the leading German-American merchants. He joined the Episcopal Church. Julius Mann followed his friend's invitation to join him in the ministry in the New World a year after Schaff's own emigration. He soon became a staunch advocate of Lutheran confessionalism and a friendly but persistent critic of the so-called mediating theology of his learned friend. Since the divergent development of these two friends had sprung from the same fertile soil of the Württemberg Awakening, it is the more regrettable that of their extensive, lifelong correspondence only Mann's letters to Schaff have been preserved.[29] In 1884 Schaff dedicated the third volume of his *Church History* to these trusted friends and fellow-emigrants, all of whom had received the best part of their education in their youth in Württemberg.

The deepest and spiritually most fruitful friendship, however, young Schaff established with Meta Heusser-Schweizer (1797-1876), the sensitive, lyrical voice of the Awakening in the German-speaking part of Switzerland.[30] This publicity-shy woman viewed in her poetry human life and the beauties of nature as but broken and imperfect reflections of Christ's crucified love for the sinner and of the joys which Christians will fully taste once they have entered the heavenly mansions for which their souls here on earth all the while long. As Schaff said, a "deep spirituality", "a peculiar tenderness and unction," "a holy sadness" suffused all her poetry. From their first meeting in the summer of 1837, just before he began his studies at the University of Tübingen, to her death in 1876 (the same year Schaff's birth mother died), he remained attached to "Mother Heusser," as he was wont to call her, "with filial affection," and she in turn in one of her poetic communications tenderly spoke of him as "the son of my heart, the son of eternal grace."[31] During almost every one of his European journeys he spent several days, sometimes several weeks, at Hirzel, her hospitable home near Zurich. Schaff had later the pleasure of seeing some of her poems published in an English translation.[32] To him she represented that combination of poetic talent and religious sentiment to which he himself aspired. After all, as Schaff once remarked, "poetry has ever been to me, next to religion, my richest source of spiritual enjoyment."[33] "Mother Heusser" and the Kornthal pastor Sixtus Carl Kapff, his "spiritual father," were obviously quasi-parental figures in Schaff's life, filling the void created by the absence of his birth parents, a void he must have painfully felt in his childhood and youth.

In his study of Ferdinand Christian Baur (1792-1860), Schaff's great teacher at the University of Tübingen, Wilhelm Dilthey (1833-1911) correctly observed that the religious milieu of Baur's youth--"the ancestral, purely theological and church-related mode of thinking which could be traced to his supernaturalistic point of origin"--adhered to Baur wherever later his revolutionary researches into the origin and history of Christianity would take him. This inherited mode of thinking "formed, as it were, the background of his

33

world of thought. Quite indestructible: for this background had become his character."[34] Of Schaff it can be said with equal justification that the imposing scholarship and churchmanship of his later years are unthinkable apart from the background of the Württemberg Awakening: "Quite indestructible: for this background had become his character." The "childlike faith" of his youth--a warmly emotional piety that firmly clung to the supernatural beliefs of traditional Christianity, expressed itself in moral rectitude, and was intent on the active pursuit of whatever charitable, missionary and scholarly tasks appeared to hasten the coming of God's kingdom--came to imbue and control permanently Schaff's life and scholarship. The Württemberg Awakening added in particular four other elements, as we have seen, to the formation of his religious and theological outlook: an emphasis on the "converted" heart as the true mark of the Christian and of Christian fellowship and, the other side of the coin, a broad-minded ecumenical outlook and outreach that downplayed denominational particularities in favor of the spiritual unity of all of God's true children; an eschatological realism; and an ambiguous, moralizing attitude toward human culture that was at all times to be subservient to and informed by the knowledge and love of Christ. Schaff had every right to call Württemberg his "second fatherland," for, as he later declared: "To Württemberg I owe, under God, my spiritual life and the best part of my education."[35] But this remark also refers to the two years he spent at the University of Tübingen, where he began the study of theology after graduating from the Stuttgart *Gymnasium*.

Many years later, Meta Heusser-Schweizer described her first encounter with Philip Schaff in the summer of 1837, at the very time when he was about to venture forth into the exciting and challenging world of the German university: "The whole being of the young man carried an imprint that made me at once have the presentiment of a great future for him, and yet he was, despite the seal of a higher world he carried on his forehead and in his eyes, so youthfully shy, so modest, however much it shone forth from his every word that he was far advanced .... for his age." And she added a friend's later comment: Schaff's

34

cheerful and versatile personality was like "an open window into all directions" ("*offenes Fenster nach allen Himmelsgegenden*").[36] How true this was already during the years of his university studies!

Chapter 3

German Theology in the 1830s

Schleiermacher's and Hegel's Long Shadow

When Schaff enrolled at the University of Tübingen in 1837, one of the most extraordinary ages in the history of German culture was drawing to its close. One only needs to remember that Hegel had died in 1831, Goethe in 1832, Schleiermacher in 1834 and Beethoven in 1827. They had towered above their age, giving voice to its aspirations, commanding its attention and shaping its intellectual, literary and musical culture. It appears to be nearly impossible to find a common designation for this age on which all could agree. It is the Age of Goethe, the Age of German Idealism. It is the towering culmination of what the historian Friedrich Meinecke (1867-1953) has simply called "the German movement," from Leibnitz to Goethe, and has hailed as the second great achievement of the German mind after the sixteenth-century Reformation.[1] According to Ernst Troeltsch (1865-1923), it is the age that created "the second great type of modern thought," besides the Enlightenment.[2] Its most elemental and often divisive forces were the classicism of Goethe and Schiller, the romantic movement, the idealistic philosophy from Kant to Hegel and the so-called Historical School, represented most brilliantly by the jurist Friedrich Carl von Savigny (1779-1861) and the historian Leopold von Ranke (1795-1886). To be sure, much of what was new in this age had been drawn from previous periods of European intellectual history, but only at this time were certain powerful ideas, however deep and widespread their historical roots, developed to perfection and turned into potent cultural forces. Friedrich Meinecke has thought it possible to reduce the multiplicity of seminal new thoughts to just two: the concepts of "individuality" (romanticism) and of "identity" (idealistic philosophy). Together they produced the revolutionary new picture of life and the world that arose in early nineteenth-century German culture, in sharp contrast to Enlightenment thought. As Meinecke summarized:

> The whole world now appeared to be filled with individuality, each individuality, whether personal or supra-personal, governed by its own characteristic principle of life, and both Nature and History constituting what Friedrich Schlegel called an 'abyss of individuality'.... Individuality everywhere, the identity of mind and nature, and through this identity an invisible but strong bond unifying the otherwise boundless diversity and abundance of individual phenomena—these were the new and powerful ideas which now burst forth in Germany in so many different ways.[3]

In the setting and under the impact of this extraordinary age German Protestantism underwent a remarkable transformation, for it now made the transition from the age of the Enlightenment, in which it had lost much of its dogmatic substance and of the intensity of its faith, to a new religious climate and a new theology that were to continue to shape the century until World War I and that even today, on both sides of the Atlantic, still influence and challenge theology and the churches. Although the most various forces combined to bring about this change, three in particular were epoch-making and therefore merit a more detailed discussion: the Awakening, the theology of Schleiermacher and the philosophy of Hegel.

The early nineteenth-century revival of religious interest in Germany, commonly referred to as the *Erweckungsbewegung* or Awakening, had its centers in Württemberg (as we have already seen), in Bavaria, along the Lower Rhine, in Berlin and Pomerania.[4] It sometimes drew its strength from what was left of the old pietism, as in Württemberg, or from a few individuals, like Johann Georg Hamann (1730-88), Johann Heinrich Jung-Stilling (1740-1817), Johann Caspar Lavater (1741-1801) and Matthias Claudius (1740-1815), lonely eighteenth-century voices of protest against the dreary rationalism prevailing in their time. In some areas it was strongly influenced by the romantic movement, or it was nourished by the patriotic uprising that under Prussia's leadership led to the Wars of Liberation and Napoleon's defeat. With its roots spread so widely, the Awakening was not sociologically homogeneous: in southwestern and northwestern Germany it took hold primarily among the farmers and townspeople, in Prussia among the lower classes and the nobility, but it had everywhere the hearty cooperation of "awakened" ministers and theology professors. Neither was its theology of one piece; it was instead characterized by what has been called a "hazy diversity."[5] All the "awakened," however, had in their own lives experienced the truth of many of those Christian doctrines that in the previous century had been placed before the bar of human reason and found wanting—e.g., the doctrine of sin, of Christ the Savior and of the transcendent, almighty God, who actively and compassionately effects his judgments and displays his mercy in the destinies of individuals and of nations. The "awakened" believed to be able to see the divine providence visibly at work in the historical upheavals of their time as well as in the mysterious course that an individual's life was so often made to follow. All had known the anxiety of being separated from God, before they had felt themselves miraculously embraced by the divine love proffered in Christ and reborn to a new life that henceforth was to be determined by deeply felt and cherished religious convictions. Thus the Awakening led back to the supernaturalism of orthodox Christianity that in the previous century the "enlightened" had tried to discard. This supernaturalism, however, was now firmly anchored not only in the Bible, but also in each individual's experience of "conversion" or "rebirth," as it was also often enriched by the wealth of new ideas hailing from recent developments in German theology, philosophy and literature.

The strength of the Awakening, however, did not lie in theology; after all, to the "awakened" the Christian faith was not primarily "thought," that is doctrine, but "experience" and "life," and many of the rising German theologians, who had once been "awakened," like Richard Rothe (1799-1867), later turned either away from, or even against the Awakening. Only Friedrich August Gottreu

39

Tholuck (1799-1877) at Halle and August Neander (1785-1850) at Berlin represented the Awakening in positions of academic responsibility to the end of their careers, propagandizing its aims in the lecture halls of German universities and introducing its spirit into various compartments of theology. This lack of intellectual substance and interest may help to explain the failure of the Awakening to extend its influence to the ever growing educated classes of the German bourgeoisie. Important, on the other hand, were the contributions of the Awakening in foreign and home missions, for this religious revival sharpened the individual's sense of moral and social responsibility and stressed the necessity of an active faith. Thus the Awakening—running here parallel to the revivals in the British Isles and the United States—not only revitalized personal religion and nourished back to life orthodox beliefs, but by eagerly organizing its various activities it also helped to usher in the "societal age" in nineteenth-century Protestantism. One must finally add that the Awakening failed to direct its reforming energies toward the whole social fabric of the German nation, it was in particular blind to the coming of the industrial revolution, and it soon aligned itself, sometimes unwittingly, with the reactionary social and political forces on the German scene.

The second force that helped to determine the character of nineteenth-century German Protestantism was the theology of Friedrich Daniel Ernst Schleiermacher (1768-1834).[6] In 1799 he had published his trail-blazing *On Religion: Speeches to its Cultured Despisers*, when the romantic poet Novalis (1772-1801) had hailed him as "the heartbeat of the new age."[7] August Neander, his colleague at the University of Berlin, announced his death in 1834 to his students with the prophetic words that "in future days a new era in theology will be dated" from him.[8] In a necessarily brief summary of Schleiermacher's significance as "the father of modern theology," we might first emphasize his ability to rise above the stalemated confrontation between the rationalism of the Enlightenment and the supernaturalism of the orthodox Christian tradition, while he retained creatively the truth that each, he believed, had imperfectly embodied.

40

He agreed with the Age of Reason that the Christian faith is founded in personal conviction and not in blind submission to an external authority, be it that of an inerrant Bible or an infallible church. He insisted on the inwardness of truth; no sacrifice of the intellect can ever be rightfully demanded of the believer. But Schleiermacher rejected the notion that the essence of religion consists in the three ideas of the "natural religion" of the Age of Reason or even of Immanuel Kant's (1724-1804) "practical reason": freedom, immortality, God. For he held with the orthodox Christian tradition that the source and center of the Christian religion is the redemption accomplished by Jesus of Nazareth. He insisted that Christianity is rooted not in some timeless truth common to all humans, but in an historical event, the life, death and resurrection of Jesus Christ as recorded in the Scriptures. However, in opposition to the orthodox position he claimed that the Christian faith does not consist primarily in dogmas and doctrines as formulated by the church in earlier centuries, but, to use some of his own technical terms, in the "religious self-consciousness" (*frommes Selbstbewusstsein*), in the "Christian religious affections" (*christliche fromme Erregungen*) that is, in Christian piety. Religion, he claimed, is neither "knowing" (as in Christian orthodoxy) nor "doing" (as in rationalism) but "feeling" (as in pietism and romanticism). It is, as he stated more precisely, the human feeling of being absolutely and unconditionally dependent upon God. In short, the starting point of Schleiermacher's theology was the Christian consciousness, the pious feeling that is centered in Jesus of Nazareth. Thus Schleiermacher's novel understanding of religion not only transcended the rationalistic-supernaturalistic bifurcation of eighteenth-century theology, but it was also equally removed from the moralism of Kant, who had taught that religion consists "in the heart's disposition to fulfill all human duties as divine commands,"[9] and from the intellectualism of Hegel, whose position will concern us shortly.

Schleiermacher's new understanding of the nature of religion was bound to effect a new and revolutionary understanding of the nature and task of theology. If the "Christian religious affections" come always first, both logically and chronologically, then theology is essentially nothing but the systematic and descriptive presentation of the Christian consciousness as it develops and changes in the course of time. In short, theology was declared by Schleiermacher to be no longer normative but descriptive: it does not tell us what Christians ought to believe but analyses and presents systematically what Christians actually do believe. And that, of course, means that as our religious experience changes in the course of time and in the context of an evolving culture, so too is our theology bound to change.

With its emphasis on the primacy of religious experience, this new theology accorded well with the aims and the spirit of the Awakening—some in fact claimed to have been "awakened " by Schleiermacher. In a famous passage, however, Schleiermacher called himself "a Herrnhuter but of a higher order" (the allusion here was to his boyhood education among the followers of Zinzendorf).[10] For it was far from Schleiermacher's mind to belittle the necessity of theology, as pietists were wont to do, or to assign to theology no other task than that of repristinating the biblical and traditional Christian vocabulary and doctrines. Indeed, his major work, *The Christian Faith, Systematically Presented According to the Principles of the Evangelical Church* (1821; 2d ed. 1830-31), became the greatest and most ingenious account of Protestantism's faith since Calvin's *Institutes of the Christian Religion* (1559).[11] Schleiermacher set out to derive substantially the entire traditional system of Protestant dogmatics from the source of all of his theological considerations: the "Christian religious affections," the Christian consciousness. In *The Christian Faith* Schleiermacher presented Christ again as the Savior, and not as the Enlightenment's great teacher of common-sense moral precepts. He took again full account of sin and grace as the two poles around which all Christian piety and theology revolve. And he replaced the shallow rationalistic notion of the church as an association of like-minded individuals for the practice of virtue and the betterment of humanity with the traditional understanding of the Christian community as the invisible-visible bearer of the corporate life that flows through history from Christ and finds its necessary but ever changing expressions in the Christian churches. However, under the touch of his creative genius these traditional Christian doctrines underwent a sometimes subtle, sometimes clearly discernible transformation and modification. They were presented, so to say, in a modern key, in order to make the old faith understandable and credible in the context of the intellectual culture of his own time. Most obvious was Schleiermacher's inability to find the dogma of the Trinity directly implied in the Christian religious consciousness, hence he assigned it to an Appendix of *The Christian Faith*, or to continue to affirm the necessity of retaining the Old Testament as a part of the Christian canon of sacred scriptures. A few years before his death, in 1829, he even wrote that he anticipated "that we must learn to do without what many are still accustomed to regard as inseparably bound to the essence of Christianity."[12]

There can be no doubt that Schleiermacher was the first Protestant theologian to provide a truly creative intellectual response to the modern challenge to Christianity's traditional system of thought. He was haunted by the question: "Shall the tangle of history so unravel that Christianity becomes identified with barbarism and science with unbelief?"[13] And so he immersed himself fully in the higher culture of his time, while he remained steeped in the traditions of Protestant Christianity. In doing so he seemed to have brilliantly succeeded in convincing the cultured that they do not need to be despisers of religion and the Christian believers that they do not need to fear to be cultured. He was convinced that the sixteenth-century Reformation had initiated the great task of effecting "an eternal covenant between the living Christian faith and completely free, independent scientific inquiry, so that faith does not hinder science and science does not exclude faith."[14] It was to the completion of this task that Schleiermacher, truly a "prince of the Church," devoted his life.[15] He successfully renewed Christian theology in his time, because he "restored the confidence of the Christian consciousness in its own content." And, adds Brian Gerrish: "After the Enlightenment, the Age of Reason, that was no small achievement."[16]

Schleiermacher's theology was bound to produce countless fruitful trends. Indeed, in his time and later his persuasive influence was felt among Christians of more liberal tendencies, who strove toward greater freedom from external authorities, who sought the religious truth in the depth of human consciousness, and who were eager to participate fully in the cultural progress of their time, as well as among those more conservatively inclined Christians, who desired to anchor the Christian life and faith once again firmly in the biblical and sixteenth-century Reformation norms. Thus many of the progressive and conservative tendencies in nineteenth-century Protestantism proceeded from, or attached themselves to, his work. It was to be Schleiermacher's fate that to a less distinguished posterity he soon appeared as one who had gone either too far or not far enough. Schaff was to belong to that later generation that honored Schleiermacher as the nineteenth century's greatest Protestant theologian but almost in the same breath always criticized him for having indeed strayed too far from the orthodox essence of the Christian faith.

While the Awakening breathed new life into the Christian faith and while Schleiermacher brilliantly reconstructed theology, Protestant Christianity received aid from still another and quite unexpected quarter—the philosophy of Georg Friedrich Wilhelm Hegel (1770-1831).[17] Reacting to Kant's transcendental system of philosophy and following in the footsteps of Johann Gottlieb Fichte (1762-1814) and Friedrich Wilhelm Joseph Schelling (1775-1854), Hegel's philosophy—if we may once more attempt a brief summary of a very complex system of thought-- was erected on the twin pillars of the Absolute Spirit and the dialectical method. His philosophy was the bold attempt to show how, in time and space, the Absolute--Schelling's postulated Identity of Nature and Spirit-- enters and passes through the opposites of organic nature and the spiritual and historical life of the human race, until it has finally developed and actualized itself fully as the synthesis of both Nature and Spirit, that is, as the Absolute Spirit. He was convinced that this dynamic process of the self-realization of the Absolute Spirit in the universe conforms to the lawfulness that Fichte had first formulated as the dialectical method. A concept unfolds its full meaning only by passing through conflicting stages, each of which, as the negation of the previous stage, is at the same time also a manifestation of an additional aspect of the full truth contained in the concept. As Hegel's dialectical method has generally been identified with the triad of thesis-antithesis-synthesis, it should be pointed out that Hegel himself only once used this triad.[18] It is more correct to say that Hegel's dialectical method embodied the novel and exceedingly fertile notion of the progressive development of truth. Thus he helped to make the principle of development central in the nineteenth century in all thinking about life and the world. Truth, Hegel believed, is something moving, developing, fluid; moreover, it makes its way only through sharp conflicts and hard contrasts. Since truth in its movement through conflicting stages, none of which can be taken in isolation, important as each one is in and by itself, preserves and combines the elements of truth of all of these stages, it follows that "the true is the whole," which properly understood, also means that everything is "only in the end what it is in truth."[19]

In short, Hegel's "speculative" philosophy staked out the titanic claim that the philosopher can comprehend all reality, all truth, provided that he take as his starting point the single, simple idea of the Absolute Spirit and that he use the logical tools of the dialectical method in tracing the explication of this idea in time and space. Speculation"—a term which at that time gained an uncommonly wide currency—implied therefore, at least in Hegel's sense, that the philosopher can construe in his own mind a total picture of the world that is at bottom independent of all empirically observed data, though, of course, it should never be found to contradict them. The presumed congruence of subject and object, of thought and being, in the act of thinking was indeed a fundamental principle of Hegel's "speculative," idealistic philosophy.[20] With excessive self-confidence Hegel boldly, even arrogantly, asserted: "Speculation, indeed, understands common sense, but common sense does not understand the workings of speculation."[21] One might also want to quote words from one of Hegel's letters, written in 1805: "I should like to say of my aspirations that I shall teach philosophy to speak German. Once that is accomplished, it will be infinitely more difficult to give shallowness the appearance of profound speech." In view of the formidable difficulties that the language of Hegel's "speculative" philosophy has ever since presented to the student of his thought, one is tempted to add Goethe's remark which was prompted by the writings of one of Hegel's disciples: "What are the English and the French to think of the language of our philosophers when we Germans do not understand it ourselves?"[22] Schaff was to learn to speak German, and later English, at least for a time, with Hegel's heavy accent, and after his arrival in the United States he was no doubt surprised to discover that American "common sense" stubbornly refused to concede the deeper insights to German "speculation." Moreover, he was chagrined to discover that most of his American contemporaries found the language of Hegel's philosophy as confusing and incomprehensible as did Goethe.

Hegel, however, like his great contemporary Napoleon (1769-1821), did not only stake out imperial claims for himself but was equally imperious in his efforts to apply the principles of his philosophy to all realms of human knowledge. There is the telling story of Hegel in Jena in 1806 putting the final touches to the manuscript of *The Phenomenology of Spirit* (1807), on the very day when the French inflicted a crushing defeat on the Prussian army near Jena. Later that day, after he had seen the victorious Napoleon ride by his house, he wrote to a friend, indifferent to the fate of Prussia: "It is indeed a wonderful feeling to see such an individual who, concentrated in a single point, sitting on a horse, reaches out over the world and dominates it."[23] We can apply these words to Hegel himself, if the reference is not to the political but the intellectual sphere, and not to the French Emperor's horse but the German professor's desk and lectern. Hegel had issued to his age the quaintly worded summons to undertake "the exertion of the Concept" (that is, of conceptual analysis).[24] He himself followed this summons into many fields, providing profound and brilliant analyses of the state, right, art, history and religion. Hegel's philosophy of history will become a powerful influence in Schaff's understanding of the history of Christianity, but here our concern is with Hegel's philosophy of religion.

In his philosophy of religion, Hegel had set for himself the great goal "to reconcile reason and religion."[25] How startled both the "enlightened" and the "awakened" must have been by his assertion that philosophy and religion, far from being enemies, "are identical; indeed, philosophy itself is worship, is religion." For philosophy and religion have in common the same subject-matter, which is "the eternal truth in its objectivity, God and nothing but God and the unfolding of God."[26] What then distinguishes the philosopher from the believer? It is a difference, Hegel replied, not in the truth which each one possesses but in the manner in which the truth, common to both, is comprehended by each. The story is told of Hegel's wife asking her husband to explain to her his philosophy. He surprised his wife by encouraging her to continue reading the Bible, because the Bible, he said, contained all that she would learn from his philosophy.[27] However, in Hegel's philosophical system the devout Christian who reads her Bible has the truth, God as the Absolute Spirit, in the form of *Vorstellung*, that is, as pictorial, figurative thought, some would soon say "myth." The idealistic philosopher, on the other hand, has the same truth as *Begriff*, he alone knows God in the highest and ultimate form of comprehension, which is abstract, conceptual thought. But if, according to Hegel, philosophy, properly understood, is religion, then the reverse holds equally true, that religion, properly understood, is philosophy, that faith is knowledge. Hence the intellectualism of Hegel's philosophy of religion. Philosophy and religion are, indeed, reconciled in Hegel's idealistic philosophy, if the terms of reconciliation that Hegel had laid down are accepted by both parties in this ancient dispute.

Hegel even made himself the champion of the orthodox Christian dogmas, proudly asserting that now "the fundamental truths of Christianity are being upheld and preserved" by philosophy.[28] He turned the tables on the theologians by blaming them for the nearly universal indifference toward the dogmas of the church in his time, and he even insisted on going beyond the theologians of the

47

Awakening and beyond Schleiermacher himself, since a theology "that describes only feelings, limits itself to what is empirically given, to history, and to similar contingencies; it does not yet deal with thoughts that have a content," that is, it does not yet truly know God.[29] Thus Hegel's "speculative" philosophy upheld precisely those fundamental Christian dogmas—the Trinity and the Incarnation—that in the previous century had so greatly embarrassed the theologians and that even Schleiermacher had not taken as seriously as Hegel deemed necessary. According to Hegel, the trinitarian dogma expresses the truth that God's self-manifestation follows the laws of the dialectical method. God as spirit and as love is this: "To distinguish himself from himself, to be object to himself, but to be completely identical with himself in this distinction."[30] The dogma of the Incarnation meant to Hegel that the unity of the divine and the human, of the infinite and the finite, of time and eternity, had already once been concretely achieved in history--in Jesus Christ, in whose death and resurrection all these opposites of the divine and the human, the infinite and the finite, time and eternity had been fully reconciled. Hence when the church designated Christ as the God-Man, it was precisely this "prodigious combination," so "utterly contradictory to the understanding,"[31] that expressed a central tenet of Hegel's philosophy. And in his philosophy of history Hegel pointed to the coming of Christ as the decisive turning-point in history: "God is only comprehended as Spirit, if he is known as the Triune. This new principle is the axis around which the history of the world revolves. History proceeds to it and from it."[32]

It is certainly not too difficult to understand that Hegel's philosophy of religion should have been hailed as "the greatest hymn to Christianity ever sung in the world of learning."[33] Here, after the Age of Reason, was a philosopher who proudly claimed to have effectively terminated modern philosophy's opposition to Christianity, even turning a former enemy into a powerful intellectual ally of the Christian church. It is true that Hegel and Schleiermacher, colleagues at the University of Berlin, were bitterly opposed to each other and that in their opposition the old enmity between rationalism and pietism was revived under new forms. Nevertheless, both men were one in their attempts, so characteristic of their whole age, to establish a lasting "reconciliation," an "eternal covenant" between faith and reason, theology and philosophy, dogma and history, Christianity and secular culture.

If we remember the stirring historical events surrounding the Napoleonic Wars in Germany and carefully weigh the achievements of Germany's higher culture at that time, we are prepared for the proud claim that Germans were now witnessing the birth of a new age of universal significance. In 1799 the poet Novalis saw the "traces of a new world" all around him.[34] In 1841 the philosopher Schelling declared categorically that "in Germany the fate of Christianity will be decided."[35] These were voices that expressed the epochal intellectual self-consciousness and self-confidence of early nineteenth-century German culture, a sense that it was the "manifest destiny" of German Protestantism to decide the fate of the Christian faith in the modern world by conquering the ever expanding spaces of the modern intellect—just as across the Atlantic Ocean in 1845 the editor of the *Democratic Review* proclaimed a "manifest destiny" for white settlers to conquer the vast spaces of the American West.[36] Later, after the Vatican Council had decreed Papal Infallibility, a German church historian concluded in all sincerity that German Protestant theology had become "the *magistra omnium*" and now occupies "within all of Protestantism the same central position as does the papacy within occidental Catholicism."[37] German Protestantism swung in the nineteenth century from a pessimistic self-appraisal, to which it had succumbed in the Age of Reason, to the optimism and the exultant mood which early in that century began to govern "the philosophy of religion through Hegel, theology through Schleiermacher and faith itself through the theologians of the Awakening."[38]

These then were the creative forces of this extraordinary age—in particular the Awakening, Schleiermacher, Hegel and Schelling, and the new historical consciousness of German culture associated with such names as Johann Gottfried Herder (1744-1803), Wilhelm von Humboldt (1767-1835), Friedrich

Carl von Savigny, Leopold Ranke, and Hegel-- that were also to determine Schaff's whole intellectual outlook. Indeed, he was first and foremost an heir of this great age. In the academic circles during Schaff's years of study Hegel's influence in particular was all-pervasive, and for Schaff to avoid falling under Hegel's spell was nearly impossible. Small wonder that Schaff was also to share fully in the sense of superiority with which his time confronted the Enlightenment. In theology, eighteenth-century rationalism and supernaturalism were to him but past stages in the development of Protestant thought, necessary in some sense in their own time, but now obsolete in the face of the great advances brought about by the combined forces of the Awakening, Schleiermacher and Hegel. The last supernaturalist on the Tübingen faculty, Johann Christian Friedrich Steudel (b. 1779) had died in 1837—Schaff had paid him a visit the year before on his way to Switzerland—and had been replaced by the young Isaac August Dorner (1809-84), who was steeped in the thought of Schleiermacher and Hegel. At Halle, during the winter-semester 1839/40, Schaff attended, out of curiosity, one of the lectures of Julius August Ludwig Wegscheider (1771-1849), the famed rationalist, and found, to his great satisfaction, only six students present, where in past years several hundred had crowded the lecture hall.

Yet in this new cultural and religious climate Schaff belonged not even to the second, but to the third generation. The great creative period of this age--there were certain exceptions--had already run its course. The foundations for a new orientation toward the world and toward life had been laid. After 1830, as Jacob Burckhardt (1818-97) is reported to have remarked, everything had begun to be "more common."[39] The new generation was now called upon to harvest—that is, to elaborate, combine, apply, draw the consequences from, correct and even challenge—the creative thought of the period just past. An eclectic and more practical attitude began to prevail; the parting of the ways commenced. Even so, the years after the death of Goethe, Hegel and Schleiermacher and prior to the revolution of 1848 were still full of hope and the promise of greater things yet to come, and Schaff was to share fully in the exultant, optimistic mood of that time.

Nevertheless, when he applied at the University of Berlin in 1842 for the *venia legendi* (the permission to give academic lectures in his specialty), he wrote in smooth, almost Ciceronian Latin that the position of a professor of theology, to which he aspired, was not only beautiful but also difficult. Why difficult? Because, as he continued,

> Some theologians, who are endowed with brilliant powers of mind, are eager to overthrow not only parts of lighter weight but the whole historical and dogmatic foundation of our saving faith, and even those theologians who are loyal to the Sacred Scriptures and to the church disagree so greatly among themselves.[40]

What a strangely discordant note these remarks strike! Who was trying to subvert the foundation of the saving faith? Who were the friends of true Christianity who disagreed among themselves, and what was the nature of their disagreements? Schaff's remarks indicate that he had been drawn into what Karl Marx (1818-83) would later call, in a grand and singularly fitting phrase, "the decay of the Absolute Spirit."[41]

The disintegration of Hegel's school of philosophy ("the decay of the Absolute Spirit") began in 1835, only four years after the master's death and two years before Schaff commenced his university studies, with the publication of *The Life of Jesus Critically Examined* by David Friedrich Strauss (1808-74), a young instructor in theology at the University of Tübingen.[42] The book provoked immediately an acrimonious discussion of the question that had already tentatively been raised: what is the true relationship of Hegel's philosophy to Christianity? Friends and opponents alike had early been struck by certain ambiguities in Hegel's philosophy. Was Hegel's concept of God as the Absolute Spirit, who makes his way through the stages of Nature and Spirit, pantheism or not? If it was not pantheism, as Hegel himself occasionally maintained, what was a Christian theologian to make of statements like the following: "God is not God without the world,"[43] or, "God is only God insofar as he knows himself; his knowing himself is, furthermore, his self-consciousness in man and man's

51

knowledge of God, which goes on to man's knowing himself in God"?[44] Hegel also seemed to belittle the stark reality of sin by turning it into an element, both transitory and necessary, in the dialectical process of the self-manifestation of the Absolute Spirit. Above all, Hegel's distinction between religion and philosophy, which required the translation of religious notions (*Vorstellungen*) into philosophical concepts (*Begriffe*) had established philosophy as the consummation and, consequently, as the measure and standard of religious truth. Was one to believe with Hegel that his philosophy is indeed the ultimate scientific justification of Christianity? Or was it rather the final dissolution of the Christian faith? Was Hegel to be celebrated as the Protestant Thomas Aquinas (c.1225-74), or was he to be condemned as another Origen (c. 185-c. 254), another Gnostic heretic? Are those today right who call Hegel's philosophy of religion "the greatest hymn to Christianity ever sung in the world of learning,"[45] or those who claim that Hegel's philosophy of Spirit "may be safely characterized as a form of humanism"?[46]

In his *Life of Jesus* Strauss for the first time exposed brilliantly and ruthlessly the ambiguous character of Hegel's synthesis of Christian faith and idealistic philosophy. Concentrating on the christological implications of Hegel's philosophy of religion, he maintained that Hegel's philosophy, properly understood and applied, is the very opposite of being Christianity's most powerful intellectual ally; rather, it is its enemy, who is the deadlier because he operates in the disguise of a philosophical theology. Hegel had declared that the idea of the unity of the divine and human, the idea of the God-Man, had rightfully been attached to Jesus of Nazareth. Strauss, on the other hand, considered such a transition from the philosophical idea to history, from what is universally valid to a single, concrete and contingent human being, arbitrary and intellectually disreputable. Maintaining with Hegel the truth and hence the necessity of the idea of the God-Man, he asserted, in opposition to Hegel, that this idea does not take on flesh and blood in one individual alone, in Jesus of Nazareth, but in the whole human race. Although this famous assertion is found only at the end of his book,

52

it already underlay his interpretation of the New Testament record, the substance of the book. Here Strauss demolished the dominant rationalistic and supernaturalistic interpretations of the New Testament record of Christ by running both interpretations smoothly through the mill of the Hegelian dialectic, proving from their contradictions that one cancelled out the other. He then developed his own view: the gospels are merely the picturesque garb for religious ideas which, after the death of Jesus, had been propagated among his followers and consolidated around his person. Although Strauss never doubted the historicity of Jesus, he did substitute for the Christ of supernaturalism—who is a divine miracle, without analogy anywhere in human history—the Christ of myth—an ordinary human being, to whom, however, after his death the high-flung notions of Christian supernaturalism had been attached. Strauss was the first to introduce the concept of "myth", which was clearly related to Hegel's *Vorstellung* as the inferior form in which religion possesses the truth, as a hermeneutical tool into the interpretation of the New Testament. The Tübingen church historian Ferdinand Christian Baur later wrote: "One must have lived at the time when Strauss's book appeared to have any idea of the commotion it provoked."[47] Baur could have added that the same year also witnessed the publication of his own *The Christian Gnosis* and Wilhelm Vatke's (1806-82) *The Religion of the Old Testament*, two books that combined in an equally radical fashion historical-critical scholarship and Hegel's philosophy.[48]

Two events, in particular, followed upon the publication of Strauss's book. The event of greatest significance, though, strangely enough, its full impact was to be felt only in the following century, was the dissolution of Hegel's school into the Hegelians of the Right and of the Left, into the Old and the Young Hegelians, distinctions which Strauss himself had introduced.[49] The Hegelians of the Left were bent on destroying Hegel's great synthesis of idealistic philosophy, orthodox Christianity and the established political and social order of the Prussian state. They attacked in particular the theistic interpretation of Hegel's philosophy of religion--Bruno Bauer (1809-82), for example, blew noisily (though

53

anonymously) in 1841 his *Trumpet of the Last Judgment against Hegel the Atheist and Anti-Christ*—as well as the conservative interpretation of Hegel's philosophy of right. As Karl Löwith (1897-1973) has shown, the opposition between the two camps of Hegel's followers had its roots in their different readings of the master's famous dictum: "What is actual, is rational; and what is rational, is actual."[50] Hegel's conservative disciples emphasized the rationality of all that is actual and hence generally contented themselves with the task of comprehending conceptually what is actual and must therefore be presumed to be rational. On the other hand, Hegel's radical disciples maintained that only what is rational ought to be actual; hence they were intent on changing whatever they found to be actual but not yet rational. While the Hegelians of the Right thus lent the weight of Hegel's philosophy to the support of the political, social and religious *status quo*, the Hegelians of the Left drew from the master's philosophy a revolutionary call for changing and even for destroying the existing order in state and society. From among the Young Hegelians, or the Hegelians of the Left, there soon came important contributions to the emergence of political and literary liberalism on the German scene. From among them there also arose in the course of time, through the work of men like Ludwig Feuerbach (1804-72), Karl Marx (1818-83) and Friedrich Engels (1820-95), and Sören Kierkegaard (1813-55), the movements of atheistic humanism, communism and existentialism.

The other event prompted by Strauss's sensational book was of narrower scope but had an immediate effect, and, furthermore, is of greater significance for the study of Schaff's formative years. Together with the germs of dissension that were nourished by the unavoidable friction between the Awakening, Schleiermacher's theology and Hegel's philosophy, Strauss's book hastened the division of German Protestantism into the three schools of theology that dominated the German scene until the advent of Ritschlianism: the "free" or "radical" theology (sometimes also called, though less felicitously, the "liberal" theology), the mediating theology and the confessional theology of resurgent Lutheran orthodoxy.

Schaff was to hear the dark rumblings caused by the dissolution of Hegel's school, but like most of his contemporaries he was only momentarily to be disturbed by this noise and was not to understand the fateful developments in German thought that led "From Hegel to Nietzsche"(Löwith). Some Hegelians of the Left, outside the narrower circle of professional theologians like Strauss, were to come to his attention and under his attack, for they represented, as Schaff later told his American readers, "the most artful and devious form of European Anti-Christianity." But he was quick to offer a disarmingly simple explanation of the negative products of contemporary German theology and philosophy: "Since the Germans are the most profound and erudite nation in the world, their unbelief therefore takes shape accordingly."[51] In his inaugural lecture at Mercersburg he had earlier exclaimed in youthful exuberance: "Only an archangel can become a devil."[52] Marx, Engels and Kierkegaard, however, were never to rise as significant historical figures above the horizon of his mental world, primarily, no doubt, because they were among those authors who, in Friedrich Nietzsche's (1844-1910) apt phrase, are "born posthumously."[53] Those developments that were at war with the prevailing spirit of the age, although viewed by Schaff with some apprehension, were in the end to him nothing but swiftly moving clouds, casting only a passing shadow on this new and glorious age, into which the mainstream of German culture and German Protestantism had entered and in which a smugly self-satisfied bourgeoisie was soon making itself comfortably at home. Indeed, to the end of his life Schaff remained a faithful, innocent child as well as an articulate spokesman of the nineteenth century's unbounded optimism. The exhilarating experience of the New World with its seemingly unlimited possibilities for human development, of course, was to invigorate still further Schaff's cheerfully optimistic mood and outlook.

The divisions of German Protestantism after 1835, however, were to affect immediately and lastingly the life of his mind and his career. As the following chapters will show, Schaff was to learn to fear the theologians among the Hegelians of the Left, in particular Strauss, but also Baur (though Baur is more properly assigned to the "center" of Hegel's school), representatives of what has here been called the "free" or "radical" theology. For these were the scholars who, in Schaff's words, were "eager to overthrow...the whole historical and dogmatic foundation of our saving faith." On the other hand, he was to enter fully into the discussions and quarrels of those theologians and churchmen whom he considered the friends of true Christianity—the representatives of the Awakening, most of the followers of Schleiermacher, the conservative Hegelians—who at this time began to group themselves into the two schools of the mediating and the Lutheran confessional theologies.[54]

Chapter 4

Tübingen - Halle - Berlin (1837-1841)

The Mediating Theology

In an earlier chapter I discussed the impact of the Württemberg Awakening on the formation of Schaff's religious outlook. That discussion must now be expanded in several directions. First of all, there was the pietists' shocked reaction to Strauss's *Life of Jesus Critically Examined*. Württemberg pietists considered it now their main task to do battle with the intellectual opponents of Christianity. Schiller, Schelling, Hegel, Hölderlin, all of them Württembergers, had gained their cultural prominence and fame only after they had gone "abroad;" their attitudes toward Christianity, dubious or even dangerous as they appeared, were therefore of no immediate concern. It was otherwise with Strauss. After all, he had written his critical examination of the New Testament record of the life of Jesus in the very heart of pious Württemberg, as a *Repetent* (tutor-supervisor) at the venerable *Stift* in Tübingen, which is the dormitory where many of Württemberg's candidates for the Protestant ministry have been housed since 1537.[1] The pietistic response to Strauss's slashing attack against the traditional interpretation of Christian origins was quick in coming. In 1836 the *Christenbote*, the house organ of Württemberg pietism, began publishing a series of articles that sounded a shrill clarion-call to warn the faithful of the poisonous contents of Strauss's book. Nothing less than the forces of the kingdom of God and of Anti-Christ were said to have been joined in battle. The *Christenbote* also claimed that as pernicious a view of the New Testament as Strauss had offered could only have sprung from a selfish, morally depraved, evil disposition. It was a vituperative attack against Strauss, published anonymously and continued into 1837, whose author, as soon became known, was none other than Sixtus Carl Kapff, the Kornthal pastor. (He later regretted the tone of these articles as not worthy of a Christian.)[2] Schaff took his first cue from the Württemberg pietists' assault on Strauss, as in the following years and even to the end of his life he, too, would wage an unremitting war against "Straussian infidelity."

Another point, important for Schaff's development, can best be stated with the help of Carl Heinrich Stirm's (1799-1873) *Apology of Christianity in Letters for Cultured Readers.*[3] Published in 1836, it was read with great approval by the "awakened," Tholuck even claiming ten years later that this book offered the only defense and explanation of the Christian faith he could recommend.[4] Stirm has been well characterized as being "among the stragglers of supernaturalistic apologetics."[5] His book invites careful attention, because Schaff read it thoroughly in the year of its publication, as his extensive excerpts from it show.[6] Indeed, many of the book's ideas retained a permanent place in his thought, although, to be sure, most of those ideas were in the air in those circles in which Schaff then and later moved. Lucidly and persuasively written, Stirm's book demonstrates how the more cultured among the adherents of the Awakening attempted at that time to combine the piety of the Awakening with some of the new and intellectually exciting currents in German theology.

As one might expect, Stirm insisted that the Christian faith "is not so much a matter of the intellect as of the heart."[7] For, according to its very nature, faith is "a deed of the will, a reflex of the heart."[8] Those who seek religious truth must therefore be conducted to "the inner, life-giving, saving power" of Christianity, that is, they must experience Christ's saving presence, their own spiritual rebirth. This experience will then become the bulwark in which the Christian will be protected against every assault launched against his faith by modern thought. For "even if he were incapable of refuting all the arguments of the reason against his faith, the foundation of his faith would remain unshaken, because it is built upon his innermost and very own consciousness."[9] The devout were told that the truth of Christianity is sufficiently and adequately demonstrated by its power to convert sinners and to give them the Spirit-induced experience of Christ's presence, which is their salvation. The Awakening never tired of echoing Paul's words that the Christian speech and proclamation do not consist "in plausible words of wisdom, but in demonstration of the Spirit and of power" (1 Cor. 2:4). In short, the Awakening turned the experience of spiritual rebirth into an epistemological principle that was no longer subject to any higher authority; it declared the "converted heart" to be the prerequisite for understanding Christianity itself and even the final judge in deciding the great intellectual issues that stood between Christianity and its contemporary opponents.

Schaff made this point of view wholly his own. He immediately applied it --it was the obvious occasion--to Strauss's *Life of Jesus*, as is evidenced by some of the notes he wrote at Tübingen. To the question, What is the best authority against Strauss?, he replied: "An honest soul filled with Christ, whose life of faith hid with God shows that Christianity is not an idea hanging in the air, but that forth from the prophet of Nazareth there continues to go power which overcomes the world and also life for all sympathetic hearts."[10] And shortly before leaving Tübingen he confided into his diary that during the past year Christ "has been wonderfully present,...proving to me indeed that he lives and that his holy Gospel is not a garland of myths which abortive effort has sought to bind around his brow, and keeping me from erring in the labyrinth of the wisdom of the age."[11]

But after having urged the faithful to entrench themselves in the bulwark of their experience of Christ's saving presence, almost in the same breath Stirm maintained (turning to another metaphor) that the ship of faith, laden with the inviolable freight of the personal experience of salvation, must sail "with the bright light of reason" and not "in the twilight of exuberant emotions."[12] And he went on to claim that it was "the urgent demand of the present time in which the intelligence has made such great progress, that the heart's beliefs be justified before reason's bar, that religion and science, reason and faith be ever more intimately reconciled with one another."[13] In the 1830s even some of the cultured

59

adherents of the Württemberg Awakening began to aim at that grand synthesis of faith and reason, theology and philosophy, Christianity and the higher culture of the time, which was to characterize so prominently the era dominated by Schleiermacher and Hegel. True, Stirm insisted that the Christian faith is irrational in the sense that it draws its ultimate justification from the heart's experience of the divine; but he also maintained, and no less forcefully, that faith, far from being anti-rational, eagerly enter into an enriching alliance with the best elements of the contemporary intellectual culture. Stirm's *Apology* itself was greatly indebted to Schleiermacher's theology. It was to be the biographical and historical significance of this insistence that it enabled many of the "awakened," who went on to study for the ministry, to make an easier and safer transition into the mainstream of German academic theology than might otherwise have been the case. For them, as Schleiermacher had hoped, the Awakening became in fact "but a transition to a worthier freedom of the spiritual life."[14] This was certainly to be true of young Schaff. Stirm's book must have been a welcome bridge for him that enabled him to leave, with greater ease than one might have expected, the pietistic surroundings of Kornthal and Stuttgart and enter confidently into the bracing air of the German university.

Finally, Stirm's book holds still another significance for Schaff's life. For here, in chapter 6, he very likely encountered for the first time the novel ecumenical notion that Roman Catholicism and Protestantism, whatever the regrettable shortcomings of the Roman Catholic Church, represent chronologically sequential and legitimate stages in the history of Christianity. Moreover, they are, Stirm insisted, to a certain degree even now already complementary manifestations of the Christian faith. He even was bold enough to envision a future when Catholicism and Protestantism will become one in a higher kind of Christian unity, provided that both will have shed their remaining imperfections. The following year Schaff might well have read in the *Christenbote* (January 15, 1837) the letter of a German immigrant in Ohio that mentioned a seminary of the German Reformed Church at "Merilsburg." Though horribly misspelled, here then, so early in Schaff's life, a letter in a journal and Stirm's book had first joined together Mercersburg and the ecumenical ideal of "evangelical catholicism"!

The expectations and hopes, but also some of the fears and apprehensions, with which Schaff began his university studies, are indicated in the advice he later gave to American students of German theology:

> To plunge boldly into the whirlpool and to swim through it, not merely to sip of the cup of doubt, but to empty it to the dregs. He who studies German theology and philosophy only superficially can very possibly harm his simple, childlike faith; but he who strives with it with manly courage and labors through the long and complicated process of probing down to the very depths of our most sacred faith will come out of the struggle more firmly grounded in orthodoxy than ever. [15]

Tübingen (1837-1839)

Schaff would fondly remember Tübingen as "a town of small size and hilly streets, but beautifully located on the banks of the Neckar, 18 miles distant from Stuttgart."[16] Many years later he claimed that he never lived at a place where there was more intense study than at Tübingen's university in this lovely setting. Following a traditional curricular pattern, during the first year of study he was introduced to the problems of philosophy from Kant to Hegel. This was done with the proverbial Swabian thoroughness, for, as Schaff complained, the student almost became convinced that "the weal of the world depended upon the abstruse categories of metaphysics."[17]

Once past this hurdle, Tübingen proved to be a most exciting place, for the opposition of theological schools was at this time more pronounced here than at any other German university. In 1818 a Roman Catholic divinity school had been added to the venerable Protestant divinity school. The great literary discussion between Johann Adam Möhler (1796-1838), the dominant figure on the Roman

Catholic faculty, and Ferdinand Christian Baur had by 1837 already run its course. Möhler had published his *Symbolics or Presentation of the Dogmatic Opposition of Catholics and Protestants According to their Public Confessional Writings* in 1832; he had left Tübingen in 1835, three years before his untimely death.[18] The second and final edition of Baur's reply to Möhler, *The Opposition of Catholicism and Protestantism According to the Principles and Major Dogmas of the Two Doctrinal Types*, had appeared in 1836.[19] Since Möhler represented a quest for the renewal of the church the spirit and aims of which show several striking similarities to the Mercersburg Theology that Schaff and his colleague John Williamson Nevin (1803-86) later developed, one is tempted to assume that Möhler already influenced Schaff during his two years at Tübingen. However, there is no evidence supporting this assumption; Schaff obviously read Möhler only later in the course of his German studies. But when at Mercersburg he surprised and even shocked his fellow-Protestants by claiming that "the true evangelical Christian ..... often feels tempted to join hands with the pious Catholic, in opposition to modern scepticism and infidelity," he was, one can be sure, thinking of someone like the Roman Catholic Möhler and of a modern sceptic like Baur,[20] though, to be sure, not the Baur who in his reply to Möhler had made himself the skillful expositor of the Reformation and Protestant orthodox dogmatics, but the Baur who by 1837 had become well known for his radical historical-critical scholarship and his Hegelianism.

When Schaff later wrote that his years at Tübingen fell "in a period of extraordinary intellectual activity and commotion, which left a permanent impress upon the theological development of Germany and the whole Protestant world,"[21] he had internal Protestant differences in mind. For here at Tübingen he first confronted the question that was nearly all-important at that time: whether and to what extent theology may have recourse to Hegel's philosophy? It must be remembered that most of Hegel's writings were published posthumously: his *Philosophy of Religion* and the second edition of his *Phenomenology* in 1832, his *History of Philosophy* in 1833 and his *Philosophy of History* in 1837 (the very year when Schaff began his university studies). After Strauss had returned from his trip to Berlin in 1831 (where he had learned the news of Hegel's sudden death in Schleiermacher's study, wounding Schleiermacher with his spontaneous response: "But for his sake I had come to Berlin"), his lectures on Hegel's philosophy had attracted ever larger and enthusiastic student audiences. Hegel's influence on Baur was for the first time clearly noticeable in Baur's *Christian Gnosis* of 1835. Although the authorities had forced Strauss to give up his teaching position at the university only a few weeks after the publication of the first volume of his *Life of Jesus*, Hegel's philosophy by that time held sway over the university. Indeed, Baur could assert that in the late 1830s "at no German university was its reputation more firmly established and more widespread than at Tübingen."[22] This is confirmed by Schaff's remark that, while he was at Tübingen, "the philosophy of Hegel ruled without a successful rival among the students and filled them with enthusiasm for absolute knowledge."[23]

A second and equally portentous question also caused internal strife at Tübingen's Protestant divinity school at that time: how is the new historical-critical method to be applied in the study of the origins and history of Christianity? According to Schaff, faculty and students were aligned in "two hostile camps" that he dubbed felicitously the "critical" and the "evangelical."[24] It is obvious that Schaff lost no time in joining the "evangelical" camp, and of this camp he remained a lifelong member. The "critical" camp was gathered around the dominant figure on the faculty, Ferdinand Christian Baur, the head of the "Tübingen School," the master of the historical-critical method, very likely the greatest theologian between Schleiermacher and Albrecht Ritschl (1822-89).[25] Although the mass of his enormous literary output was to appear after 1840, in the late 1830s he had already distinguished himself (apart from his controversy with Möhler and some other writings) by publishing the results of his sensational researches into the New Testament. During Schaff's second year at Tübingen, Baur brought out his *Christian Doctrine of Reconciliation in its Historical Development from the Oldest to the Most Recent Times*, which a few years later was followed by the three volumes of his *Christian Doctrine of the Trinity and the Incarnation of God in its Historical Development* (1841-43).[26] Thus, the "Tübingen School" of Baur and his disciples, of whom Strauss was the most prominent one, had already shown itself to be a major voice of the "free" or "radical" theology: independent of all dogmatic presuppositions in its search for truth, dedicated solely to the strictest application of the critical tools of historical scholarship to the sources and history of Christianity, and, in pursuing these goals, employing boldly the categories of Hegel's philosophy of Spirit. In particular, Baur insisted on treating the biblical source of Christianity historically, that is, as a part of the natural flow of events and not as a divine miracle interrupting the historical sequence. Furthermore, his researches into the New Testament led him to assign most of the canonical writings to the post-apostolic era; he accepted, for instance, only the first four letters of Paul as authentic. He also had shown the necessity of interpreting the apostolic writings as factors in the controversy between Petrine and Pauline tendencies in the early church, a controversy that in the second century had issued in the formation of the Catholic Church. In investigating the history of Christian doctrines, he had begun to "speculate" brilliantly by applying the Hegelian concept of dialectic development to the historical data and by making the pursuit of the Spirit's inner movement and development in these data the primary object of historical scholarship. Schaff heard Baur's lectures on Symbolics from the Point of View of the Lutheran-Protestant Church and on the History of Christian Doctrine.

Schaff, like his pietistic friends always inclined to seek the root of wrong doctrine in wrong living, was somewhat puzzled by Baur's imposing personality. He found Baur's character beyond reproach, his integrity, sincerity and diligence as a scholar and teacher inspiring, his learning truly impressive--all qualities that Schaff, though somewhat grudgingly, came to admire in his teacher. Nevertheless, he considered it a frightful anomaly that so radical a theologian as Baur, by his state-controlled appointment to the theological faculty, should have been entrusted with the training of future ministers of the Church. He regarded Baur's call to Tübingen's divinity school as one of the unfortunate consequences of the fateful alliance between the German Protestant churches and the state. He most likely had the Kornthal congregation with its freedom from state control and Baur's professorship in mind, when later, in the United States, he claimed that ever since his student years he had an "insuperable aversion" against any kind of church order "that limits the independence and the dignity of the church."[27] One may safely argue that Schaff was incapable of admitting the force of Baur's counter-blast against his pietistic accusers:

> [It is said] that the more recent speculative theology, because it deviates in so many respects from biblical Christianity, that is, from the letter of the Bible, abolishes the foundation of practical religiousness.....What is this other than the arrogant pietistic prejudice that everything that belongs to the calling of the practicing clergyman can be pursued only in pietistic fashion?[28]

Baur's domination of the faculty, however, did not go unchallenged. Heinrich Georg August Ewald (1803-75), the Old Testament professor (since 1838), fiery, loquacious, gifted, outspokenly opposed Baur. Schaff heard his lectures on Genesis and on the Theology of the Old Testament, and in his "Autobiographical Reminiscences" related more anecdotes of this professor than of any other of his teachers. The head of the "evangelical" camp at Tübingen, however, was Christian Friedrich Schmid (1794-1852), who represented a moderate biblical supernaturalism and attracted all those students who were revolted by Baur's critical scholarship and Hegelianism. Schaff was convinced that Baur had been prevented from causing even greater damage among the students by the "excellent, devout as well as erudite" Schmid,[29] who, it must be added, published little--as Schaff put it, he was "modest to a fault"[30]--and was no match for Baur as a scholar. His *Biblical Theology* appeared posthumously in 1853 and was later also published in an English translation.[31] Schaff was especially impressed by Schmid's distinction of the four apostolic doctrinal types of James, Peter, Paul and John, the more so as he later encountered a similar interpretation of the New Testament in August Neander's writings. He sincerely believed that Schmid's (and Neander's) explication of these doctrinal types was, in opposition to the Baur school, "a triumphant and profoundly scientific defense of the historical nature and the divine origin of Apostolic Christianity."[32] The Schmid-Neander distinction of apostolic doctrinal types will later play a prominent role in Schaff's own understanding of the history of the apostolic church and even in his ecumenical theology.

Among the circle of students gathered around Schmid Schaff struck up a friendship with the gifted Heinrich Wilhelm Josias Thiersch (1817-85). After having completed his course of studies elsewhere, Thiersch had came to Tübingen for further work in the winter semester 1837/38. Already then Schaff detected "a visionary side" to his friend's piety.[33] Indeed, a few years later Thiersch ended a promising academic career, when he joined the newly founded Catholic Apostolic Church (more commonly known as Irvingism, after its founder Edward Irving [1792-1834]), which Schaff later esteemed so highly that he called it "the most churchly, catholic, hierarchical, sacerdotal and liturgical" of all Protestant sects.[34] He continued to correspond with Thiersch, his "esteemed and beloved friend and fellow-student," even in Mercersburg,[35] and eagerly learned from the Irvingite liturgy as he prepared the controversial New Liturgy of the German Reformed Church.[36] One should note an interesting parallelism in the early scholarly publications of these two fellow-students, which might suggest a critical comparison of their development and theological program, since it would call attention both to common features and pronounced differences and thus throw additional light on Schaff's own distinctive theological contributions.[37]

Of still greater influence on Schaff than either Baur or Schmid, if we can trust Schaff's own words, was the young Isaak August Dorner (1809-84). A tutor (*Repetent*) at the *Stift* since 1834 and a one-time student of Baur, he had been called in 1838, against Baur's will, to a vacant chair in the faculty. In this position he stayed for only one year, when Schaff had the good fortune of hearing his first lectures on Dogmatics and Apologetics. He was apparently one of only five students who took this course.[38] According to Schaff, Dorner labored "to prove the harmony of Christian theology and sound philosophy" and made "the dialectics of Schleiermacher and Hegel subservient to the defense of the truths of revelation, while Dr. Baur employed his genius and learning, and the same categories of Hegel, for the opposite purposes of undermining the historical foundations of Christianity."[39] Thus Dorner succeeded, in Schaff's estimate, in satisfying "the wants of those advanced students who wished to master the speculative and critical problems of the age without losing their Christian faith."[40] Schaff also praised Dorner's *History of the Development of the Doctrine of the Person of Christ* (1839), because, once again, it was "the most triumphant refutation of Baur's investigation in the same field."[41]

In summary, we can say that at Tübingen Schaff was repelled by Baur's critical scholarship and Hegelian "speculation" in the study of the origins of Christianity, because it seemed to him to destroy the supernatural foundation of Christianity. But neither was Schaff entirely satisfied with Schmid's biblical theology, at least in the sense that he desired his own theology to be more than a systematic explication of the biblical world of thought, important as biblical Christianity was as a foundation for all theology. Dorner showed Schaff the necessity as well as the possibility of developing a theology that held on to the supernatural elements of the faith of Schaff's youth, but was also scientific, that is, "critical" and "speculative", by opening itself to the historical temper of the times and by trying to absorb and utilize selectively the stimulating and exciting new thoughts of Schleiermacher and Hegel. In this way Dorner was the first to introduce Schaff, already at Tübingen, to the aims of the mediating theology (*Vermittlungstheologie*), which in due time would become Schaff's own position. It was in the spirit of such mediation that Schaff allowed himself to be crucially influenced by Baur at Tübingen in at least one important respect. From Baur he took over Hegel's concept of dialectical development. As Schaff wrote, Baur "gave me the first idea of historical development or of a constant and progressive flow of thought in the successive ages of the church."[42] Hegel's idealistic philosophy of history was to shape permanently Schaff's understanding of the history of Christianity.

Halle (1839/40)

Following the German tradition of studying at more than one university, Schaff spent the winter-semester 1839/40 at Halle. He found Halle to be "one of the ugliest and most repulsive cities of Germany, full of old-fashioned uncomfortable dwellings, narrow crooked streets, wretched muddy pavements, gloomy air, and intolerable smell arising from peat bogs and salt springs."[43] The city's great attraction, however, was the university. In the late 1830s its ornaments were the historian Heinrich Leo (1799-1878), the philosopher Johann Eduard Erdmann (1805-92) and the theologian Friedrich August Gottreu Tholuck. Once, under August Hermann Francke, the university had been the academic citadel of pietism; two generations later, under Johann Salomo Semler (1725-91), the divinity school had become famous as a stronghold of rationalism. Tholuck, who in 1826 had been forced upon the predominantly rationalistic faculty by the Prussian Minister of Public Worship and Education, had almost single-handedly managed to give Halle its latest and well-deserved reputation as a stronghold of the Awakening. At the time of Schaff's arrival only Julius August Ludwig Wegscheider (1771-1849) and Justus Genesius (1786-1842), the lexicographer of Old Testament Hebrew, still represented the rationalistic theology of a bygone age, though they were lecturing to no more than a handful of students. Tholuck had through skillful maneuvers in 1839 prevented Baur's call to Halle and succeeded in winning Julius Müller (1801-78) as his colleague. Both men had been "awakened," Tholuck by the devout Baron Hans Ernst von Kottwitz (1757-1843) in Berlin, Müller by Tholuck himself. While in Berlin, both had kept close to the church historian August Neander. They had suspected Schleiermacher of not having the true faith, while Schleiermacher had disliked these youth for their somewhat tumultuous return to the narrow confines and pious language of supernaturalism. Tholuck had won early and lasting fame through his *Doctrine of Sin and of the Reconciler, or the True Consecration of the Sceptic*, a brilliantly effusive and inspiring account of his conversion.[44] As a teacher, he had developed an uncanny ability to attract, guide and inspire students, always more concerned about their growth in Christian piety than about their scholarship. He was the missionary of the Awakening to the academic world, the counselor to students perhaps without a rival in the history of the German university. Well-equipped with letters of introduction from the "evangelical" camp in Württemberg, Schaff had the good fortune of being at once employed by Tholuck as his *amanuensis* (an academic and social assistant) and of being offered lodging in Tholuck's house. Since Tholuck, a brilliant linguist, also drew foreign students to Halle, Schaff met in his house his first American, George L. Prentiss (1816-1903), who became his lifelong friend and later his colleague at Union Theological Seminary in New York. Other distinguished Americans who studied with Tholuck at various times were Edward Robinson (1794-1863), Charles Hodge (1797-1878), Henry B. Smith (1815-77) and Edwards A. Park (1808-1900).

At Halle, the question of the relationship of Hegel's philosophy to Christianity was again the great topic of discussion. Here three options for following Hegel were well represented. (1) Arnold Ruge (1802-80), later a radical social activist, edited, since 1838, the *Hallische Jahrbücher für deutsche Kunst und Wissenschaft*, the major organ of the Hegelians of the Left. (2) Johann Eduard Erdmann, the philosopher, had published in 1837 his *Lectures on Faith and Knowledge as an Introduction to Dogmatics and the Philosophy of Religion*, in which he had argued persuasively and in lucid prose (he was one of the few Hegelians who did not murder the German language) that Hegel's philosophy is the crowning consummation and the most faithful intellectual ally of the Christian faith. Erdmann, as Schaff reported, "lectured without notes in the most fluent style and made the metaphysical speculations of Hegel as clear as day light."[45] (3) Hermann Ulrici (1806-84), another philosopher (in whose house Prentiss was staying), edited the *Zeitschrift für Philosophie und spekulative Theologie*, which

Immanuel Hermann Fichte (1796-1879), the great philosopher's son, had founded, also in 1837. These men, charging Hegel with pantheism, thought it nevertheless possible to develop his idealistic philosophy in the direction of an unequivocal Christian theism. Hence they were known as "speculative theists."

It was precisely during Schaff's months at Halle that even Tholuck publicly entered the debate about Hegel's philosophy. It is worth remembering that the Awakening and the idealistic philosophy had at first sought each other as allies in opposition to rationalism, the common foe. While Schleiermacher had strongly resisted Tholuck's call to Halle, Hegel had warmly supported it and had proposed a *pereat* ("may it perish") to Halle's rationalism at the party in celebration of Tholuck's appointment. Now, in 1840, Tholuck flatly asserted: "Rationalism is a dead dog, Hegelianism prowls around like a roaring lion."[46] The "roaring lion" in 1 Peter 5:8, one remembers, refers to the devil. In the Preface for 1840 in the *Literarische Anzeiger für christliche Theologie und Wissenschaft*, which he edited until 1849, Tholuck tried to defend himself against the suspicion apparently alive in some theological circles that he was a closet Hegelian. For the first time he now found publicly fault with Hegel himself, even though he showed the same double-edged and ambiguous attitude toward Hegel's and Schleiermacher's new thought that we had already noticed in Stirm's *Apology*. Tholuck, of course, also regarded the "rebirth" of the individual as the prerequisite of all religious knowledge. But he did by no means want to limit theology to the role of merely analysing and describing the religious affections, as he thought Schleiermacher had wrongly done, for theology must also present the content of the religious affections "as something necessary to the thinking mind." Theology, Tholuck boldly asserted, "'can therefore not do without speculation." It was his right as a Christian theologian to apply even to Hegel's philosophy Paul's words (1 Cor. 3:22), "'All are yours,' provided that I do not forget what follows, 'And you are Christ's'."[47] In short, even Tholuck found it worth his time to "speculate," on the assumption, of course, that Hegel's "speculation" could be yoked to the task of explaining and enlarging intellectually the piety of the Awakening. But

70

wherever Tholuck found Hegel's philosophy to be destructive of the Christian faith and piety, he brusquely rejected it. In his critique of 1840 he rejected, in particular, the "pantheistic" and "panlogistic" features of the Hegelian system. He accused Hegel of having tried to destroy Christian theism and morality, for he had sadly failed to ascribe to God a free, self-conscious personality and to conceive of the human being as a free, moral agent. Tholuck equally rejected Hegel's "panlogistic" tenet that history can be fully reconstructed through the application to the past of the dialectics of speculative thought. Hegel had misused philosophy by arrogantly obscuring the individually diverse forms of human life with the conceptual net of his speculative thought. Nevertheless, even Tholuck whole-heartedly embraced Hegel's concept of dialectical development as a means, if properly applied, for achieving a true and complete understanding of the history of Christianity.

Small wonder that Hegel had already in 1828 characterized Tholuck as merely another "representative of the twaddle about pantheism."[48] And the young and keen-eyed Albrecht Ritschl, who arrived as a student at Halle two years after Schaff, would later report: "Tholuck is scientifically incommensurable. I have heard him talk like formerly the *Hallische Jahrbücher*, and then again like a Herrnhuter."[49] Schaff, however, found no reason whatsoever to quarrel with Tholuck's position. Indeed, the same ideas stated so forcefully in the *Literarische Anzeiger* in 1840, will constantly recur in his later writings.

Similar ideas were expounded by Müller, whom Schaff thought to be "less widely learned and brilliant, but more deep and solid" than Tholuck.[50] He had just published the first volume of his great monograph *The Christian Doctrine of Sin* (1839), in which he labored to show that the stark reality of sin cannot be comprehended as a somehow necessary element in the seamless synthesis of divine and human life and thought, as Schleiermacher and Hegel, he claimed, had attempted to do.[51] Nevertheless, Müller himself "speculated" no less brilliantly about the nature of sin, only, as he believed, with a firmer biblical and experiential footing. Thus Müller's book was really an attempt to mediate between the dialectics of Schleiermacher and Hegel and the piety of the Awakening, even as the book displayed the Awakening's characteristic uneasiness toward the thought of these two men. Schaff, who took Müller's course in Dogmatics, continued under his guidance his studies in systematic theology.

Berlin (1840-1841)

Founded in 1810, the University of Berlin had quickly acquired the well-deserved reputation of being Germany's foremost institution of higher learning. The brilliance of its faculty and its location in the heart of Prussia's capital were attractions that Schaff, like so many other young men at that time, was unable to resist for long. With Tholuck's blessing and in his and his wife's company, Schaff traveled by carriage from Halle to Berlin during Easter Week of 1840. The next semester a fellow-Swiss arrived in Berlin, Jacob Burckhardt, who was destined to become an even greater historian than Schaff, and a year and a half later Sören Kierkegaard and Friedrich Engels also were students in Berlin. Engels was to remark enthusiastically in 1841 that at the University of Berlin "there are daily spoken words to which the boundaries of Prussia, yea of all the German-speaking countries cannot set a stop."[52] Someone else has observed that in these years "the elite of young men studying theology" flocked to Berlin "for the stimulating ideas that were to remain with them all their lives."[53] How true this was, certainly also for Schaff! For he was to encounter in Berlin stimulating ideas that were to remain with him all his life, and in his own way he would prove the truth of Engels's observation, when he would bear many of the words spoken at Prussia's great university far beyond the boundaries of Germany, even across a vast ocean to America. The various departments of the university had brilliantly capable scholars--the historian Leopold Ranke (1795-1886), the geographer Carl Ritter (1779-1859), the jurist Friedrich Karl von Savigny (1779-1861), the professor of physics and philosophy Henrik Steffens (1773-1845), a follower of

Schelling, and, coming in 1841, Schelling himself. Schaff heard lectures by most of these men and eagerly sought to make their acquaintance.

In the theological faculty Schleiermacher and Hegel were ably represented by disciples who taught in their spirit. Philip Konrad Marheineke (1780-1846), a Hegelian of the Right, continued the master's influence. Many considered him at this time "the head of the school, which, similar to Mohammed's disciples after the prophet's death, had gathered around his widow."[54] Hegel's widow, a faithful follower of the Awakening, did her best to convince her many visitors, Schaff among them, that her husband, were he still alive, would have had nothing to do with the Hegelians of the Left. She assured Schaff that her husband was a good Christian, though she admitted that he refused to attend with her the church of her favorite preacher, Johannes Evangelista Gossner (1773-1858) at the Bethlehem Church. One Sunday morning, she told Schaff, he excused himself with the words: "My dear child, thinking too is worship."[55] Henry B. Smith, later Schaff's colleague at New York's Union Theological Seminary, similarly reassured his parents in 1839 that Mrs. Hegel spoke of her husband "as a Christian, said that in him there was no contradiction or strife between his philosophy and his faith, that he led her from rationalism to embrace the doctrines of Christianity, and showed me some verses written by him expressive of most pious confidence in Christ."[56] While Schaff frequently visited Frau Hegel (she was the aunt of Tholuck's wife), he had apparently little contact with Marheineke, an uninspiring, somewhat pompous lecturer, and had little use for his ponderous Hegelian theology. Marheineke, however, gave a farewell party for Schaff shortly before his departure for the United States.

Much more impressed was Schaff by August Twesten (1789-1876), Schleiermacher's successor, who derived, like his great teacher, the Christian doctrines from the religious self-consciousness, but emphasized, unlike Schleiermacher, as Schaff was quick and pleased to notice, the doctrinal aspects of the Christian faith, "and, what was still more important, of the orthodox faith."[57] Indeed, Twesten derived from the religious self-consciousness what was essentially the dogmatic system of seventeenth-century Lutheran orthodoxy. Moreover, in the spirit of the Prussian Union, the merger of the Lutheran and Reformed Churches effected by royal fiat in 1817, he demonstrated the essential agreement of Lutheran orthodoxy with the doctrinal position of the Reformed Church. Schaff later characterized Twesten's theology most felicitously: "The scholastic Lutheran orthodoxy of the seventeenth century made fluid and modified by Schleiermacher's scientific influence and by the spirit of the Prussian Union."[58] Schaff also drew close to the court preacher Gerhard Friedrich Abraham Strauss (1786-1863) and to Franz Theremin (1780-1846), who both taught practical theology in the spirit of the Awakening. Two other members of that distinguished faculty, however, made the most profound impression on Schaff: August Neander, the church historian, and Ernst Wilhelm Hengstenberg (1802-69), the professor of Old Testament and the editor of the influential *Evangelische Kirchenzeitung*, who was the leader of the "evangelical" camp in Berlin. But since the significance of these two men for Schaff's theological development manifested itself fully only after the conclusion of his course of studies, a more detailed discussion of them will be left to the next chapter.

Hengstenberg obtained at once for Schaff the position of tutor to the only son of the widowed Baroness Sophia von Kröcher, a position that provided Schaff with the necessary financial security and allowed him sufficient leisure for the completion of his studies. He spent the summer of 1840 at the castle of the von Kröchers at Cöthen near Berlin and the following winter in Berlin. In the spring of 1841 he completed the required course of studies with the presentation of his dissertation to the Berlin faculty. Already in Tübingen he had set his mind on an academic career in theology, and in pursuing this goal he had received the encouragement of Schmid, Tholuck, Müller, Neander, Twesten and Hengstenberg, a galaxy of names that was convincing proof of young Schaff's scholarly attainments and of his success in gaining the support of a truly distinguished group of scholars. Because of time pressures--he wanted to take his degree before starting out in June on an extended Italian journey with Frau von

74

Kröcher and her son--he could submit in February only the first seven proof sheets (about two thirds) of his dissertation. The faculty found them adequate. His examination took place a few weeks later in the presence of Marheineke, Hengstenberg, Neander and Strauss, with Twesten presiding. Schaff passed it with the grade: *non sine laude* (not without praise).[59]

Schaff's dissertation, *The Sin Against the Holy Spirit*, deserves our special attention, for it reveals for the first time the character of his scholarship and the nature of his theological position, it may even yield some clues as to his future development.[60] The youthful author, barely twenty-two years old, had tackled a subject that enjoyed at the time a certain popularity. Immediately preceding Schaff, a number of other theologians, among them Tholuck, had offered their answers to what is no doubt one of the more vexing problems of New Testament exegesis: just what is the meaning of Matt. 12:31-33, the passage that speaks of the unforgivable sin against the Holy Spirit?

One is immediately struck by the author's youthful eagerness to display his learning and the encyclopedic range of his interests. The work, dedicated to Theremin, has both an exegetical and a dogmatic-ethical section, a chapter of pastoral suggestions and an "Historical Appendix Regarding the Sad End of Francesco Spiera." Schaff was obviously more interested in the dogmatic-ethical than the exegetical aspect of his subject, for the first section is only one-half the length of the second section. Moreover, he failed to offer a thorough exegesis of Matt. 12:31-33; instead, he was content to arrive at his own conclusions by comparing critically the exegetical investigations of his predecessors--a characteristic methodology that will distinguish all of his later contributions to biblical exegesis as well. Twesten, who missed in the dissertation "a method that satisfies the demands of the grammatical-historical interpretation," very properly took exception to Schaff's approach.[61]

Before Schaff launched into the discussions of the dogmatic-ethical section, he presented, on three pages, a theological program that was of a disarmingly straightforward simplicity.[62] He acknowledged three authoritative sources in theology--the religious self-consciousness, Holy Scripture and the tradition of the church--and he welcomed philosophy as an important ally. He explained that he desired to conduct his discussion "from the point of view of the Christian consciousness, but certainly not from a purely subjective consciousness that might even go so far as to elevate itself above objective Christianity." How sadly Strauss, for instance, had gone astray by taking his stand in the purely subjective religious self-consciousness! The theologian must therefore both acknowledge the New Testament as "the inexhaustible source" of the Christian consciousness and recognize the doctrinal tradition of the church as his "mother." As to the relationship of Scripture and tradition, Schaff maintained that the tradition of the church is "the explication of the doctrinal content deposited in fresh immediacy in Holy Scripture, which explication approximates ever more closely and faithfully, even though it moves through opposites and hence through one-sided positions, the absolute knowledge of the objective truth." Schaff then assigned an indispensable role to philosophy in theology in terms that are likely to strike us as naive. If the dogmatic theologian knows what is to his advantage, he will avail himself "gratefully" of all of philosophy's "true advances as a means of confirming revelation." For reason and revelation are by no means absolute opposites. Rather, "they sound like harps, occasionally out of time, but never out of tune," and together they are moving toward that goal where, as Schaff contended in a self-confident and characteristic reversal of the relationship that Hegel had posited between the two, "reason will be totally transfigured by the light of revelation and the one will be perfectly comprehended by the other." All of these ideas Schaff will develop repeatedly and more fully in his later writings.

To what specific results these theological principles led Schaff he showed by his subsequent treatment of various questions that occurred to him in connection with the concept of an unforgivable sin. Of particular interest to us is Schaff's attempt to prove that the concept of an unforgivable sin calls for an understanding of human freedom that is possible only from the point of view of Christian theism. Here he eagerly involved himself in a detailed discussion of

Hegel's alleged pantheism. Frau Hegel had apparently not succeeded in persuading him of the entirely Christian character of her late husband's philosophy, for he, too, asserted that Hegel was a pantheist. He objected in particular to Hegel's seemingly pantheistic dictum: "God is not God without the world."[63] Still, it was far from his mind to reject out of hand the categories of Hegel's philosophy. On the contrary, he viewed in particular as a true philosophical advance Hegel's notion that "all life is essentially process, mediation of distinct moments," development through antithetical stages.[64] He even agreed that this notion must be applied to the Absolute, to God. But he cleverly managed to avoid Hegel's alleged pantheism by assigning the second person of the Trinity to the place that the world held in Hegel's scheme. That is to say, he combined the Hegelian notion of life as process and development with the doctrine of the ontological Trinity, thereby demonstrating, no doubt to his own great satisfaction, that he, too, was capable of "speculating"--an academic obsession of those years--even as he upheld and explained the traditional theistic and trinitarian positions. We should note that Schaff's position in this discussion resembles most closely that of the speculative theists and their theological allies, Tholuck and Müller, at Halle.

Another question that drew Schaff's interest was related to the statement in Matt. 12:32 that the sin against the Holy Spirit will not be forgiven "either in this age or in the age to come." Schaff polemically denied that this statement proves the Catholic doctrine of purgatory. But he favored the novel doctrine of a "middle state" (*Mittelzustand*). If only "from compassion," he protested against the assertion that "all those yearning spirits in the pagan world who put innumerable Christians to shame" should perish. Dividing all of humanity into three groups--the believers, the undecided and the unbelievers--he had all of them enter a middle state between death and the Last Judgement. There, however, the possibility of conversion is left open only to the undecided, to all those who had not already here on earth been confronted by the Gospel, "particularly pagans and Turks, and those Christians who belong in the category of pagans, e. g., the

Armenians and Abyssinians."[65] In entire accord with the Reformation principle of *sola gratia*, the undecided, during their sojourn in the middle state, however, will be saved only by faith in Christ. Little did he know that a few years later, on another continent, these statements about a "middle state" would bring down upon him the charge of heresy.

The most satisfying impression left by Schaff's work derives from the historical appendix, even though the necessity for its inclusion remains somewhat obscure--until one discovers that a priced sixteenth-century publication of Spiera's story was in Hengstenberg's possession, who loaned it to Schaff, perhaps with the words: "See what you can do with it."[66] With a good eye to what was thematically important and historically illuminating, Schaff told the story of Francesco Spiera (1502-48), a lawyer in northern Italy at the time of the Reformation, whom the Jesuits forced to deny his Evangelical faith. To Spiera this denial was the sin against the Holy Spirit, and soon after, broken in body and spirit, he died. Schaff thought it likely that Spiera was in fact the living example of an unfortunate one guilty of the unforgivable sin, though he conceded that in the end only God knows the true condition of the human heart.

Several features clearly stand out in Schaff's dissertation. Numerous footnotes and references on almost every page testify to the prodigious number of books he had read. Apparently without hesitation or confusion, he was able to draw upon a mass of materials, collected from centuries of church history and from contemporary literature and well organized in an orderly mind. This helps to explain the lucidity and fluency of his style as well as the care and thoroughness with which he probed to the depth of every problem. But he was less sure-footed when he ventured into the realm of abstract thought. Marheineke may have had this weakness in mind when he complained that the dissertation "lacked in certain definitive concepts, such as freedom, spirit, love."[67] Even though Schaff had labored with particular diligence to present himself at the beginning of his academic career as a philosophical theologian, already this dissertation showed him less capable of philosophical-abstract thought than of a descriptive approach

78

to the factual and concrete, which is the stuff of history. This may be taken as an indication of Schaff's turn, which was soon to come, from philosophical and dogmatic theology to church history, from Twesten to Neander, while he would always continue his interest in Biblical scholarship and further develop his encyclopedic ability of ranging freely over the whole field of theology. When Schaff submitted his dissertation to the Berlin faculty in 1841, he named New Testament exegesis and dogmatic theology as his principal interests.[68] Two years later, in his reply to his appointment to the faculty of the Theological Seminary at Mercersburg in Pennsylvania, he declared himself competent and interested primarily in biblical exegesis and church history.

The thoroughness of Schaff's investigations showed up yet another weakness, which was a lack of creative judgment. Schaff's ability to absorb materials drawn from all kinds of sources was truly astounding, but it outweighed his creative powers to the extent that, as a rule, he arrived at his own conclusions only after a critical and exhaustive study of all the available options, when he would finally agree with one of these options or a combination thereof. This is the method of the eclectic. And it is this fusion of eclecticism, erudition, and a marvelously retentive memory--the outstanding feature of his first scholarly publication--that was to characterize Schaff's scholarship throughout his whole career. Toward the end of his life his friend Julius Mann wrote him: "If you had as much imagination and creative-active power as you have memory and the critical and organizing ability of assimilation, you would today be without a rival."[69] Already Schaff's first little book provided ample evidence that his "memory and the critical and organizing ability of assimilation" outweighed his "imagination and creative-active power."

Finally, this dissertation--because of its eclecticism and the sources the young author used--allows us to conclude that at the end of the required course of study Schaff was firmly and securely anchored in the position of the mediating theology (*Vermittlungstheologie*). Among his teachers this school of theology was represented by Dorner at Tübingen, Tholuck and Müller at Halle and Marheineke and Twesten at Berlin.[70] In this group we must also include Carl Ullmann (1796-1865) at Heidelberg, even though he was not one of Schaff's academic teachers. Ullmann, whom Schaff had met for the first time at the centenary celebration of the university in Erlangen in 1843, strongly influenced the young scholar not only through his writings but also as the editor of *Theologische Studien und Kritiken*, the major organ of the mediating theology.[71] The name of this broadly based and influential school of theology in nineteenth-century German Protestantism goes back to a programmatic statement, made in 1827 in launching this periodical, that at no time, and least of all at this time, there can be "too much of true mediations" (*der wahren Vermittlungen zu viel geben könne*).[72] It was this understanding of the theological task that was to become the dominant motif also of Schaff's theology and churchmanship. Indeed, the story of his American career is, in one sense, best told as the story of a *Vermittlungstheologe* who emigrated to the United States.

The *Oxford English Dictionary* offers several definitions of "mediate" that can help to illuminate the nature and aims of the mediating theology: "to form a connecting link or transitional stage between one thing or another.....to take a moderate position, to avoid extremes.....to intercede, to intervene for the purpose of reconciling." All three definitions apply, first of all, to the attempt of this group of theologians to combine the most prominent forces of early nineteenth-century German Protestantism: the Awakening, Schleiermacher and Hegel. Most of them hailed from the Awakening, or at least had come into contact with it; they considered themselves Schleiermacher's true heirs; and they were open, though in diverse ways, to various aspects of Hegel's philosophy. They were equally determined to mediate, especially in the sense of avoiding and reconciling the extremes, between the "free" and "radical" theology on the left, represented most prominently by Baur's Tübingen School, and orthodox Lutheran confessionalism on the right. Together with the "free" and "radical" theologians they affirmed the individual Christian's freedom from religious and doctrinal positions that may be faithful to the letter of the Christian faith but stifle its spirit, and they agreed that

80

the doctrinal traditions of the church must be adapted, though moderately, to the intellectual culture of the age. On the other hand, with the Lutheran confessional theology they shared the conviction that the Christian faith must remain firmly grounded in biblical and historical Christianity; hence the individual's faith must continue to be subject to the authority of the Bible and must still accept the normative guidance of the dogmas of early Christianity and of the confessions of the sixteenth-century Reformation. It was obvious to the mediating theologians that each of the other two camps had presented its position one-sidedly, to the exclusion of the truth embodied in the other position. It therefore followed that only those of a more conciliatory and moderate bent of mind were capable of upholding simultaneously the truth of what, in the theological jargon of the time, was called "subjective" and "objective" Christianity. Small wonder that these theologians were also ardent supporters of the Prussian Union, Julius Müller even speaking confidently of its "divine right."[73]

Furthermore, all of these theologians were dedicated to the daunting task of establishing the "eternal covenant" between historical Christianity and modern culture, to which Schleiermacher and Hegel had summoned the theology and philosophy of their time. But precisely at this point their position needs to be still further delimited. For, as Martin Kähler (1835-1912) has shown, we must distinguish between two alternative kinds of "mediation" between Christianity and modern culture that were propagated by nineteenth-century German theologians. Some of them aimed at bringing the great cultural achievements of the age under the dominant influence of the Christian tradition, while others were ready to transform and even diminish the substance of historical Christianity by adapting it to the highest cultural standards of modern civilization which they optimistically assumed was progressively becoming ever more truly humane. As Kähler put it, some theologians attempted to "Christianize" culture, others to "humanize" Christianity.[74] Faced with this alternative, the mediating theologians expended their best efforts and their impressive learning in carrying out the role of intermediary between Christian faith and contemporary culture *to the end* of making historical Christianity, with appropriate modifications and adjustments as called for by the progress of the human sciences, the dominant force of the intellectual culture of their time. They were repelled by those who propagated the other alternative. They even suspected Schleiermacher and Hegel of having attempted, if only secretly and perhaps even unintentionally, to make Christianity increasingly indistinguishable from the on- and upward flow of the cultural aspirations and accomplishments of modern times. Furthermore, they sincerely believed that no irreconcilable conflicts between "church" and "science" need ever arise, provided that Christians state their case wisely and moderately and modern science admit its limitations imposed upon it by the confinement of reason to the immanence of human experience. If, nevertheless, these theologians found themselves forced to choose between Christian faith and modern science, they generally were ready to side with the traditional understanding of Christianity rather than with the sciences of modern times. As Schaff stated the matter in 1848 in characteristically uncomplicated terms: If he should ever face this unhappy choice, he would rather be "too churchly at the expense of science, than too scientific at the expense of the church."[75] Moreover, as far as propositions about the relationship between God and world, faith and history, Christ and culture were concerned, the mediating theology continued to adhere to a moderate supernaturalism, all attacks of modern science against this position notwithstanding. The traditional supernaturalism of these theologians is the more surprising in light of their claim to be the true heirs of Schleiermacher. But in their theology, as Emanuel Hirsch (1888-1972) has pointedly observed, they had done away "with the heart of all of Schleiermacher's new concepts, his doctrine of God."[76] Most of them accused even Schleiermacher, and not only Hegel, of "pantheism." It is also true of these theologians that in arguing the case for the traditional understanding of the Christian faith, as Ernst Troeltsch has pointed out, "at the decisive moment the 'inner experience' had to take the place of the biblical-orthodox dogma."[77] Thus they gave a characteristic twist to Schleiermacher's and

Hegel's insistence on the inwardness of truth, thus they showed their roots in the Awakening.

Finally, the mediating theologians characteristically combined polemics and apologetics, skillfully attacking their opponents to the left, such as Baur's Tübingen School, and the stiffening orthodoxy of Lutheran confessionalism to the right, while they boldly and imaginatively employed many of the potent cultural ideas and concepts of their time as persuasive apologists of evangelical Christianity. It should be pointed out that the very concept of mediation is unthinkable apart from its roots in the fertile cultural soil of the romantic-idealistic era, as is the habit of these theologians to focus on polarities in order to combine them in some higher synthesis. Ullmann offered a telling definition of "mediation," when he claimed that it is "the scientifically executed reduction of relative antitheses to their original unity, through which an inner reconciliation of them and a higher standpoint are won, in which they are sublimated (*aufgehoben*)." And he affirmed that "the scientific position, which results from this mediation, is the true, healthy middle."[78] By making "mediation" the primary goal of their theology and by always aiming to position themselves in the "middle," these theologians sincerely believed that they had succeeded in reconciling the conflicting forces of their time, or would at any rate soon succeed. Drawing the sum of it all, we may conclude that the mediating theology can be best characterized as representing a progressive orthodoxy or liberal evangelicalism in nineteenth-century German Protestantism.

Their critics, however, then and later, accused these mediating theologians of having in the end fallen woefully short of attaining those challenging and ambitious goals which they had set for themselves. To these critics they appeared to have been evasive and vague at the points of real intellectual conflict and too often ready to settle for what later turned out to be, at best, a temporary truce. Baur spoke contemptuously of their "insipid and flat theology which availed itself of Schleiermacher's name merely to cover its scientific shortcomings."[79] Troeltsch referred even more acidly to the "petty harmony and unctuous inaccuracies of the so-called mediating theology which fraudulently used Schleiermacher's name for its own purposes."[80] And Karl Barth (1886-1968) judged the theology of Alexander Schweizer (1808-88), whom he called a typical mediating theologian, to be "tedious" and concluded that during the reign of this theology in German Protestantism systematic theology tended to hibernate and consequently the liveliest minds gave up dogmatics for historical studies[81]--as did indeed Schaff! Most of these theologians came to represent in their work an eclecticism that in the end proved to be unstable, for "the personal union (*Personalunion*) of theological motifs did not lead to an actual, substantial union (*Realunion*)."[82] Nevertheless, it also needs to be said that the mediating theology, whatever its shortcomings, "kept open all questions and decisions and in the breathing space thus gained (did) helpful intellectual work according to its best abilities" (and, adds Hirsch, what more can be asked?). It is certainly to the lasting credit of these theologians and churchmen that to a large extent Germany's higher culture remained allied with Protestant Christianity far into the nineteenth century, even in the face of increasingly powerful intellectual and social tendencies hostile or indifferent to Christian institutions and beliefs.[83]

One must agree with some final observations that Hirsch has offered in fairness to these men. Most of them were scholars and churchmen, who conscientiously tried to mediate between the scholarly and the active life and who therefore devoted themselves whole-heartedly, and often with notable success, to many of the practical tasks in church and state. Equally characteristic and praiseworthy were their historical interest as well as their ability and eagerness to harvest the rich results of the scholarship of the age. They also deserve credit for having "awakened an appreciation and understanding for the fact that there is a world-wide Protestant community."[84] And no one was to bear out the truth of this last observation more so than Philip Schaff!

A most convenient summary of the views and concepts of the mediating theology can be found in an essay Carl Ullmann first published in *Theologische Studien und Kritiken* and which later grew into a book, *The Essence of*

Christianity.[85] This book has been called "a nearly complete collection of all the catchwords of the mediating theology."[86] One notes with interest that John Williamson Nevin, Schaff's lone colleague at Mercersburg, found Ullmann's essay so admirable that he added a compact English translation of it as the introductory chapter to his *The Mystical Presence* (1846).[87] We may not be too far from the truth when we call the Mercersburg Theology of Nevin and Schaff an American variant of Germany's mediating theology.[88]

We can conclude our discussion of this important chapter in Schaff's life by affirming, in his own words, that during his years of study the "child-like faith" of his pietistic youth in Württemberg had indeed survived without impairment "the long and complicated process of probing down to the very depth of our most sacred faith" and had emerged from it "more firmly grounded in orthodoxy than ever," though one would search in vain for any evidence that this self-assured young scholar ever even had come close to emptying "the cup of doubt to the dregs."[89] However, as the following chapter will show, the theological orientation that Schaff had come to embrace--the progressive orthodoxy or liberal evangelicalism of the mediating theology--was to be still further developed and expanded in some important respects during the next two years, when he began his career as an academic teacher at the University of Berlin.

Chapter 5

Privatdozent at Berlin (1842-1844)

The "Church Question"

Johann Wolfgang von Goethe's Italian journeys had first inspired among young Germans the tradition of seeking the crowning completion of their education in a pilgrimage to Italy. The Italian journey, on which the von Kröchers and Schaff embarked in the early summer of 1841, was, therefore, a fitting conclusion to the years of Schaff's academic apprenticeship.[1] One gathers from Schaff's diary that the journey had many highlights: the trip through Sicily on a donkey's back, the visit to the Waldensian settlements near Turin, and the many hours passed in animated conversation with some of the leading Protestant theologians at Geneva and Lausanne. The most memorable weeks, however, were those spent in Rome--it was the Rome of the reactionary Pope Gregory XVI (1831-46)--where the von Kröcher party arrived during the first days of 1842. Here Schaff officiated for several weeks as the chaplain at the Prussian embassy, a position held before him by Tholuck, and stayed long enough to be able to participate in the solemnities and the excitement of Passion Week. He even was received in audience by the pope himself.

No doubt, the von Kröchers found Schaff a delightful companion. Well versed in the history of classical antiquity and the Middle Ages, he was also already an accomplished linguist: at Chur he had grown up speaking German and some Italian, and at Kornthal and the Stuttgart *Gymnasium* he had acquired his basic knowledge of Latin, Greek, Hebrew and French (to which, beginning in 1843, he would add English). Moreover, he now showed fully his native ability of associating easily with all kinds of people--high and low, peasants and church dignitaries, artists and theologians, Protestants and Catholics--, passing freely from one to the other and always eagerly drawing out from each what was instructive and would increase the pleasures of sociable companionship. One gathers further from his diary that in the lively enjoyment of the natural beauty and the historical splendor of the Italian landscape he perceived with particular vividness the contrasts between nature and art, paganism and Christianity, Catholicism and Protestantism. After having watched a stunningly beautiful sunset in Italy, he exclaimed, echoing a well-known romantic sentiment, that he had now "no hesitation about giving nature the preference over art." Leaving Rome and passing through the Campagna, he recorded his vivid sense of how the Italian landscape with its numerous historical monuments reminded him of the stark contrast between paganism and Christianity, "the bloom and decay of the first, the energy of the latter, which defies the powers of destruction." The service on Palm Sunday at St. Peter's in the presence of the pope, a service which Schaff thought made a dramatic appeal to the senses and the imagination, also prompted him to remark with Protestant sobriety: "A plain pungent sermon on the atoning sufferings of Christ would be more worth than all the gay, perishable pomp." He was also Protestant enough, during his audience with Pope Gregory XVI, to find it hard to kiss the pope's red slippers (which he did). And since the pope chose to tell his visitor stories of some recent Protestant conversions, Schaff, to whom making conversation came always easily under less trying circumstances, for once had to admit that he had "little to reply and was ill at ease." But when he witnessed the Catholic service of scourging on Wednesday of Passion Week, he perceptively and irenically observed that the service, "indicating the heart's discontent with itself and its longing after the death of the old man, represents what the Protestant doctrine of justification stands for." And he thought prayer on one's knees before and after a lecture, as he witnessed it at a Jesuit seminary, "a very appropriate and beautiful custom."

Near the end of his life, in 1890, Schaff returned once more to Rome for an extended visit--it was now the capital of a united Italy, the Rome of Pope Leo XIII (1878-1903). Leo XIII had recently for the first time opened the Vatican archives to Protestant scholars, and this time Schaff came to Rome in a determined effort at bringing the volumes of his *History of the Christian Church* up to the end of the Protestant Reformation. He was, in fact, the first Protestant to be admitted to this great library. A year later, at the assembly of the Evangelical Alliance in Florence, which he himself was unable to attend, his paper "Renaissance and Reformation" was presented, calling forth words of praise from Catholics and Protestants alike on account of its irenic and scholarly spirit. This same irenic and scholarly spirit, we are certainly justified to conclude, already animated Schaff during his first Italian journey.

Schaff resigned from his post as tutor to the young von Kröcher upon their arrival in Stuttgart, in the summer of 1842. After his return to Berlin, he immediately set to work to prepare the second dissertation required by German universities of all those who desire to venture forth on an academic career. His treatise, *The Relationship of James, the Lord's Brother, to James, the Son of Alphaeus, Anew Exegetically and Historically Investigated,*[2] failed, however, to find the faculty's full approval. He had again merely surveyed whatever solutions had been offered in previous attempts at solving what is certainly a very minor problem of New Testament research: who are the various men called James in the New Testament? Twesten, once again in charge, noted, no doubt with some satisfaction, that Schaff's view "on the whole agrees with my own." But he informed his colleagues that since Schaff "has neither produced anything new, as far as the question under discussion is concerned, nor has he followed an original approach in his treatment, this treatise might as well have remained unwritten without loss to scholarship." He added, however: "But since we have already declared to the Ministry that we consider him worthy otherwise, I therefore do not find anything in this treatise that might prompt us to change our opinion." Neander, who for lack of time had not even read Schaff's dissertation, was equally magnanimous: "Since, in any case, the opinion I have already formed of Schaf (sic) will hardly be changed and since he is in a hurry to qualify himself, I do not want to cause a delay."[3] Schaff delivered his German trial lecture "The Different Types of Apostolic Doctrine" on December 3, 1842, and his Latin trial lecture "*De Notione Theologiae*" four days later. Some thirty years afterwards he still sighed: "I passed safely through the ordeal of the professorial examinations."[4]

In the winter-semester of 1842/43, Schaff, now twenty-three years old, proudly began his academic career as a *privatdozent* (a non-tenured assistant professor whose sole source of income are the fees paid by the students he is able to attract) in the theological faculty of Germany's most famous university. Most of the courses he taught were in the field of New Testament studies, but he also offered courses on the History of Protestant Theology and the Theological System of Schleiermacher.[5] He counted five students in his first class and was pleasantly surprised when thirty students joined his class the next semester. Among his hearers was even an American professor, Edwards Amasa Park (1808-1900) of Andover Seminary, visiting Germany at that time, of whose stature in his homeland Schaff, of course, had no inkling. During the second year he was fortunate enough to receive a special grant of 800 Prussian thalers from the Ministry of Public Worship and Education. This money helped to provide financial security in what Schaff called the "literary purgatory" of the life of an unsalaried *privatdozent*, whose hope to succeed in an academic career depended almost entirely on his forthcoming publications.[6]

But during these last months that Schaff was to spend in Berlin he was suddenly caught up in the exciting discussions of what came to be known as the "church question:" what is the nature and order of the church, its relationship to the individual Christian, to society and to the state? Once more Schaff participated in a dramatic change in the theological climate of German Protestantism. One of Schaff's teachers at Halle, the philosopher Erdmann, had in 1837 still categorically asserted: "The question as to the relationship of faith and science, or religion and science, has attained a kind of notoriety that has rarely ever been accorded to an intellectual problem."[7] This statement, coming as it did two years after the publication of Strauss's *Life of Jesus*, may be considered a fair indication of what was at that time uppermost in the minds of most German Protestant theologians: the grave issues which some of the more radical theologians had raised by their seemingly destructive application of Hegel's philosophy and historical criticism to the Christian faith. Only two years later, however, Theodor Kliefoth (1810-95), soon to emerge as a leading spokesman of Lutheran confessionalism, advanced the novel claim that nineteenth-century Protestantism "will have its special task in the doctrine of the church."[8] Combining elements of Schleiermacher's theology and of Hegel's philosophy of history with the orthodox Protestant insistence on the Bible as the complete and final depository of the Christian truth, he maintained that this truth is to be developed fully, and defined as dogma, in the historical sequence of five periods, of which each is preoccupied with one particular aspect of the Christian faith. Since the Greek church had fully developed theology, that is, the trinitarian and christological dogmas, the Latin church anthropology, and the Protestant Reformation soteriology, Kliefoth boldly assigned to nineteenth-century German Protestantism the formidable task of pronouncing the final word in ecclesiology. Eschatology he left to a still later age.

In the 1840s, signs began in fact to abound that the "church question" was to be the major preoccupation of large segments of German Protestantism. The titles of a few books published in these years testify, albeit in a somewhat curious manner, to the increasing intensity of the ecclesiological discussion: Wilhelm Löhe's *Three Books about the Church* (1845) was followed by Franz Delitzsch's *Four Books about the Church* (1847) and Kliefoth's own *Eight Books about the Church* (1854). However, since Kliefoth published only the first of his projected two volumes and a few years later Bernhard Wendt his *Two Books about the Church* (1859), one might take this latter sequence of publications as an indication that interest in the "church question" began to ebb in the late 1850s. Still, in 1845 Wilhelm Löhe (1808-72) spoke the truth, though hardly the whole

91

truth, when he exclaimed: "Everybody is talking about the church in our time."[9] A century later, Emanuel Hirsch would agree:

> The history of the evangelical theology and church in the nineteenth century has the peculiarity that the church itself--its nature, its task, its structure and order, its relationship to the state and to the common life in general--become the object, if not the center, of the theological and ecclesiastical consideration and activity and this to an extent which was not known to an earlier age, not even to the age of the Reformation.[10]

And Schaff, too, was now "talking about the church." In 1843 he wrote two articles for the Berlin *Literarische Anzeiger*. The first, "A Word Regarding Theological Criticism," still tried to blunt the sharp edges of historical criticism as Baur and Strauss had applied it to the New Testament; the second, "Catholicism and Romanism," was his first literary contribution to the "church question."[11] Less than a year later, only a few weeks after his arrival in the New World, he remarked jubilantly in his diary that he had found his Mercersburg colleague Nevin to be in full agreement with his own views on the church, with which he had been preoccupied "for one year."[12] Schaff and Nevin now echoed Kliefoth's insistence that the solution of the "church question" is the unique task of nineteenth-century Christianity. The first two of the "Theses for the Times," which Schaff appended to his *Principle of Protestantism* in 1845, read, in Nevin's translation, as follows:

> (1) Every period of the church and of theology has its particular problem to solve; and every doctrine, in a measure every book also of the Bible, has its classical age in which it first comes to be fully understood and appropriated by the consciousness of the Christian world.
> (2) The main question of *our* time concerns the nature of the church itself in its relation to the world and to single Christians.

In order to gain a better understanding of this remarkable further development in Schaff's theology--this lively, even passionate engagement in the

92

contemporary quest for the renewal of the church that was to characterize the young professor's first decade at Mercersburg--we return once more to the larger German scene, before we focus our attention on the Berlin circles in which Schaff moved during the final months of his sojourn in Berlin. For at the very time that he began his academic teaching career, he came under the powerful influence of the party of theologians and Prussian aristocrats gathered around Hengstenberg's *Evangelische Kirchenzeitung*. At the same time he also became a disciple of the church historian August Neander.

Previous chapters have described, in the broader context of the dawn of the romantic-idealistic era in German culture, the transformation of German Protestantism primarily under the impact of the Awakening, Schleiermacher's theology and Hegel's philosophy. Now we note that these important developments had in due time also resulted in a recovery of the biblical and traditional understanding of the nature of church as a corporate entity that, far from being a mere historical or even "Catholic" accretion to the Christian faith, was now once again perceived to be an integral part of Christianity's proper life. This new "church consciousness" developed along lines generally at variance with the previous century's prevailing rationalism. Rationalistic theologians had conceived of the church as a human association or society differing from other such human associations or societies not in principle but in kind. Further accommodating themselves to the spirit of the age by reducing religion to morality, they had declared the church to be an association of like-minded individuals who have voluntarily and on a contractual basis joined themselves together for the practice of virtue and the moral betterment of society. This was a shallow notion of the Christian church, and correspondingly minimal was the interest these rationalistic theologians took in the doctrine of the church. They were generally content to uphold the traditional distinction between the "invisible" and "visible" church by relegating the "invisible" church to the abstract, ideal realm and by defining the "visible" or empirical churches as useful expedients for human betterment—unless they were even convinced that the institutional churches with their superstitious beliefs and outdated rituals were an impediment to human progress or even contradicted the true spirit of the Christian religion. Even Kant, in his attempt to define "Religion Within the Limits of Reason Alone," declared the goal of human progress to be the establishment of a community where the victory of good over evil will bring about the "kingdom of God" as an ideal moral commonwealth. On this understanding the churches represented no more than a transitional stage on the road toward that ultimate goal.[14]

The romantic movement, with its all-pervasive notions of the mystery of life and of the indwelling of the divine in the universe, as well as with its powerful organismic thought, created a new cultural climate that inspired and helped both Roman Catholic and Protestant theologians to conceive once again of the church as a supra-individual, spirit-filled community, the members of which are linked organically to each other and to Christ, the Savior and Head of his Church. This church is indeed a unique "fellowship of believers," it is indeed the "Body of Christ." Among Protestant theologians Schleiermacher, influenced not only by the romantic movement but also by his earlier experience of Christian fellowship in Zinzendorf's pietistic communities, was the first to channel the wealth of new ideas into the doctrine of the church. In his systematic presentation of the Christian faith he insisted that the interpretation of Christianity stands and falls "with the doctrine of the union of the divine Essence with human nature, both in the personality of Christ and in the common Spirit of the Church," and that therefore the church must be understood as being "the Bearer and Perpetuator of the redemption through Christ."[15] The church was the invisible-visible bearer of the divine life that flows from Christ through history. It was the center, organ, and sphere of God's saving activity in the world, a communal manifestation of the continuing activity of the Spirit. Hence it should never be debased into an organ of the state or an instrument merely for the achievement of moral and cultural ends, though it most certainly was to be a leaven for all human life. Friends and foes would later freely acknowledge that it was Schleiermacher's great merit "that he again established the church in its full importance."[16] Hegel, too, inspired among his contemporaries a new appreciation of the church, when he regarded the church as the necessary historical embodiment of the Christian "idea," that is, of the union of the divine and human, first fully realized in Christ and then continued through the generations in the Christian community under the power of the Spirit. And when his philosophy made itself the advocate of orthodox dogmas such as those of the Trinity and the duophysic Christ, it encouraged Protestants to be attentive also to the orthodox doctrine of the church. It is true that the Awakening was initially indifferent toward the established churches, especially their institutional and confessional differences. But from the beginning the Awakening had been permeated by a warm sense of Christian fellowship of all those who knew themselves miraculously rescued by God's grace and mercy as shown in Christ. In due time many of the "awakened" abandoned the earlier preference for the fluid forms of Christian fellowship and then also developed a lively interest in the institutional church as the proper and necessary receptacle of the religious life of the individual Christian.

But no less important were external changes and events in drawing the attention of German Protestants to the "church question." The Napoleonic Wars had had a profound effect on the political landscape of continental Europe, so that in the wake of Napoleon's final defeat a reorganization of the several German states and the territorial churches within their new boundaries became an urgent necessity. These changes in the ecclesiastical structure of German Protestantism forced churchmen, theologians and jurists alike to reflect seriously on the nature of the church, its constitution and administration, its ministry and the significance of its sixteenth-century confessions. Additionally, as has been well observed, the enthusiasm engendered by the Wars of Liberation, especially in Prussia, filled not only patriots with a desire for a state but also Christians with a desire for a church—often, of course, the patriot and the Christian were one and the same.[17]

But even greater and more far-reaching was the impact of two events in 1817, the year of the tercentenary celebration of Luther's Reformation. King

Friedrich Wilhelm III of Prussia--who was Reformed as his ancestors had been since 1613, while most of his subjects were Lutheran--inaugurated by royal fiat the union of the Lutheran and Reformed churches in his kingdom. Such union was soon to be effected also in a number of other German states, like the grand duchies of Hessia and Baden. But the same year also witnessed, already in reaction to this union, the resurgence of Lutheran confessionalism, when Claus Harms (1778-1855) published Ninety-Five Theses (Luther's and his own), intended as a first clarion-call to arms in defense of Lutheran orthodoxy against the twin threat of rationalism and the Prussian Union. It is no exaggeration to claim that these two events became the concrete causes for the importance and notoriety accorded the "church question" among German Protestants during the second third of the nineteenth century. In Prussia, further actions by the king and his advisers proved to be controversial, even provoking determined resistance to the union. The early introduction of the designation "Evangelical" for the new Prussian union church, replacing "Lutheran" and "Reformed", still left open the controversial question of the precise nature of this church. Was it to be an administrative union only, or was this union intended to create a church with a common confession, and if so, in what sense, given the fact that the Lutherans and Reformed both had their own distinctive sixteenth-century confessions? The royal introduction of a new liturgy, the so-called *Agenda*, in 1822 proved even more controversial, especially when finally its use was made mandatory and was enforced, where necessary, by the police and the military. This happened in Silesia, where it led to the open rebellion of Lutheran pastors and laity, henceforth known as the Old Lutherans. Some of them joined later other disgruntled Lutherans from Saxony, Prussia and Bavaria in emigrating to the United States, where Schaff would soon encounter these stalwarts of confessional Lutheran orthodoxy and do battle with them. At the same time in those German states where there were only Lutherans, as in Bavaria and Saxony, the Awakening had promoted the growth of a church consciousness that soon evolved into a determined Lutheran church consciousness. Thus, beginning around 1840,

96

Lutheran confessionalism became a powerful religious and ecclesiastical force in these and other German states.

It was therefore unavoidable that the growing "church consciousness" of German Protestantism began in these years to crystallize into two antagonistic concepts of the church that Emanuel Hirsch has dubbed "neo-Protestant" and "neo-orthodox."[18] It is true that both parties were influenced, though to varying degrees, by the main cultural and intellectual currents of their time--romanticism, idealism, the Historical School—as well as by the Awakening and diverse elements in Schleiermacher's and Hegel's complex systems of thought. Both parties also conceived of their common quest for the renewal of the contemporary church as a way of continuing or even completing the sixteenth-century Reformation. And both opposed the free-church tradition with its implied denominational fragmentation of the Lutheran, Reformed and United churches, an opposition so entrenched in German Protestantism that it initially was almost impossible for Schaff to accommodate himself to the denominational diversity of American Christianity. Nevertheless, conflict ensued between two different conceptions of the church's nature, ministry, confession and place in society and the state. And it should be obvious that this conflict contributed to, as well as manifested, the deepening party divisions in German Protestantism that followed upon the publication of Strauss's *Life of Jesus* in 1835. Indeed, a more elaborate discussion of the quest for the renewal of the church in mid-nineteenth-century German Protestantism could well focus on *three* different programs that roughly correspond to our distinction of the three camps of the "radical and "free" theology, the mediating theology and the Lutheran confessional theology.[19]

Hirsch has called attention to the remarkable fact that the *neo-Protestant* understanding of the church issued from the combined strength of the three hostile forces of the Enlightenment, Schleiermacher and Hegel. In a telling romantic analogy, the church was held to be as essential to Protestantism's proper life as the body is to the soul. But this church, as the Enlightenment had insisted, was to be free of all authoritarianism, dogmatism and narrow confessionalism. Instead, it was to manifest the Christian faith in broad, universal terms and to keep traditional Christianity responsive to every authentic aim and insight of contemporary culture while simultaneously trying to imbue modern culture with the Christian spirit. It also was to support all unitive efforts of German Protestantism.

Moreover, the neo-Protestant concept of the church tried to emphasize equally the divine and human aspects of the church's nature. The church was to be viewed not only as a unique community drawing its life from the presence of the divine Spirit who works primarily through the ministry of Word and Sacrament, but also as a part of the ever changing fabric of history. Consequently, such expressions of the church's on-going life as the dogmas of early Christianity and the confessions of the sixteenth-century Reformation, even the Bible itself, were to be accorded only the relative authority of historical witnesses to the one absolute truth, which is Christ. Once again it was Schleiermacher, who offered the most succinct and telling definition of the neo-Protestant view of the Christian church, when he insisted that we must think of the church "as a whole that is capable of motion, progress and development, with the single restriction without which Christianity would collapse ... namely, that such progress is nothing but a better understanding and a more perfect appropriation of what is founded in Christ."[20] It was also Schleiermacher who, when he considered the church in practical and legal terms, conceived of the church not as an authoritarian institution standing over against the individual and the congregation but as an association of regenerate individuals who regulate and administer their own affairs, with the Spirit indwelling in their community. As he put it succinctly in *The Christian Faith*: "The Christian Church takes shape through the coming together of regenerate individuals to form a system of mutual interaction and co-operation."[21] With this understanding he made himself the advocate of the so-called collegial system of church government that is commonly traced back to Christoph Matthäus Pfaff (1686-1760).

It is finally noteworthy that this understanding of the church allowed for great diversity; after all, it drew its substance from so wide a theological and cultural terrain and had such broad aims. Hirsch maintains that even Richard Rothe's singular theory of the gradual and ultimate disappearance of the church into the ideal state as the perfect form of the kingdom of God, which he set forth in his *The Beginnings of the Christian Church and its Constitution* (1837), was an ultimately consistent, though extreme, consequence of the neo-Protestant understanding of the church.[22] This book, we should add, surprised his friends and shocked the defenders of orthodoxy almost as much as Strauss's attack on the New Testament record of the life of Jesus had done two years earlier. (Rothe did not dare to publish a projected second volume.) But all expressions of the neo-Protestant view of the church, however diverse their nature, were one in their opposition to those "hierarchical," "clerical," "orthodox," "reactionary" and—as it was soon to be called—"catholicizing" or "romanizing" tendencies that appeared to be, at least to its antagonists, the very marrow of the "neo-orthodox" concept of the church.

Those who represented the *neo-orthodox* point of view were Protestant churchmen and theologians who were deeply troubled by what they perceived to be the destructive forces of modernity. Hence they tended to view the church as a fortress necessary and even indispensable for the survival of the Christian faith in modern times. Their main foe was modern "subjectivism," the autonomous human self. It first manifested itself in the rationalism that flourished during the previous century and continued in various ways in their own time. Even more destructive and objectionable were the ideas that emanated from the Hegelian Left. After all, Strauss's *Life of Jesus Critically Examined* (1835) had "put in question the historical object of faith, Jesus Christ," as a few years later Ludwig Feuerbach's *The Essence of Christianity* (1841) "put in question the metaphysical object," when it made God out to be an illusion produced by a projection of human consciousness.[23] And when Rothe in 1837, as already mentioned, advocated the dissolution of the church into the ideal state, a man like

Hengstenberg condemned Rothe's book as an even greater threat than Strauss's book, for here the last bastion against the destructive forces of modernity, the Christian church itself, was put in question.[24] Even though the faithful firmly believed that these contemporary assertions—no Christ, no Church, no God—had at once been convincingly repudiated or were so outrageously absurd that they repudiated themselves, still they were a part of the dark background against which the fortress mentality of the representatives of the neo-orthodox concept of the church becomes understandable. In the broader social and political context there was also the shattering and continuously reverberating impact of the French Revolution, the Spirit of 1789, with its ideal of popular sovereignty and the parliamentary system. It led to the growing strength of bourgeois liberalism in the German states and the futile and bloody revolutionary uprisings of 1830 and 1848. To these neo-orthodox churchmen the ecclesiastical analogy of the ideals of the French Revolution, of Rousseau's *contrat social*, was the collegial system of church government now sanctioned again by Schleiermacher. Friedrich Julius Stahl (1802-61), the most brilliant spokesman for the emerging conservative understanding of church and state, wrote his important *The Constitution of the Church According to Doctrine and Right of the Protestants* (1840) as a repudiation both of Rothe's book and of the collegial system of church government, whose parallel, as he never tired of repeating, to the "pernicious political doctrine of popular sovereignty is plainly visible."[25] Years later he uttered the words for which he is often best remembered: "authority not majority" as the ruling conception in both church and state. The church as well as the state are to be established and governed "from above" and not "from below." Hirsch is convinced that the historical and theological impact of Stahl's book of 1840 can hardly be overestimated, for it provided a "genuine intellectual and spiritual support for the growth of neo-Lutheran ecclesiastical thinking and striving" in the 1840s.[26]

Drawing mostly upon this book, Hirsch developed the main features of the neo-orthodox concept of the church. At its heart was the belief in the indissoluble unity of Christianity and the church, that is, the institutional church. Over against the "subjectivism" not only of rationalism but even of pietism and of much contemporary theology, Schleiermacher's included, Lutheran orthodoxy set out to revive and stress the "objective" aspects of Christianity: ministry, sacraments, liturgy, church order and government, the binding authority of the sixteenth-century confessions. Back of this emphasis was the belief that the church is the "Body of Christ," a social organism whose lifeblood is the continuing presence of Christ the Savior. The Enlightenment's social contract theory was here supplanted by romanticism's powerful idea of organism which allowed for unity and difference, life and development, continuity with the past, and, perhaps most importantly, placed the whole above its individual parts. In this high view of the church the church could even be viewed as the *Christus prolongatus*, an affirmation that had been set forth most beautifully by the Roman Catholic Möhler in his *Symbolics* (5th ed., 1835).[27] To the opponents this affirmation in particular revealed the "catholizising" or "romanizing" tendency inherent in the neo-orthodox concept of the church. These churchmen and theologians did certainly not conceive of the church as an association of regenerate individuals, established by the believers themselves, but as an authoritarian institution that is prior to and stands over against the individual believer and the congregation. It follows that the believer is subject to this church just as the citizen is subject to the state, for both are established by God and ruled by God's will. Equally characteristic and important was the neo-orthodox Lutheran affirmation of the visibility of the true church as the "Body of Christ." The traditional distinction between the invisible and visible church was generally so understood that the fellowship of true believers, who are known only to God, was identified with the invisible church, while the institutional church was identified with the visible church--neither one, however, being ever without the other!

But there was diversity in the neo-orthodox Lutheran camp as well. For once the church had become the main topic of an intensifying discussion in the late 1840s, differences developed especially in the more precise understanding of

101

the nature of the church, the ministerial office and the meaning of the sixteenth-century confessions. These differences need not concern us, for they developed only after Schaff's departure for the United States in 1844. Only then is it necessary to distinguish more clearly between three parties: Hengstenberg's *Evangelische Kirchenzeitung*, a group of high-church Lutherans that included Löhe and Kliefoth, and the more moderate Erlangen School centered around *Die Zeitschrift für Protestantismus und Kirche* in southern Germany. This journal had been founded in 1838 in opposition, as its motto proclaimed, "to a church which knows nothing of Protestantism and a Protestantism which knows nothing of the church." Thus it announced its intention to confront an increasingly aggressive Roman Catholicism centered in Bavaria and the Rhineland and Protestant "subjectivism" in its several contemporary manifestations. It should be noted, however, that these three parties, whatever their differences, continued in common to uphold the normative and authoritative character of the Lutheran confessions. Since they embody the biblical truth, they are the most highly prized possession of the Christian church, they are the church's one foundation. Not "mediation" between Christianity and modern culture but "confession" of the old, orthodox faith, as enshrined in the sixteenth-century confessions, was the watchword as well as the goal toward which all neo-orthodox Lutheran thinking and striving remained oriented.

Enough has been said about the neo-orthodox concept of the church in general to make it necessary only to highlight some of the most characteristic positions and features of the Hengstenberg circle as they had developed prior to Schaff's departure for the New World. Moving among those theologians and aristocrats associated with the *Evangelische Kirchenzeitung*, what in particular impressed Schaff so deeply that these last months in Berlin marked a final and important phase in his German education, indeed a phase so important that it helped to shape the distinctive Mercersburg Theology that he and his colleague Nevin developed during the following decade.[28]

While the Awakening in Württemberg had found most of its adherents in the villages and among the petit bourgeoisie, the Berlin Awakening had its greatest impact upon the lower classes and the aristocracy.[29] During the early years the center of the Berlin Awakening had been the Baron Hans Ernst von Kottwitz (1757-1843), and even Schaff was still a frequent visitor of the old Baron, sharing in the admiration of this "John-like disciple of Jesus."[30] In the Awakening many Prussian junkers had been won over to a vital Christian faith, after the Wars of Liberation and the romantic movement had been important experiences in their early manhood. In 1827 some of these "awakened" Prussian aristocrats, among them the brothers Otto (1801-49) and Ludwig von Gerlach (1795-1877), founded the *Evangelische Kirchenzeitung* and asked Hengstenberg, who just a year earlier had gained a permanent position in the Theological Faculty of the University of Berlin, to be the journal's editor. In this way Hengstenberg and his journal, with the strong backing of members of the Prussian nobility, assumed leadership of the Berlin Awakening and soon wielded a powerful influence throughout the Prussian Church and even in other parts of Germany. The journal's immediate goal was twofold: to revive vital piety and to wage a fierce battle against rationalism in the universities and churches. A shrill battle cry was sounded in 1830 by the journal's anonymous, scandalous attack, drawn from student lecture notes, on two rationalistic professors (Wegscheider and Gesenius) at the University of Halle.[31] The article's author, it soon became known, was Ludwig von Gerlach. Later in the 1830s the journal attacked Hegel's philosophy and especially the radical Hegelians, Hengstenberg adding poison to his arrows by declaring that Hegel's philosophy celebrated a triumph in Strauss's *Life of Jesus*, "like that of Satan when he descended into Judas."[32] But in 1840, just at about the time of Schaff's arrival in Berlin, a significant change in the theological orientation of the *Evangelische Kirchenzeitug* party was announced by Hengstenberg in the always eagerly awaited Preface he wrote for the journal's first issue of each new year —a change from the Awakening's traditional emphasis on individual piety and the fluid forms of Christian fellowship to doctrinal orthodoxy and the institutional church. According to Ludwig von Gerlach, this change "away from the character of the times, to make the heart the center of all things," had already occurred much earlier, but this changed attitude broke only now dramatically into the open.[33] Now Hengstenberg renounced both the old and the new pietism. He could see no difference, he now declared, between rationalism and pietism, because, with their concentration on the individual's reason or piety, both were "subjective," that is "unchurchly." And thus even pietism, "though unaware, had become a servant and precursor of indifference and unbelief."[34] Hengstenberg in particular attacked and rejected pietism's notion that the true church was "invisible." Already earlier (against Richard Rothe) he had pointed to the doctrine of the invisible church as "the main cause of the downfall of the church."[35] Pietism's great error was the depreciation of the doctrines and the ministry of the church, for, so wrote now Hengstenberg, pure doctrine (and not living piety, we add) is "the foremost and most important treasure of the church."[36] While the Awakening in Württemberg had embraced a conciliatory and broad-minded Lutheranism, the Berlin Awakening increasingly tended belligerently to revive the tenets of sixteenth- and seventeenth-century Lutheran orthodoxy, and with its emphasis on the "objective" character of Christianity and its high-church views it became a major representative of the neo-orthodox concept of the church. In the larger context of the history of theology this development must appear curious, for it meant that pietism helped to revive its former foe, orthodoxy, while a revived orthodoxy then turned against pietism, its own progenitor.

The year 1840 also witnessed the ascension of Friedrich Wilhelm IV (1840-61) to the Prussian throne, and since the new king was an ardent supporter of the Awakening, the party of the *Evangelische Kirchenzeitung* through its aristocratic members now also gained political power and influence at the Prussian court. It is for these later years that Hans Joachim Schoeps (1909-80) has designated this group of churchmen and aristocrats with their conservative views in both church and state as the Prussian High-Orthodoxy.[37]

One of the king's first efforts was directed toward fighting the dominance of Hegel's philosophy and its radical disciples by calling to the University of Berlin the philosopher Schelling and the jurist Friedrich Julius Stahl, the author of *The Constitution of the Church According to Doctrine and Right of the Protestants* (1840). But Stahl became the brilliant spokesman of the conservative, reactionary party in church and state in Prussia only after the revolution of 1848. In the early 1840s no one had developed and presented the position of the Prussian High Orthodoxy more clearly and fully than, oddly enough, another jurist, Ludwig von Gerlach.[38] In the 1830s and 1840s he contributed in fact more articles to the *Evangelische Kirchenzeitung* than anybody else, though always anonymously.[39]

Ludwig von Gerlach appears to have exerted a magnetic attraction on young people in particular, who, as Schaff's fellow-student August Kahnis (1814-88) reported, succumbed to his personality without resistance.[40] This is confirmed by so unlikely a witness as Charles Hodge (1797-1878), later Princeton's crusty opponent of the high-church views of Schaff and Nevin. While studying in Berlin in 1827, he recorded in his diary: "Returning home, I walked with Ludwig von Gerlach, a man who has excited more love and respect in me than almost any other I have seen here."[41] Schaff too now came under the spell of this Prussian aristocrat, for, by some strange coincidence, Ludwig von Gerlach was present in Berlin precisely during those two years when Schaff began his teaching career.[42] After having held several judicial posts elsewhere in Prussia, von Gerlach was recalled to Berlin in 1842 to join a royal commission established for the reform of the Prussian law code. Two years later, he left Berlin (like Schaff) to assume his new appointment as the president of the Magdeburg appeals court (a position he held until 1874). It was, therefore, primarily through Ludwig von Gerlach, as well as through Hengstenberg, that Schaff absorbed many of the peculiar ideas and aims of the Prussian High Orthodoxy. We know that he attended the weekly soirées of Ludwig von Gerlach and of Hengstenberg. His theology now evolved still further, and, when compared with the pietism of his youth in Württemberg, was changed rather drastically.

The majority of von Gerlach's political views can hardly have held much appeal for Schaff, a native of republican Switzerland. In one of the few later references to von Gerlach in his published writings, Schaff spoke of him as "a statesman of brilliant genius" who can defend with the greatest plausibility the oddest propositions.[43] This may have been an oblique reference to some of von Gerlach's extreme political views which in the reign of Friedrich Wilhelm IV, especially after the revolution of 1848, characterized this brilliant publicist who helped to found and lead the reactionary conservative party in Prussia. As a Prussian statesman, Ludwig von Gerlach was guided by the principle that "We must give our consciousness of God a political form."[44] Thus he gave voice to what critics have called the "romantic political theology" of the Christian conservative circles in Berlin.[45] As a principled enemy of all revolutions he opposed popular sovereignty and democracy no less than royal absolutism and the omnipotent state, the revolution "from below" and "from above," while at the same time he continued to defend the feudal privileges of the landed aristocracy as grounded in God's will. Only when he finally accepted Stahl's more advanced principle of the constitutional monarchy did he, like most of his like-minded fellow-aristocrats, "abandon the wilderness of private law relationships for the broad plain of constitutional government."[46] But even then he faulted Stahl for not knowing "that the eternal God was the king of Prussia in accordance with the law of the state."[47] He strove to make Prussia a Christian state governed by the norms of the gospel, but his understanding of the Christian state was such that, for instance, he called it the victory of a "preposterous principle" when in 1849 "Jews, pantheists, atheists" were admitted to public office in Prussia.[48]

Ludwig von Gerlach, however, was really at heart more concerned about the church than the state. In the Awakening he had become an individualistic pietist, but he participated in, and even hastened, the evolution of the "awakened" circles in Berlin "from pietism to the institutional church, from the individual to

106

the Basileia," as he put it in his review of the past that has already been mentioned.[49] Like Hengstenberg, he embraced and tirelessly publicized the doctrine of the visible church as well as a high view of the church as the "Body of Christ." Lutheran orthodoxy and the romantic idea of organic growth were fused in his affirmation of the indissoluble unity of Christ and the church. The church is the body of Christ as Christ is its head. Therefore, as Christ is never without the church, so the church is nothing without Christ. It might even be said that von Gerlach perceived of the church as being "not only in organic, real, but in almost magical connection" with Christ.[50] As a social organism the church undergoes in the course of time development and growth yet remains always the same, the "Body of Christ," with the divine life emanating from Christ continuously flowing through its veins. Obviously this church, representing God's will and authority as does the state, requires the individual Christian to be subordinate to the authority of the church, for the church is the mother (one of von Gerlach's favorite metaphors) who nourishes and guides all believers. "First Christ, the apostles, the ministries of the church; only then the faithful and the faith."[51] This church was certainly not a "platonic state," invisible, but the institutional church, with its legal constitution, sacraments, ministerial office and confessions. Von Gerlach could go so far as to claim, as he did in 1853, that the salvation of a Christian depends upon his (or her) obedience to the authority and constitution of the church.[52] Furthermore, like all these neo-orthodox Lutherans he emphasized the confessional character of the church. But it is important to note that he supported, as did Hengstenberg during Schaff's time in Berlin, the Prussian Union Church, for the differences between the sixteenth-century Lutheran and Reformed confessions, he believed, do not touch the essentials of the Christian faith. He affirmed the sole authority of the Word of God and held the Bible and the three ecumenical creeds to be the true foundation of the universal church.

As to von Gerlach's complex understanding of the relationship of church and state, he argued that both, founded by God, represent God's authority, though each in its own sphere and with its own authoritarian form of government. The

107

church, however, is to be independent of the state, even the Christian state, though never separate from the state, for both together are to serve the realization of God's kingdom on earth. But since von Gerlach conceived of the relationship between church and state analogous to the relation between law and gospel in Pauline and Lutheran theology, he held to the firm belief that the church (and not, for instance, Rothe's and Hegel's state) is to be the ultimate goal in the divine plan for ushering in the kingdom of God. As he argued in the *Evangelische Kirchenzeitung* in 1836, the perfect theocracy is the ultimate goal of the Christian churches and of all Christian states.[53] Ludwig von Gerlach has the unusual distinction of being the only modern politician, certainly in Germany, who can be called "a consistent theocrat."[54]

What must have especially appealed to Schaff, besides von Gerlach's high-church views, was therefore the remarkable fact that this Prussian aristocrat, in his thought and action, was motivated by the overriding conception of the "kingdom of God," Augustine's *civitas Dei*. Von Gerlach read Augustine's book repeatedly and firmly believed that all political and religious striving must in the end be directed toward the establishment of the kingdom of God on earth. He was twenty years old, when in 1815 the Holy Alliance was created by bringing together Eastern Orthodox Russia, Roman Catholic Austria and Protestant Prussia for the promotion of Christian principles in European politics. This event profoundly impressed him. He always viewed the Holy Alliance (which subsequent history showed up as ineffective) as "the greatest idea and tendency of our century," as his century's greatest achievement.[55] The league of three sovereigns representing the three great Christian traditions was to him a manifestation of the fact that "our Lord and Savior is the foundation of the European system of states," he saw in this league the beginning of the royal reign of Christ![56]

It was this grand vision of the kingdom of God that made this Prussian aristocrat an outspoken opponent of German nationalism. In Bismarck's German Empire he declared in a parliamentary debate: "I am in all the relations of my life nothing else but a Prussian, but for me Prussia and Germany rank far below the kingdom of God." Earlier he had stated in even simpler terms his conviction that the German cannot be a nationalist: "The kingdom of God is his fatherland." And when in 1842 the celebration of the building and restoration of the Cologne cathedral under the leadership of the Prussian king and with the support of Roman Catholics and Protestants alike stirred up nationalistic fervor, he warned in the *Evangelische Kirchenzeitung* that it was not Germany's mission to strive to become a powerful nation state. For Germany was distinguished by its religious profundity and should not give it up "and forget the ecclesiastical oppositions which it is its very own mission to examine, to live through, and to struggle to resolve."[57] We should note that, in a similar vein, Stahl said of the German nation that "it caused the division of the church, it and it alone contains the seeds for the reunion," and he called this ecumenical quest "the mission of the German people."[58] This notion of a German mission in the quest for Christian unity Schaff appropriated and incorporated into his Mercersburg program for the renewal of Protestantism. It can be argued that Ludwig von Gerlach became first interested in the quest for Christian unity in order to provide the necessary ecclesiastical corollary and support for the Holy Alliance. In any case, his idea of Christian universalism was no doubt the counterpart to his political universalism.

This quest for Christian unity manifested itself in what Schaff's Berlin mentors liked to call an "evangelical catholicity" which they strove to bring about--as did Schaff throughout his life, inspired by the initial guidance he received in Berlin![59] This remarkable openness toward Roman Catholicism and the desire to work toward the reunion of Protestantism and Roman Catholicism set the Prussian High Orthodoxy apart from the other centers of nineteenth-century Lutheran confessionalism. Even Friedrich Wilhelm IV, the "lay theologian" on the Prussian throne, aimed at "the realization of a true evangelical catholicity—a concept that shows up time and again and is difficult to grasp rationally."[60] One may also want to ponder Theodor Kliefoth's remark in 1845, that "evangelical catholicism" was "for the time being only a word, a formula, a manner of speaking," the hollowness of which becomes apparent the moment "one tries to imagine what such a church must be like, or tries to adjust even a single point of ecclesiastical life along its lines, or to use it as an arbiter for settling even one of the unresolved controversies."[61] Nevertheless, the ideal of "evangelical catholicism" in its application and elaboration in the ecclesiastical setting of his time made Ludwig von Gerlach, this remarkable Prussian aristocrat, a pioneer of the ecumenical movement of our time.[62]

The roots of the ideal of "evangelical catholicism" reached back to the Awakening, when Roman Catholics and Protestants had been drawn together by their common religious experience and their common indifference toward the external forms of the church. After the visit of a French Catholic in 1832 von Gerlach wrote he "felt a burning desire for a union of believing Catholics and Protestants."[63]. When he and the other members of his circle later developed their understanding of the visible church as the "Body of Christ," they were deeply impressed by the ideal of the one, holy, catholic and apostolic church, an ideal with which the disunity of Christianity, and in particular the fragmentation of Protestantism, now appeared to be irreconcilable. They therefore set out to heal the Roman Catholic-Protestant division and in particular the disease of Protestant "subjectivism" in an attempt to help restore the visible unity, catholicity and historical continuity of the church. In this aim they were deeply influenced by the romantic rediscovery of the Catholic Middle Age; indeed, they came to believe that the ideal of Christian universalism was most clearly embodied in medieval Catholicism.[64] In 1848 Ludwig von Gerlach wrote that he "honored and loved" the Roman Catholic Church "as the mother of all Latin Christianity, therefore also as the mother of the Protestant churches, and thus as his own mother." The Reformation, he asserted, was the organic outgrowth of medieval Catholicism, it was "one of the most exquisite blossoms" of the medieval Church.[65] For his own time he pleaded for a new attitude among Roman Catholics and Protestants for the good of the universal church of Christ: Protestants must affirm God's creative activity in the Roman Catholic worship of God *until* the Reformation, as the

Roman Catholic Church must affirm God's creative activity *since* the Reformation. And both churches must be animated by the spirit of penitence, for only a penitent Protestantism has a future, and likewise only a penitent Roman Catholicism. "Without penitence both will retain nothing but their errors."[66]

But there were political reasons as well for pursuing the ideal of "evangelical catholicism." The members of the Prussian High Orthodoxy, like their king, who in several of his early decisions favored the Roman Catholic Church, realized that this church and conservative Protestantism could unite in a common cause against the common foe, the spirit of revolution and unbelief alive in their time. This strategically important political alliance, however, was founded on the conviction that orthodox Protestantism and Roman Catholicism agree on the fundamental doctrines of the Christian faith. Schaff later described the attitude of the *Evangelische Kirchenzeitung* party in the person of Hengstenberg, who, to be true, as a strict Lutheran showed a certain reserve toward the ecumenical ideal of "evangelical catholicism." Hengstenberg, Schaff wrote,

> holds most firmly to the basic teachings of the Reformation, but he believes....that at the present time not the papacy but rationalism and unbelief in its various forms is the greatest and most dangerous enemy of the Evangelical Church. Hence his inexorable hostility to the spirit of rebellion and revolution, which he regards as a product of modern unbelief, while he views the Catholic Church, notwithstanding its errors, as a great conservative power, whose fundamental doctrines of Christianity agree with orthodox Protestantism.[67]

To call Roman Catholicism the "Anti-Christ," Hengstenberg insisted, is an "actual blasphemy."[68]

But von Gerlach did speak his mind where criticism of the Roman Catholic Church was called for. He opposed the dogma of the Immaculate Conception of 1854. He called it an error of Roman Catholicism "to seek in the authority of the church a substitute for the absent God, to forget over the body of the church the spirit which animates it." Infallible is only the Holy Spirit, he declared, who cannot be identified with any empirical church.[69] At times he lamented the lack of penitence in the Roman Catholic Church. For Ludwig von Gerlach the road did not lead from Herrnhut to Rome, as some critics prophesied, even though in Bismarck's Empire he joined the Catholic Center Party. He remained rooted in Protestant piety, declaring later in life that nothing can be "a substitute for the altar in the heart, for the fire of the spirit, for the intimate, secret intercourse with the Lord." He mentioned that the English and Americans speak of 'personal religion' and 'sacramental religion,' and he concluded: "Both intimately one is the truth."[70] But the hope for the coming unity of all the Christian churches remained. In 1853 he set down his ecumenical creed: "The unity of the whole church of God is the lofty goal toward which the developments of the world run. This goal stands still far behind the year 1900. But it is nevertheless beginning to become visible at the remotest horizon of time for the eye of faith."[71]

It should finally also be mentioned that von Gerlach's ecumenical aspirations helped to create the favorable climate for one of the Prussian king's favorite ecclesiastical projects, the establishment by the Prussian Union Church and the Church of England of a Joint Episcopate in Jerusalem in 1841. But, somewhat surprisingly, in the end he opposed this ecumenical venture for personal, theological and political reasons.[72]

In the spring of 1843 Schaff preached a sermon in the Berlin cathedral, which can serve as an illustration of the extent to which he had embraced the religious and political conservatism of the *Evangelische Kirchenzeitung* party. The text, 1 Cor. 2:2, prompted him to compare the "Jews" and "Greeks" in Paul's letter with the liberals of his day. They want freedom and equality—so do we.

> But by this they do not mean the true freedom from sin and guilt, not the lofty equality of all of God's saved children....They want to be free of all bonds, even that of God's authority, free from humility and the silent subjection to God's law and order, free from everything that hampers the impetuous urgings of their passions.

His hearers in the Berlin cathedral were hardly surprised when the zealous young preacher next pointed to the contemporary "Greeks."

> Do not the leaders of our time use wisdom and science as their slogan? Has not reason once again become the golden calf?....Does not their innermost being rebel when we still preach that reason should be taken captive by the obedience of faith, faith in a personal God, in personal immortality, in a personal Christ in whom the fullness of God dwelled and who, through his bitter suffering and death, gained for us forgiveness of our sins, peace, and eternal life?[73]

The centrality of the church as the "Body of Christ" and the bright ideal of an "evangelical catholicism" for the renewal of Protestantism were fortunately for Schaff a more significant and lasting part of the legacy of the *Evangelische Kirchenzeitung* than that journal's narrow-minded, pious opposition to the progressive social and political aspirations of the growing German middle class.

A full evaluation of Hengstenberg's influence on Schaff must, of course, consider his dual role as editor of the *Evangelische Kirchenzeitung* and as professor of the Old Testament in the Theological Faculty in Berlin.[74] Hengstenberg was unswervingly orthodox in upholding the Scripture as the inspired and unerring Word of God and in interpreting the Old Testament throughout christologically as pointing to Christ. His acceptance of the Old Testament in its entirety and in every detail as the Word of God and his rejection even of textual criticism, not to speak of the historical-literary criticism then coming into vogue, was of one piece with his journal's opposition to everything in church and state that the editor and his circle of supporters perceived to be rebellion against God's authority and will. As the orthodox champion of the inspiration and authority of the Old Testament, he was, as Schaff soon discovered, besides Tholuck and Neander the best known and most highly regarded German theologian in America.[75]

But during these unusually rich and stimulating last months in Berlin the young docent encountered two other men who were to have a lasting influence on him--the church historian Neander and the philosopher Schelling.[76] It is true that Schaff heard only Neander's lectures on modern church history, and heard these lectures, which were never published, already in the summer semester of 1840. But he immersed himself in Neander's writings and now that he was a docent he was a frequent guest in Neander's living quarters, so admirably presided over by a faithful sister. Neander, like Tholuck in Halle, continued to represent the Awakening, though he was also deeply influenced by his faculty colleague Schleiermacher, with whom he came to share the understanding of Christianity as primarily "life" rather than "doctrine" or "ideas" or even ethics. In 1830 he broke with the *Evangelische Kirchenzeitung* after its anonymous attack on the two rationalistic professors at Halle. Ever since the Hengstenberg circle suspected Neander of being too liberal, Ludwig von Gerlach, for instance, recording in his diary that Neander was "definitely in favor of the liberals."[77] Neander's *Life of Christ* (1837), written to refute David Friedrich Strauss, strengthened this impression. Schaff, too, thought that of all of Neander's publications it was least satisfactory as far as the demands of orthodoxy were concerned, though he was willing to excuse Neander's unnecessary concessions to the rationalistic point of view as merely "some wounds" that the great church historian brought away from his battle with this latest and most dangerous form of German unbelief.[78] Nevertheless, Schaff considered Neander next to Schleiermacher the greatest theologian of the nineteenth century.[79]

Neander's writings and his personal association with the great church historian aroused Schaff's interest in the study of the history of the Christian church and in the end helped to determine his character as a church historian. When fifty years later the Theological Faculty of the University of Berlin honored his church history as "the most important monument of universal history from the School of Neander,"[80] then it deserves to be emphasized that the seeds for Schaff's distinguished work as a church historian were planted during these last months in Berlin. He was particularly impressed by Neander's "comprehensive liberalism and evangelical catholicity," which was the outcome of the broad-

114

mindedness of the Awakening and of Schleiermacher's influence.[81] Obviously, "evangelical catholicity" meant something else to Neander than to Ludwig von Gerlach. Characteristic is Neander's assertion that "The voice of the whole church warns against all that could force the spirits into one dogmatic form and hinder the freedom and diversity of the development of the spiritual life."[82] Neander found in every period of the history of the Christian church the same principle at work: unity in diversity. He disliked the straight-jacket of doctrinal orthodoxy as much as he disliked polemics—with at least one notable exception, for he grimly and passionately polemicized privately and publicly against Hegel's philosophy, what he perceived to be its pantheism and panlogism. No less impressed was Schaff by Neander's ability to combine personal piety and the scientific spirit. Masterfully employing the best tools of historical research, the great church historian aimed at describing Christian piety in all the diversity of its historical expressions with the goal of inspiring vital piety in his own time. He wanted to write the history of the Christian church "as a living witness of the divine power of Christianity; as a school of Christian experience; a voice sounding through the ages, of instruction, of doctrine, and of reproof, for all who are disposed to listen."[83] The pietism of his youth drew Schaff irresistibly to this church historian whose well-known motto was *pectus est quod theologum facit* ("It is the heart that makes the theologian"). And it is obvious that he was drawn more to this "pectoral theologian" than to Baur in Tübingen. Yet he learned to combine eclectically Hegel's powerful principle of dialectical development, as Baur was applying it to the study of the history of the Christian church, with the organological method of German romanticism which in Neander's application led to the interpretation of the history of the Christian church as a self-unfolding organic process in which Christ's life becomes individualized in his followers. One might say that as a budding church historian Schaff, influenced by Germany's two greatest church historians, "grafted Baur on Neander."[84]

For the time being he also grafted the doctrine of the visible church of the Hengstenberg circle on Neander's church historiography, for in keeping with the spirit of the Awakening Neander, as the historian of Christian piety, endeavored to trace the manifestations of the "invisible church" or the "kingdom of God" through history. If in Schaff's agreement with the basic orientation and aims of Neander's church historiography we hear the voice of the Awakening, then we hear in his criticism the voice of the *Evangelische Kirchenzeitung* with its doctrinal orthodoxy and high-church views as well as of Hegel's philosophy, at least in so far as Schaff thought it necessary to utilize Hegel's philosophy in his own theological endeavors. Schaff's reminiscences of 1851, which were prompted by Neander's death the year before, are of particular interest because they accurately reflected some of the theological currents that were swirling around Schaff in Berlin. Schaff took exception to Neander's lack of doctrinal orthodoxy and his insufficient recognition of the "objective" and "churchly" character of Christianity. He did not join the circle of students who met weekly in Neander's quarters, but instead attended, as already noted, the weekly soirées of Ludwig von Gerlach and Hengstenberg. He was revolted, as he wrote, by "the everlasting criticism which several of (Neander's) uncritical worshippers heaped on Hegel, on the one hand, and on Hengstenberg (whom I personally learned to esteem highly and to love), on the other hand." And he continued:

> Anyway, my own position toward speculative theology and churchly orthodoxy was one he could not entirely approve of. My position toward speculative theology seemed and still seems to me solely suited to solve adequately certain problems of our time, in particular the christological question, or at least to offer an approach to a final solution. As for my relation to orthodoxy, I consider it not merely a dam to hold back the destructive tendencies of unbelief, but also a salutary supplement to the one-side subjectivism from which all modern Protestantism suffers.[85]

This revealing passage once again shows that at the end of his German years of education Schaff had learned to combine creatively and in the manner of an eclectic some of the most prominent currents in German Protestantism in the late 1830s and early 1840s.

Our survey of Schaff's years in Berlin would be incomplete, if we were to fail to mention Schelling's role in the Prussian capital. He had been called from Munich to Berlin by Friedrich Wilhelm IV with the full support of the conservative Christian circles in Berlin in the hope that one of the founders of idealistic philosophy in his old age would not only break down the omnipotence of Hegel's philosophy but also fill the ugly ditch that Hegel's radical disciples had dug between philosophy and theology, the sciences and Christian faith. Schelling's inaugural lecture in the winter semester 1841/42 turned into one of the great academic events in the history of the German university. For everybody of prominence came and crowded the auditorium, including foreign ambassadors and among the theologians Twesten and Neander. Even more noteworthy was the attendance of four young students, all of whom were to offer their comments on Schelling's inaugural lecture and the whole lecture course that first semester: the German Friedrich Engels, who only a few years later would publish with Karl Marx the "Communist Manifesto," the Russian and later anarchist Mikhail Bakunin (1818-97), the Swiss Jacob Burckhardt, who in Basel would rival Berlin's Leopold von Ranke as one of the nineteenth century's greatest historians, and the Dane Søren Kierkegaard, who had escaped to Berlin after breaking off his engagement to Regine Olsen.[86] Schaff missed Schelling's inaugural lecture since he was still traveling in Italy, but after his return, in the winter semester 1842/43, he heard Schelling's lectures on "The Difference between Negative and Positive Philosophy."[87]

Schaff knew Schelling especially as the author of *Lectures on the Method of Academic Studies* (1803), which some have called his most influential book.[88] In these lectures of the twenty-seven year old, brilliant professor at the University of Jena, which were published the next year, is to be found an important source of the romantic principle of organism that became all-pervasive in German culture and especially in theology at that time.[89] Furthermore, these lectures also helped to establish the principle that characterized the whole century, that history must be viewed, in one sense or another, ultimately as the revelation of God. Schelling presented a romantic metaphysic of history that taught his contemporaries to conceive of history as "sacred," as "a great mirror of the world spirit, an eternal poem of the divine mind. Nothing should be protected more carefully from the touch of unclean hands." And he declared that "History does not satisfy reason until the empirical causes that satisfy the understanding have served to disclose the workings of a higher necessity. Treated in this way, history cannot fail to strike us as the greatest and most marvelous drama, which only an infinite mind could have composed." How impressed Schaff also was when Schelling spoke of the necessity of "the historical construction of Christianity" and, furthermore, asserted: "On account of the universality of its idea, the historical construction of Christianity presupposes the religious construction of history as a whole."[90] This romantic metaphysic of history, reinforced by Hegel's idealistic philosophy of history, would underlie Schaff's own understanding of history.

Schaff himself mentioned the fifth and sixth of these lectures which had taught him that *Vernunft* (reason) comes from *Vernehmen* (perceiving), and that what reason, when properly used, perceives is the revelation of God in Christ. And since both reason and faith come from God, they are finally destined to unite again in Him. The goal of historical development is therefore theosophy, the merging of reason with the Christian faith. Schaff pieced these ideas together to form a comfortable pillow on which his philosophical reflections could slumber for the rest of his days without ever stirring again. His interest and competence did not lie in philosophical theology but lay elsewhere.

Now in Berlin Schaff had the opportunity of meeting the last great representative of German idealism in person and of hearing from his own lips the philosophical justification of traditional Christianity and the proclamation of the fundamental harmony between reason and revelation, philosophy and theology. After having kept silent for two decades, Schelling's Berlin lectures presented the final stage of his intellectual odyssey. As Schaff put it in 1845, for the benefit of his American readers: The greatest living philosopher "in the evening of his days has again come forth like the sun from behind the clouds, and is now pouring the last splendid rays of his genius from Berlin over the philosophical horizon of Germany."[91] In his old age Schelling had turned away from a "negative" philosophy-- termed "negative" because it relies exclusively on a rational approach to the mysteries of God, Self and the World—to the task of setting forth the "positive" philosophy which in its quest for truth is guided and determined by God's revelation. That revelation occurred first in the religions of the world (*mythology*) and finally and ultimately in Christianity (*revelation*). But the sanguine hopes for the success of Schelling's lectures in Berlin that many of the devout entertained--among them Neander who in 1842 dedicated the 2d edition of his *General History of the Christian Religion and Church* to Schelling--were to be disappointed. Schelling never published these lectures and a pirated edition in 1842 of his "Philosophy of Revelation" by the rationalist theologian Heinrich Eberhard Gottlob Paulus (1761-1851) at Heidelberg, a passionate enemy of Schelling, who relied on student lecture notes, embittered Schelling's final years in Berlin.[92] Ernst Troeltsch has given a succinct and critical résumé of the content of Schelling's Berlin lectures and their impact in the nineteenth century: The old Schelling "makes Christianity, whose traditional dogmatics are interpreted in gnostic-evolutionary fashion, the goal of history and the foundation of science, the state, morals and art. This theory has found adherents only in small circles, above all in ecclesiastical and pietistic circles, but has had scarcely any effect on the wider public."[93] As another critic put it, Schelling's Berlin lectures were bound to become "the green pasture of the mediating theology, " because one of the greatest philosophers had here offered once more (and, as it turned out, for the last time) the desired fusion of idealistic philosophy and biblical Christianity.[94]

Nevertheless, these lectures were to be of lasting importance for Schaff because of Schelling's bold ecumenical vision of the history of Christianity which he presented in what in the posthumously published version are the concluding thirty-sixth and thirty-seventh lectures of his *Philosophy of Revelation*.[95] Like the Cistercian abbot Joachim of Floris (circa 1130-1202), Schelling used an allegorical interpretation of biblical personages as a means of discerning and foretelling the historical development of the Christian church, distinguishing three ages that he identified with the apostles Peter, Paul and John. In the dialectical development of Christianity the first age of the Petrine Church or Roman Catholicism was followed by that of the Pauline Church or Protestantism; he then posited their coming reconciliation in the Johannine Church of Love, which will be followed by the return of Christ in his glory. And he concluded:

> If I were to build a church in our time, I should dedicate it to St. John. But sooner or later a church will be built which will unite the three princes among the apostles, for the last authority does not annul or exclude what has gone before, but transfigures and absorbs it. This church would be the true pantheon of the history of the Christian church.[96]

To be sure, Schaff did not hear these lectures himself, for at the time of their delivery, March 1842, he was still in Italy. But he must have quickly acquainted himself with their general content, most likely through some of those who heard Schelling—fellow students, or Neander, or even Ludwig von Gerlach, who chanced upon Schelling's lecture on March 15 and, curiously enough, as the great champion of "evangelical catholicism," recorded at the time no deep impression, still scenting in Schelling's philosophy only the dreaded "pantheism" of idealistic philosophy.[97] Schaff first mentioned Schelling's ecumenical vision at the conclusion of his *Principle of Protestantism*.[98] In 1854 he visited the dying Schelling in Ragaz in Switzerland. Asked whether he still held to his ecumenical vision of the history of Christianity, Schelling, according to Schaff, "emphatically replied in the affirmative, but added that he had, on further reflection, made room for James as the representative of the Greek Church, in distinction from the Roman or Petrine Church."[99] Toward the end of his life Schaff summarized his response to Schelling's scheme once more: "It is, like all philosophical constructions which anticipate the future known only to God more or less fanciful; but it is certainly grand and ingenious and involves a truth which illuminates the past and casts light on the future. It impresses itself indelibly upon the mind."[100] In Berlin this philosophical construction of the history of Christianity, however fanciful it was, as Schaff at once conceded, first became important for him because it did three things to the grand but somewhat empty notion of "evangelical catholicism" of the Prussian High Orthodoxy: it grounded it in Scripture, filled it with historical content, and marked the reunion of Christendom as the *telos*, the goal, of all history.

It was in Berlin at this time that Schaff met Frédéric Godet (1812-1890), a fellow-Swiss, who enthusiastically attended Schelling's lectures and who became Schaff's closest friend. He was the tutor of the crown prince Friedrich Wilhelm, the future ill-fated emperor Friedrich III (1888), and later was a distinguished theologian in the French-speaking part of his native country. To the end of their lives the two remained close friends and admirers of each other's work.

It is finally necessary to place the Prussian High Orthodoxy once more into the larger context of the theological currents in the mid-1840s, for only then can we hope to understand more precisely the nature of the influence of the high-church and ecumenical views to which Schaff was exposed in Berlin. Prior to his departure for America those German Protestant circles which were "church-conscious" agreed on the essential point that Christianity must have a body, that Protestantism cannot exist without a church, and that therefore the "subjectivism" of contemporary theology, however it may manifest itself, must be opposed. Of course, there were already indications of differences among them in their ecclesiologies and church politics, but these differences had not yet advanced to the point of producing a divisive, exclusive Lutheran confessionalism. Löhe, who would become the leader of Lutheran confessionalism in Bavaria and whose influence would soon extend to the Middle West of the United States, published his trail-blazing *Three Books about the Church* only in 1845. Kliefoth had not yet emerged from out of the shadow of Schleiermacher and Hegel as the influential leader of Lutheran confessionalism in Mecklenburg and other North German states. But even more important was it for Schaff that Hengstenberg did not challenge the Prussian Union in the *Evangelische Kirchenzeitung* until 1846. It is true that his attitude toward the Prussian Union was ambiguous, that it did not follow a straight line.[101] In the controversy between the Prussian Union Church and the Lutheran separatists, the "Old Lutherans," in the 1830s, the *Evangelische Kirchenzeitung* sided with the Union, by speaking up for the established church against sectarian separation. And when Schaff in the New World in 1845 praised the Prussian Union as "a great step toward the catholicity and unity which are necessarily implied in the idea of the church," he included Hengstenberg in a long list of theologians who were decidedly for the Union.[102] But this positive attitude toward the Prussian Union of the Hengstenberg circle changed dramatically in 1846, when the king convened the Prussian General Synod for the purpose of consolidating the Union by giving it in addition to a common administration and liturgy also a common creedal formulary for ordination. The General Synod, it turned out, was dominated by "liberal" delegates, mediating theologians in particular. The ordination formulary that Dorner and Karl Immanuel Nitzsch (1787-1868), who was called to Berlin as Marheineke's successor the next year, prepared (ridiculed by opponents as the "Nitzschenum," in contrast to the "Nicaenum") was unacceptable to the orthodox party. Hengstenberg opposed it in the *Evangelische Kirchenzeitung*; Ludwig von Gerlach later added the remark to his diary: "My whole activity at that time was directed toward breaking up the Synod and then the non-confirmation of its resolutions; the latter was achieved."[103] The king did indeed not confirm the resolutions of the General Synod. The revolution two years later turned these conservative Prussian aristocrats and churchmen then decisively into the reactionary, exclusivist party that dominated both church and state in Prussia for more than a decade. The end of that era is marked symbolically by the death in the same year, 1861, of both Friedrich Julius Stahl and his king, Friedrich Wilhelm IV.

One can therefore hope to understand the precise nature of the influence of the Prussian High Orthodoxy on Schaff as well as his own formulation and proposed solution of the "church question" only if one keeps in mind that before 1844 the Hengstenberg circle, and in particular Ludwig von Gerlach, were still both Lutherans and ecumenical Christians. They had set themselves the twofold task of reviving the orthodox traditions of Lutheranism and of restoring the historical and catholic wholeness and oneness of the Christian church. This was what has been called the paradoxical position of the Prussian High Orthodoxy at that time.[104] Only after 1846/48 did these theologians and Prussian aristocrats embrace an exclusive and even belligerent Lutheran confessionalism, except that von Gerlach's and even Stahl's quest for the unity of the universal church, though strictly on the basis of orthodox Lutheran principles and in opposition to the Prussian Union, never flagged. In short, Schaff did not come in contact with the exclusive Lutheran confessionalism that asserted itself and spread in Germany around the middle of the century, and when it then became a force in the United States as well, Schaff turned against both. In 1857 he finally publicly distanced himself from Hengstenberg's political and theological position: "It is evident that Dr. Hengstenberg has no sympathy whatever with religious and political freedom, which must necessarily result from Protestantism, wherever it is fully and consistently developed." And Schaff now spoke of

> the defect in the high-churchism of Hengstenberg and his school. The churchly tendencies which are indeed needed, should not flow in the narrow channel of Lutheran denominationalism, or any ism or sect, but be as broad and comprehensive as the kingdom of Christ, and in harmony with the deepest wants and movements of the age that hates despotism and loves freedom in church and state.[105]

Though these words obviously reflect Schaff's "Americanization" during the intervening years, they can also help to recall to our attention Hirsch's discussion of the conflict between the "neo-Protestant" and "neo-orthodox" concepts of the church. For that discussion concludes with a brief sketch of a third position, that of the mediating theology, which Hirsch explicates by drawing upon the writings of Schaff's lifelong friend Dorner.[106] Typically, Dorner tried to mediate between what the mediating theology had come to consider the one-sided extremes of the other two parties: confessional orthodoxy and doctrinal freedom,

123

Lutheranism and the Union Church, a church order "from above" and "from below," the "visible" and the "invisible" church, deftly trying to steer the ship of the church between the extremes of hierarchy and anarchy. It now merely needs to be stated that this "mediating" third way was to be Schaff's own position, with the emphasis placed on the "churchly" and "objective" character of Christianity during the first decade at Mercersburg, as he had learned it from the Hengstenberg circle prior to 1844.

There is no better way to end this important chapter in Schaff's life than with the words that conclude the brief chapter on the Berlin years in his "Autobiographical Reminiscences": "The three years I spent in Berlin are among the happiest in my life. I enjoyed all the educational advantages of the metropolis of Germany and the daily intercourse of men devoted to the highest pursuits of life." But then he added: "I had the best prospects of promotion when I unexpectedly received a call to America."[107]

An American by Choice

Chapter 6

Called to Mercersburg Seminary in Pennsylvania

The German Reformed Church in the United States, whose members were mostly immigrants or the descendants of immigrants primarily from the Palatinate region in southern Germany, was one of the smaller denominations in this new nation then barely fifty years old.[1] In the early 1840s it claimed 75,000 members, 600 congregations and 180 ministers. It had established two institutions of higher learning, a college and a seminary, both located since 1837 at Mercersburg in western Pennsylvania. Far removed from Prussia's capital and its illustrious university, Mercersburg was a small town of about 1,000 inhabitants that had recommended itself as the ideal site for the seminary and college because of the scenic beauty of its location in the western foothills of the Appalachian mountains, its safe distance from urban distractions and a road passing through the town that was much traveled by the stage coach. In 1840 this small immigrant denomination had called the Presbyterian John Williamson Nevin to join Frederick A. Rauch (1806-41) to teach both at the seminary and the college. A native German, Rauch had been educated at the University of Heidelberg and had first introduced the new German philosophy and theology into the German Reformed Church. It was his untimely death at the age of thirty-five that prompted, early in 1843, a special synodical conference to invite the famed preacher of the Awakening from the Lower Rhine, Friedrich Wilhelm Krummacher (1796-1868), to join Nevin as the other professor on the faculty of the isolated and struggling Mercersburg Seminary. The Seminary's enrollment at the time was small, between 10 and 20 students. This call was certainly an act of faith on the part of the synodical fathers, for the synodical treasury was once again empty. Moreover, Krummacher, then forty-seven years old, stood at the height of his fame as one of Germany's most eloquent pulpit orators—four years later he succeeded Marheineke at Berlin's Trinity Church and in 1853 he was appointed preacher at the Prussian royal court at Potsdam. The denomination's two envoys, Theodore L. Hoffeditz and Benjamin S. Schneck, proceeded at once to Krummacher's church at Elberfeld, where they presented the Synod's call. Krummacher pondered the matter for some time but in the end refused the call "with a bleeding heart."[2] He wisely realized that his proper sphere of activity was the pulpit and not the professor's lectern. Moreover, he considered it a nearly hopeless task to prevent the German immigrants from becoming fully "Anglicized." Among the mission-minded Christians in Germany the feeling at that time was wide-spread that German immigrants in the United States should retain not only their religious but also their ethnic and linguistic identity. Wilhelm Löhe's eloquent appeal to the Lutheran immigrants, for instance, equated Lutheranism with the German language and customs as well as with the true and saving faith.[3] Since Krummacher conceived his American task primarily in these terms but was less sanguine than Löhe in his hope for success, he declined to join his life to a lost cause.

Undaunted, the American envoys continued their search, traveling first to Halle and then to Berlin, where in each place their attention was drawn to Philip Schaff. Encouraged by Krummacher himself, by Tholuck and Müller, Twesten, Neander and Hengstenberg, they approached Schaff sometime in July 1843 and quickly secured his permission to present his name for the Mercersburg vacancy at the next synodical meeting of their church. Upon their return, in the fall of 1843, the Synod of the German Reformed Church officially extended its call to Philip Schaff.

And Schaff accepted this call as "a divine call that came to me with irresistible force."[4] To be sure, he must have felt tempted to remain in Prussia's capital, where, as he told the synodical members of the German Reformed Church in rural Pennsylvania a year later, "my academic career had just begun under favorable auspices, in the society of so many cultivated, profound, and noble

128

minds, well-fitted to enlarge and invigorate my inexperienced powers, and under the fostering care of a pious and highly gifted monarch."[5] But Schaff, no doubt, also realized that he could hardly expect to further his academic career at Berlin (rumors already circulated, however, that he was in line for a professorship at Zurich). The university counted just then an unusually large number of *privatdozenten*, twenty-seven in the summer of 1843, which prompted Johann Albrecht Friedrich Eichhorn (1779-1856), the new Minister of Public Worship and Education, to instruct the faculties to separate the wheat from the chaff by scrupulously examining each *privatdozent's* performance.[6] Moreover, in the theology department several aspiring young scholars had already qualified themselves, or were in the process of qualifying themselves, for an academic career. Curiously, all of them were church historians, and most of them belonged to Neander's school, as it is interesting to note that only during the last decade of his life Neander attracted a group of gifted young followers eager to prepare themselves for an academic career. Besides Schaff, those aspiring church historians in Berlin were Wilhelm Heinrich Erbkam (1838), Ferdinand Karl Wilhelm Piper (1840), Justus Jacobi (1841), Karl Friedrich August Kahnis (1842), Hermann Reuter (1843) and Wilhelm Rudolf Chlebus (1844). One should also mention H. Rossel, Neander's favorite pupil, "the only one who perhaps would have become his equal," had it not been for his untimely death due to overwork, at the age of 26, in 1846.[7] Only Piper, who was appointed an associate professor the same summer Schaff finished his degree work, remained at Berlin for almost fifty years, even though—a Berlin academic curiosity—he was never promoted to a full professorship. At Neander's death in 1850, Jacobi had every hope of being appointed his teacher's successor but was passed over in favor of the undistinguished Johann Karl Lehnerdt, Hengstenberg's choice. All then, except for Piper and Chlebus who also died young, accepted academic positions elsewhere in Germany. Erbkam (1810-84), Jacobi (1815-88) and Piper (1811-89) remained in Neander's camp; Kahnis (1814-88), at Berlin close to Hengstenberg and Schaff, became a strict Lutheran, but later embraced the mediating theology;

Reuter (1817-89) maintained an independent position. All were from northern Germany, which made Schaff from republican Switzerland stand out and doubtlessly helped to induce his Berlin teachers to consider him better qualified for an appointment in the new republic across the ocean than the others.

But Schaff was not inclined to decide the future course of his career on so mundane a level. Motivated, as he was, by the spirit of the Awakening, he endeavored, more conscientiously than ever, to surrender himself entirely to the divine guidance, so that in the end he could face the synodical members of the German Reformed Church with the "consoling conscience" that in the matter of his removal to the United States he had "not pursued a road cast up by my own hands."[8] He was moved by the unanimity with which his teachers had recommended him for the Mercersburg position. Hengstenberg, for instance, had praised his serious Christian spirit, lively mind, his gifts of teaching and attracting the young, and his youth which, far from being a deterrent, vouched for his adaptability to new and challenging conditions.[9] Even more decisive was for Schaff the impressive unanimity by which the Synod of the German Reformed Church in the fall of 1843 confirmed the initiative of its two envoys in inviting him to Mercersburg. Now, at last, his eyes were fully opened to the divine nature of his American call. As he wrote in his reply:

> I sunk down upon my knees, I may say involuntarily, and breathed forth thanksgiving and praise for that unbounded Grace of my God, which has followed me from my earliest years...and I therefore hasten with all the fullness of a grateful and glowing heart, to say Yea to that call.[10]

However, Schaff was no less powerfully motivated by the Awakening's missionary and ecumenical impulses. Martin Schmidt (1909-82) has shown that the mid-nineteenth-century efforts of German Christians to care for the destitute Germans abroad was inspired by the piety of the Awakening, in which "the dynamics of the Word of God and the profound conception of the diaspora situation as the Christian's pilgrimage on earth" had been fused.[11] Already in his youth Schaff had seen the missionary impulse at work in the Kornthal community, which from its beginning had sent many of its students to the Basle Mission for training as missionaries in foreign fields. The Basel Mission had been founded in 1815 as an outgrowth of the Swiss and southern German Awakening, in particular through the efforts of the *Deutsche Christentumsgesellschaft*. It is a moving experience even today to visit the Kornthal cemetery, where not only the founders of Kornthal but several of Kornthal's foreign missionaries have found their final resting place.[12] Now that Schaff was about to leave for the New World, he could have echoed Löhe's beautiful word, for the spirit of the Awakening was alive in both: "Mission is nothing but the one church of Christ in its movement—the realization of the universal, catholic church."[13] The same spirit manifested itself in the short sentence Ludwig von Gerlach wrote in Schaff's album, when he bade him farewell: "The Lord turns the homeland into foreign land, and the foreign land into homeland." In the New World Schaff time and again quoted von Gerlach's album verse. He himself put it this way: "The church of the living God, who has also in America a large people, is truly the believer's fatherland."[14] The Awakening had taught Christians to think of themselves as pilgrims on earth, truly at home only in Christ's church, and for these Christians the mission of the church was unthinkable apart from the desire to manifest more fully the world-wide unity of the universal church.

These missionary and ecumenical impulses were given eloquent voice in Schaff's ordination sermon delivered in Krummacher's Elberfeld church on April 12, 1844. Baptized in the Reformed Church at Chur and confirmed as a Lutheran at Kornthal, he was now ordained to the ministry in the Reformed Church at Elberfeld, but under the auspices of the Prussian Evangelical or Union Church. After Krummacher's powerful and lengthy charge to the ordinand, which left Schaff weak and trembling with intense emotions, holding on to a table for support, he preached on the Macedonian call: "Come over and help us" (Acts16:9). This call was now addressed to him, for the Macedonian of old was the North American of today. His departure for America was therefore not "a private matter but a holy concern of the kingdom of God." Moreover, whoever averted his eyes from the German immigrants in their hour of need, still lacked the true conception of the church, "the life of the Body of Christ does not yet flow in his veins."[15] The kingdom of God and the universal church as the Body of Christ—these were the shining ideals that inspired Schaff on the eve of his departure for the New World. The condition of these immigrants Schaff painted in the darkest colors, even speaking of them as "a confluence of beggars, adventurers, freedom-cranks, criminals, and obvious blasphemers."[16] Small wonder that the German secular press in the United States, as soon as Schaff's sermon was printed in Krummacher's *Palmblätter* and in an English translation in the *Weekly Messenger* of the German Reformed Church, raised a mighty cry of outrage which reverberated unpleasantly throughout Schaff's first American years--though this hostile reaction must have reassured the fathers of the German Reformed Church that in calling Schaff they had not unwittingly imported a German "rationalist." According to the zealous young preacher, three mighty foes threatened the German immigrants and the German-language churches: paganism, Roman Catholicism and sectarianism. To do battle with them in the strength of the armor of God's biblical word and of German theology he conceived as his missionary task. But Schaff also extolled--as had some of his teachers in their letters of recommendation and Krummacher himself in his ordination charge--the much broader and daunting task of going abroad as a scholarly mediator between German and American Christianity. Schaff had at that time obviously only a very imperfect and dim conception of so challenging a task, but the gradual unfolding of its full implications and possibilities in his professional life gave in the end a truly distinctive and unique cast to his whole career. At the end of a long service, when darkness had already set in and the preacher's figure could only dimly be seen in the pulpit by a patiently listening congregation, Schaff finally lifted up the ideal of the world-wide unity of Christ's church and kingdom, ending his sermon with these stirring words:

132

What is wanted is that members of the same faith take hands as brothers, both in spirit and in body, on this and the farther shore of the great ocean. What is wanted is the firm union of all true members of the evangelical, apostolic and thus truly catholic church. What is wanted is to have Europe—and more especially its heart, Protestant Germany—with all it has achieved in eighteen centuries, live and thrive and bloom in America, and to bring the new world, pregnant with future, closer to the old and aging world, so that it be kept from decaying and be born anew out of young strength. Thus the time will come when both hemispheres will completely understand each other in their love for the One who was crucified and will take hands across the great ocean in a spirit of love and everlasting peace."[17]

Schaff was commissioned to his work by the "Evangelical Association for Protestant Germans in North America at Langenberg, Elberfeld, and Barmen," called the "Langenberg Association" for short. Founded in 1837 as an outgrowth of the Lower Rhineland Awakening, this Association was "evangelical", that is, interdenominational, in character, supporting all Protestant German language-churches in the United States. Not much later, the Association also commissioned August Rauschenbusch (1816-99), who in America joined the Baptists and was the father of Walter Rauschenbusch (1861-1918). Schaff and the elder Rauschenbusch were to be the Association's most distinguished envoys to the New World.

Schaff had traveled from Berlin to Elberfeld on a circuitous route that took him first to southern Germany and Switzerland, ostensibly for the purpose of taking leave from his former teachers and his many friends, as well as from his mother. But, as his diary reveals, foremost on his mind was his eagerness to secure a bride in Württemberg, who would follow him to the New World.[18] In Tübingen the most important call he made was therefore not on Professor Schmid, who in parting five times prevented his favorite student from leaving, but on a minister's daughter to whom Schaff proposed marriage. The proposal, however, was brusquely rejected. Yet five days later his diary records: "Yesterday may well be the most important day of my whole journey." What in all the world had happened? In the post coach from Tübingen to Reutlingen, another young Swabian woman had won his eager heart, a chance meeting he reported as follows: "She is not yet a completely devoted disciple of the Lord, and her parents seem even farther removed from Him. But what she said, and the way she behaved toward the end, testify that the Lord has begun His work of grace within her. How wonderful it would be, if I were to act as His tool!" Courtship and evangelism rolled into one! In Mercersburg, on November 22 of that same year, the diary groaned with the news: "Dreadfully disappointing letter from Reutlingen, dated September 20th." A month later, the young professor spent the Christmas holidays in the midst of the German Reformed congregation in Frederick City, Maryland. There he made the acquaintance of Mary Elizabeth Schley. Here again is his diary entry: "This is the first time that Cupid's arrow has struck me in America." But here too he paused to muse: "She is neither rich nor beautiful but uncommonly attractive...But since I do not know enough about her character as a Christian, that impression is not sufficient to bring about a decision. At any rate, I shall not undertake the slightest step in this important matter until spring and wait for further signs of the Lord." The following spring the local pastor invited the young professor back for a second visit, an invitation that Schaff must have interpreted as that hoped-for "sign of the Lord." For he called on the young woman's uncle, and, as he wrote, "oddly enough, she herself soon appeared" and delighted him with some beautifully presented songs.[19] On December 10 of that same year he and Mary were married. Adolf Hausrath (1837-1909) has shown in the person of Richard Rothe the sad results that the pietist's religiously motivated approach to courtship and marriage so often entailed.[20] Philip and Mary Schaff, however, were more fortunate. David Schley (1852-1941), the son, dedicated his father's biography to his mother, "who intimately shared for nearly fifty years the joys, cares, and hopes" of her distinguished scholar husband.[22] The couple had eight children, of whom five died at an early age.[22] Mary survived her husband by eight years.

Finally, one cannot help but wonder how much this young immigrant theologian already knew about the New World prior to his emigration. It is true that he had made the acquaintance of some Americans, as already mentioned: at Halle he had gained his first American friend, George L. Prentiss, and in Berlin one of his students was Edwards Amasa Park of Andover Seminary. The first English book he owned was apparently Andrew Norton's *Evidences of the Genuineness of the Gospels* (1837-44), a present of the American ambassador in Berlin. It is also noteworthy that Hengstenberg's *Evangelische Kirchenzeitung* carried from time to time unusually well-informed articles about important religious developments in the New World. Schaff might even have read the letter which the fathers of the German Reformed Church had sent in 1841 for the purpose of soliciting fraternal interest in the centennial celebration of their church, hinting at past difficulties but prophetically concluding: "A sunnier and more beautiful day is now before us."[23] One may also assume that Schaff had read Friedrich Wyneken's classic appeal on behalf of the German immigrants, "The Need of the German Lutherans in North America."[24] For Wyneken, who had emigrated to America in 1838, singled out sectarianism, Roman Catholicism and paganism as the chief threats to the spiritual welfare of the German Protestant immigrants, just as Schaff did in his ordination sermon a few years later. Robert Baird's (1798-1863) important book, *Religion in America* (1843), could have been a most helpful source of information for Schaff, but an edited translation, with an Introduction by Neander, appeared unfortunately too late, in the year of Schaff's departure for the New World.[25]

Some years later Schaff would castigate German church historians for having "but a very superficial acquaintance with the religious world of the English tongue" and for being therefore unable to "duly appreciate its vast present and future importance for the kingdom of God."[26] He would complain that German scholars are often "much better at home with the most remote sources of Greek and Roman antiquity than with modern English—to say nothing of American—literature."[27] And he would warn his German readers (curiously, in an

135

English-language text) "against the ridiculous caricatures of American Christianity which abound in European works."[28] These remarks, one is tempted to conclude, may be taken to indicate also the nature and extent of Schaff's own knowledge of the religious life of the United States at the time of his departure for the strange new world across the vast Atlantic Ocean. It is interesting to note, however, that already in Germany he was optimistically conscious of going forth from an aging European civilization into a land "with a great creative activity before it, which breathes the fresh air of spring and where every tendency can develop itself unhampered from without."[29]

En route to America, Schaff spent six weeks in England, a country that was then ascending to the height of its imperial power. During this trip he laid the foundation for his thorough knowledge of English affairs, both past and present, and for his working friendship with leading representatives of England's churches and theological faculties. He also now showed to good advantage his lifelong propensity for viewing opposite forces, whenever possible, not as mutually exclusive but complementary. He was, for instance, greatly impressed by the common-sense and activist "realism" of the English national character, sharply contrasting it with the high-flying, speculative "idealism" of the Germans. Yet he concluded that both dwelt "in the same ethical sphere" and mutually needed each other, so that English "realism" would not degenerate into "bald materialism" nor German "idealism" into an "airy spiritualism."[30] This notion of the complementary character of the Anglo-Saxon and German would soon help to determine Schaff's understanding of his own American mission and even of America's mission itself. He sought out some of the best-known dissenting preachers, attending their rousing assemblies, but participated as eagerly in the stately services of the Established Church. With equal ease and impartiality he called upon two leading combatants of the day in the Established Church, Frederick Denison Maurice (1805-72) and Edward Bouverie Pusey (1800-82). He dined several times with Maurice at Guy's Hospital in London. Maurice, the author of *The Kingdom of Christ* (1838) and a chief proponent of "Broad Church" views, favorably impressed his visitor as "a man of deep feeling and a German temper of mind, who is neither an Evangelical nor a Puseyite,"[31] but is, one is tempted to add, the English counterpart of a German mediating theologian. During his brief visit to Oxford Schaff was charmed by this old university town and marveled at a university system so conspicuously different from the German. Pusey, however, aroused his greatest curiosity and interest, as well he might. Puseyism or Tractarianism, so named after "The Tracts for the Times" (1833-39) that had propagated the aims of the anglo-catholic revival, was in fact the English parallel to the Prussian High-Orthodoxy, both movements aiming at a "churchly" renewal of Christianity as a sorely needed remedy for the sectarian, subjectivist and rationalistic tendencies they both held to be rampant in modern times—and that were rampant especially in the New World, as Schaff was soon to claim. From the beginning Hengstenberg's *Evangelische Kirchenzeitung* had evinced great interest in the English "churchly" revival, offering frequent and detailed accounts of its progress. But the Lutherans at Berlin had also early noticed substantial disagreements between their own position and that of their Anglican counterparts, primarily in the matter of how best to cure the "diseases" of contemporary Christianity. Like two doctors conversing and arguing at a sickbed, they agreed on the diagnosis but disagreed about the therapy needed for the patient's speedy and full recovery. Indeed, already in 1841, two years after the publication of John Henry Newman's (1801-90) explosive 90th *Tract for the Times* but well before he joined the Roman Catholic Church, the *Evangelische Kirchenzeitung* had accused Puseyism of "romanizing tendencies."[32] How ironic! After all, that same epithet, considered most devastating by Protestants, was not much later hurled at the Hengstenberg circle itself and soon also at Schaff by his opponents in the United States. Schaff came therefore well prepared to his interview with Pusey in his study at Christ Church. Interestingly, he chose to argue, with the zeal and even pugnacity of the rising young professor, the differences between them rather than celebrate the common ground and aims they shared. Quite unlike Ludwig von Gerlach, we might add, who toured

England that same summer and had two interviews with Pusey a few weeks after Schaff's visit. Pusey, as he later wrote, "made a deep impression of genuine catholicity upon me, which accompanied me throughout my whole later life and still accompanies me."[33] Schaff, on the other hand, engaged Pusey in a spirited discussion of some of those very issues that had prompted the *Evangelische Kirchenzeitung* to charge the Tractarian movement with "romanizing tendencies." While Pusey limited the doctrinal development of Christian truth to the first six centuries, Schaff claimed for the church a continuous, maturing development under Christ's promise to be with his church to the end of time. While Pusey proclaimed the apostolic succession of the episcopacy as a mark of the true church, Schaff questioned the biblical warrants of this doctrinal position. And when Schaff pointed to the inestimable service Luther had rendered the church with his doctrine of justification, Pusey replied that Augustine and the other Fathers had stated it better and that, moreover, precisely what was peculiar to Luther passed beyond the bounds of Christian truth, eventually leading to serious errors. In the end, though, Schaff and Pusey parted amicably enough, with Pusey expressing the hope that, as Schaff wrote, "God, having led me thus far, would lead me still further," which prompted Schaff's reply, "but only not in the direction of Rome, but of the truth." Schaff in turn expressed the hope "that God would use the Tractarian movement for the good of the Church Universal and bring the leaders to an appreciation of the services of the Reformation."[34]

In his Mercersburg Inaugural Address Schaff attributed a "world-historical importance" to Puseyism and then added, in good Hegelian fashion:

> I have myself hardly ever before had such an impression of the objective power of the "idea," as during the course of my late travel through Germany, Switzerland, Belgium, England, and North America; encountering as I did everywhere, in the persons of distinguished ministers and laymen, if not precisely Puseyism itself, at least aspirations and endeavors of a more or less kindred kind.[35]

This statement is obviously sweeping enough to take in a broad range of contemporary church renewal movements and individuals, not only Pusey but also Maurice, not only the Prussian High Orthodoxy but also Germany's mediating theology, even a Roman Catholic like Möhler. However, by focusing the attention of his American audience on the anglo-catholic revival in the Church of England, Schaff brought it upon himself that he was wrongly identified by his critics with Puseyism during his first years at Mercerburg.

Toward the end of June Schaff sailed for the New World. After five weeks at sea, on July 28, he finally caught sight of the New Jersey coast and exclaimed (one detects a note of pleasant surprise in this diary entry): "The evidences of civilization are here, as in the land we left."[36] On the evening of August 12 he arrived at Mercersburg, where the students surprised him with a torchlight procession and speeches of welcome in both German and English. Thus began, in the isolation of that little town in western Pennsylvania, Schaff's remarkable American career, which would unfold over nearly fifty years, first at Mercersburg, then in New York City, where he died in his home on October 20, 1893.

On that long journey from Berlin to Mercersburg, from Europe to the beckoning New World, Schaff carried with him the letter by which the German Reformed Church had called him into its service. This letter, which marked the end of the formative years of his education in Germany and the turning point of his life, may therefore appropriately conclude this chapter.[37]

> To Dr. Philip Schaf in Berlin:
> The Synod of the German Reformed Church in the United States of North America, with complete confidence in your wisdom, gifts, and theological scholarship, as well as in your piety, has, in today's election, appointed you, Honored Sir, with pleasing unanimity, Professor in the Theological Seminary at Mercersburg, Pa., particularly in the fields of Exegesis and Church History.
>
> Herewith we inform you, Honored Sir, that we, the officers of said Synod and commissioned by it, hereby solemnly ask and exhort you in all seriousness and love, to accept this call. Should you deign to do so, the said Synod promises you the reverence due to

you and all necessary protection and assistance in the exercise of the lofty duties of your office. It also pledges you an annual salary of one thousand dollars, to be paid in quarterly installments, and free lodging, with the earnest prayer that the great Head of the Church may reward you more liberally in the life to come for your work in his vineyard.

Written at Winchester, Va. On October 19th, 1843
(Signed)   Samuel K. Fischer   J. J. Berg
Scriba   Praeses

Conclusion

Since this study of Schaff's formative years has shown how closely Schaff depended upon his German teachers and how eclectic his scholarship was, it may have created the impression of having followed a procedure that, as Goethe once remarked, "often happens in the literary world when people doubt the originality of this or that famous man and seek to trace the sources whence he obtained his cultivation." It is therefore salutary to heed Goethe's outburst, "that is very ridiculous," and to take to heart his further remark: "We might as well question a well-fed man about the oxen, sheep, and swine which he has eaten and which have given him strength. We are indeed born with talents, but we owe our development to a thousand influences of a great world, from which we appropriate to ourselves what we can and what is suitable to us." If this study should in fact have questioned Schaff too closely about all those German "oxen, sheep, and swine," it finally needs to be stated emphatically that Schaff most assuredly had what Goethe in the end considered alone important: "A soul which loves the truth and which receives it wherever it finds it."[1]

Goethe's wise counsel that what matters is to love the truth and to receive it wherever it is to be found must therefore be kept in mind when here a final backward glance at Schaff's formative years is attempted. It should be noted, first of all, how important at almost every significant turn of his life the network of the "awakened" or evangelical Christians in Switzerland and Germany had been. By supporting and directing him, they had kept him firmly within the orbit of their piety and world view. Pietists in eastern Switzerland and southern Germany facilitated Schaff's removal from his native Chur to Kornthal, Stuttgart and Tübingen. Tholuck at Halle and Hengstenberg at Berlin found employment for him and kept close to him. After the ascension to the throne of Friedrich

Wilhelm IV in 1840, even the newly appointed Minister of Public Worship and Education Eichhorn made it a matter of policy to seek out and support "awakened" and orthodox young scholars like Schaff. And soon the leading representatives of the "evangelical" camp at Halle and Berlin unanimously recommended Schaff for the Mercersburg position in the United States. In pietistic fashion Schaff saw the guiding hand of divine providence at work in all of these events. The historian, however, will simply point to the network of "awakened" Christians who firmly believed that they were doing God's will and furthering the coming of his kingdom, when they supported young men of their own persuasion for the ministry and an academic career—and withheld with equal determination their support from those of a different outlook! Richard Rothe once bitterly remarked of these pietistic churchmen: "Their kingdom of heaven is a religious fraternity."[2] No doubt, the "fraternity spirit" of the Awakening guided Schaff's early years and in the end helped to shape the character of his scholarship and his whole career.

However, as this study has tried to show, Schaff's theology evolved not only from the biblical-supranaturalistic piety of the Awakening but absorbed also many of the potent theological, philosophical and historical ideas that were alive in the German universities in the era dominated by Schleiermacher and Hegel. And facilitating Schaff's education was a brilliantly receptive and productive mind, a photographic memory, as well as an energetic, outgoing, sociable and wholesome personality. His education passed through three stages in particular, as we have seen, each in turn shaping and enriching his intellectual outlook and theology: the Awakening in Württemberg, the mediating theology and finally the Prussian High Orthodoxy, together with the growing influence of the church historian Neander. The theological program that Schaff brought with him to the New World in 1844 and publicized during the first decade at Mercersburg can therefore best be characterized as the provocative and eclectic fusion of an ecumenical high-church pietism and a romantic-idealistic philosophy of history. Still, the principles and aims of Germany's mediating theology had made the most

142

lasting impression upon his malleable mind. This immigrant scholar was, and would remain, a transplanted mediating theologian. This viewpoint alone can adequately explain Schaff's activity and thought throughout his distinguished American career and the unity underlying his whole life's work in its various stages of development.

It should therefore be emphasized that Schaff's first American publications, his contributions to the so-called Mercersburg Theology which he evolved together with his colleague John Williamson Nevin, represented nearly the sum total of what he had been taught by his German mentors and absorbed through his voracious reading in the extensive literature of German exegetical, historical, systematic and philosophical theology. After his Inaugural Lecture on "Das Prinzip des Protestantismus," especially its publication in Nevin's English translation the following year, had caused a lively controversy in the German Reformed Church, even leading to Schaff's and Nevin's trial for heresy, Schaff wrote his German friends that he had not "passed off his whole point of view as something original," but had "declared it to be essentially identical with the standpoint of the evangelical-churchly theology of present-day Germany."[3] These same words can be equally applied to all of Schaff's early Mercersburg publication. In the spirit of the Prussian High Orthodoxy *The Principle of Protestantism* (1845) set forth Schaff's provocative and controversial program for the renewal of Protestantism by recalling contemporary Protestantism to the catholic traditions of the universal church, by interpreting the sixteenth-century Reformation in its proper universal historical context, and by pointing Protestantism toward the realization of a future "evangelical catholicism," that higher synthesis of Roman Catholicism and Protestantism so alluring at that time to so many German Christians. *What is Church History?* (1846), and especially the lengthy Introduction to Church History with which he prefaced his history of apostolic Christianity, *History of the Apostolic Church, with a General Introduction to Church History* (1851/54), acquainted American Christians for the first time with the rich and complex story of recent German contributions to the study of the history of Christianity culminating in the work of Baur and Neander. His *History of the Apostolic Church* itself drew largely upon the work of Neander and his Tübingen teacher Schmid and as such was a conservative rebuttal to the rival interpretation of apostolic Christianity of Baur's Tübingen School. Finally, *Der deutsche Kirchenfreund*, the first German-language theological journal in America, which Schaff founded and tirelessly edited for six years (1848-1853), was essentially an American combination of *Theologische Studien und Kritiken*, the major organ of the mediating theology, Hengstenberg's *Evangelische Kirchenzeitung*, *Berliner Allgemeine Kirchenzeitung* and Krummacher's *Palmblätter*. The current issues of these publications Schaff received regularly at Mercersburg and utilized in his own monthly journal.[4] During the first Mercersburg decade Schaff was indeed "a missionary of science,"[5] an eloquent spokesman and tireless publicist in the New World of what he had learned in the Old World during the formative years of his young life.

To a remarkable extent Schaff's life, therefore, bears out the truth of Arthur Schopenhauer's observation which was already quoted in the Preface to this study:

> The impression which the world makes on the individual mind, and the ideas with which such a mind, after it has gone through the process of education, reacts to that impression, all this is over and done with by the thirtieth year: what comes later are only the developments and variations of the same theme.[6]

Schopenhauer's astute observation, however, becomes fully applicable to Schaff's life only when the first few years of his American career, when the impressions of the New World on his receptive and creative mind, are also included. After all, it was five years after his arrival in the United States that he turned thirty. This young immigrant scholar did indeed already during those first years at Mercersburg gradually become an "American by choice," a fact that is borne out fully by the series of lectures on his adopted country which he delivered in Germany and Switzerland on his first return trip to Europe in 1854. These lectures were soon published, first in German and then in an English translation: *America. A Sketch of the Political, Social, and Religious Character of the United States* (1855). This book—the first, it should be noted, Schaff had written free of the influence of his German mentors—provides brilliant evidence of the fact that during the nearly ten years after his arrival in America Schaff had been as ardent and observant a student of the strange new world of American society, politics and especially religion as he had been in that earlier decade of the exciting new world of German scholarship. Schaff's *America* is therefore also, as the editor of a 1961 reprint perceptively remarked, "a document of primary importance" for anyone interested in "the history of that mysterious process called 'Americanization.'"[7] The formative years of Schaff's education reached in fact their final conclusion only during those first Mercersburg years, when in his experience as an immigrant scholar the American context and his German learning met, clashed and finally began to merge in that complex and indeed "mysterious" process called the "Americanization" of the immigrant, a process that millions of newcomers to the New World have shared and continue to share. The "Americanization" of this particular immigrant scholar, however, is a topic so important that it demands a separate study.[8] The present study has intentionally limited itself to a consideration of the crucially important, formative years of Schaff's education up to the time of his arrival in the United States in 1844.

Epilogue

Schaff's American Career – An Appraisal

Note: The following review and appraisal of Schaff's American career is the major part of an article I wrote on the occasion of the 1988 Centennial of the American Society of Church History, of which Schaff had been the founder and first president until his death in 1893 (*Church History*, 59 [June 1990]:207-221). Omitted from the article is the section on Schaff's early years in Germany (207-212), the subject of this present study. Since the formative years of his German education were, as it turned out, nothing but a preparation for his distinguished American career, an appropriate way of completing this present study would therefore be a brief survey of Schaff's Mercersburg years, his "Americanization," and his further evolution as a chief spokesman and representative of the dominant evangelical Protestantism in the decades following the Civil War. The original text has been corrected in a few places, the footnotes have been renumbered.

[The Mercersburg Years]

When Schaff, barely twenty-five years old, left Berlin for the United States in 1844, he obviously carried a distinctive and substantial theological program with him to the New World. He had every reason to think of himself as "a missionary of science."[1] And he was indeed one of the first to introduce Americans to what Friedrich Meinecke has simply called "he German movement," from Leibnitz to Goethe, hailing it as the second great achievement of the German mind after the sixteenth-century Reformation, or what Ernst Troeltsch has suggestively described as "the second great type of modern thought "besides the Enlightenment.[2] Small wonder, then, that Schaff's theological program clashed with America's pre-Civil War evangelicalism, what Perry Miller (1905-63) called "its indigenous passions, that is, its virulent anti-Catholicism, its biblicism and individualism, its contrived and emotional revival techniques, and its disregard and hence ignorance of the history and traditions of the universal church.[3] The wonder, however, is that Schaff's lone Mercersburg colleague, John Williamson Nevin, had independently, through his own study of Neander's works, arrived at a position quite similar to Schaff's. Together, they were to initiate what came to be called the "Mercersburg movement" or the "Mercersburg theology," fanning not only a long-lasting controversy in the German Reformed Church but also adding a remarkable new chapter to the history of American theology.[4]

I would like to suggest, however, that some additional perspectives can be brought to bear on the Mercersburg period of Schaff's life. Historians of the immigrant experience in American culture remind us that the first phase of immigrant alienation is usually followed by the no less typical reaction of immigrant fervor. One might therefore view, for instance, Schaff's two books—*The Principle of Protestantism* (1845) and, a decade later, *America*—as literary manifestations of those two typical immigrant reactions, first of alienation and then of fervor, so that Schaff's *America*, as Perry Miller claimed, not only "by its objectivity" but also by its "affectionate power is as fine a tribute to America as any immigrant ever paid."[5] And if I may indulge for a moment in psychohistory, then one can also view the Mercersburg period in Schaff's life, in particular his high-church views, as a belated stage of rebellion in his otherwise so smoothly continuous development. It was a healthy reaction of doubt and resistance directed against the "fathers," men like Tholuck and Neander, who represented the German Awakening, so that, with his sense of adult independence and self-identity strengthened and confirmed, he later typically rejoined their company even more firmly and faithfully. In any case the Mercersburg period of Schaff's career can be properly understood only back to back with the last Berlin years of his education and as that stage in his life when in his experience as an immigrant the American context and the new German modes of thought first met—and clashed, and then began to merge.

But one more remark is called for. Lord Acton (1834-1902) is reported to have said of John Henry Newman's *Essay on the Development of Christian*

148

Doctrine (which was published the same year as Schaff's *Principle of Protestantism*) that more than any other book at the time it made the English "think historically, to watch the process as well as the result."[6] These words can be applied with equal justification to Schaff's Mercersburg publications and their impact upon American Protestants. One should therefore single out as perhaps Schaff's greatest achievement at Mercersburg that here his historical learning, rooted as it was in the romantic-idealistic philosophy of history, helped to prove Newman's famous dictum to be no longer applicable even to American Protestants: "To be deep in history is to cease being a Protestant."[7]

Schaff was to return to Europe fourteen times. None of the European journeys, however, was more significant for his own development than the first one, in 1853/54, for he returned from it, as he wrote, hinting at a further evolution in his outlook, "a better Protestant and American."[8] The inherently unstable "paradox" of the Prussian High Orthodoxy, which uneasily combined Lutheran confessional and ecumenical tendencies, dissolved after 1846/48, thereby prefiguring Schaff's own, though somewhat later and different, development.[9] His former Berlin mentors now embraced an exclusive Lutheran confessionalism, while Schaff, after his return from Europe, turned ever more firmly in the other direction of an inclusive "evangelical catholicism."

[The "Americanization" of an Immigrant Scholar]

This final stage in Schaff's development is obviously also a part of the complex story of Schaff's "Americanization." His adaptive personality and scholarly eclecticism, his Hegelian idealism and American pragmatism, no doubt helped to ease his way into the mainstream of American life. After all, Schaff was only too ready to march in the rear of what he was wont to call, in good Hegelian fashion, "the objective force of history."[10] Believing firmly that God's spirit manifests itself in the actual flow of history, Schaff's own evolution therefore became a part of the remarkable story of the evolution of American Protestantism itself: from the evangelicalism of the nineteenth century's first half, which Schaff

149

and Nevin liked to deride as "Puritan" and "Methodist," to the evangelicalism of the postbellum years. The latter became increasingly "liberal" and "ecumenical," because (among other things) it was increasingly informed by those new German modes of thought, especially the historical consciousness of nineteenth-century German culture. James H. Nichols (1915-91) correctly observed that Nevin and Schaff led the German Reformed Church through a transition that the Presbyterians and Congregationalists experienced only in the 1880s and 90s, and that therefore the Mercersburg movement should be viewed as "a kind of paradigm before the Civil War of what would happen to the American Reformed churches generally by the end of the century."[11] For it was then that the New England theology and that of the Presbyterian Old School finally collapsed. And as Schaff was a driving force in the earlier transformation of the German Reformed Church, so he was an equally active participant in the later transformation of the evangelical denominations of American Protestantism. At the same time, his own theological program evolved still further as well.

The complex story of Schaff's "Americanization" is therefore much more than an instructive example of how in the end American "facts" will overcome European "theories" in the immigrant's mind. This conclusion holds true in still another respect. Schaff, for instance, soon embraced the prevailing millenialism and messianism, even racism, of nineteenth-century American religion and society. He soon welcomed—and no longer condemned—the denominational diversity of American Christianity and then celebrated its lively, active mass of individual Christianity. These changes in outlook obviously manifested Schaff's growing accommodation to the reality of America's dominant evangelical Protestantism and his new-found appreciation of its pietistic core. But I now want to emphasize what is less obvious: these changes also revealed the renewed impact of certain German categories of thought and influences that had, as it were, for a time merely lain dormant in his mind. A single example, illustrating a shift in his ecumenical views, must suffice as evidence.

At the beginning of his American career Schaff had shouted, "Away with human denominations, down with sects!" which was the pointed expression of his rejection of the Free-Church tradition of Anglo-American Protestantism as a diseased stage in the historical development of Christianity.[12] Later, however, he drew a careful distinction between "denomination" and "sect," and he then affirmed the denominational diversity of American Christianity as a "blessing."[13] This important reorientation in his ecumenical outlook was, on its intellectual side, nothing but a shift from the dialectics of German idealism to the individualizing approach of German romanticism, both being a part of the German background of his thought.

In keeping with the logic of idealistic dialectics Schaff had at first posited the "reunion of Christendom" as the *end result* of the historical process and, moreover, had conceived of this process as the unfolding of the great European dialectic of Reformation Protestantism and Roman Catholicism. Hence he denigrated the American denominations as wild shoots on the stem of Reformation Protestantism. Furthermore, orienting his ecumenical thought at first to the high-church notion of the visible church as the "Body of Christ," he had also insisted that the coming unity of the universal church is to be made manifest in a visible structure. Later, however, he returned to Neander's (and Schleiermacher's) conception of Christianity as "life," to the romantic understanding of the whole Christian world with its multiplicity of distinct historical phenomena as being but the necessary individualization of the Christian spirit. This understanding then led him to affirm that diversity itself belongs to the very nature of Christianity and that diversity is therefore also essential to Christian unity. Hence the ecumenical battle cry of Schaff's later years would be the slogan "Unity in Diversity, and Diversity in Unity." Only those romantic notions and not the idealistic understanding of history corresponded to his own experience of the strength of evangelical Protestantism in the second half of the nineteenth century. For that strength manifested itself both in the diversity of the evangelical denominations and in their underlying unity as expressed in a common spirit and in voluntary missionary cooperation. Correspondingly, Neander's concept of the "kingdom of God," rather than the high-church notion of the church as the "Body of Christ," now became the focal point of orientation not only for his ecumenical thought but also for his conception of the nature and task of church history. Those historians who look for "the true architects of the denominational theory of the Church" should therefore not only look to the Dissenting Brethren in the Westminster Assembly or to the nineteenth-century American Evangelicals but also to Schleiermacher and Neander—and to Philip Schaff, who finally came to embrace fully and represent their views. Thus it should be obvious that Schaff's so-called "Americanization" is indeed a very complex process that should invite still further exploration.[14]

[The Years after the Civil War]

It is for these and still other reasons that roughly since his move to New York in 1863—where in 1870 he joined the Presbyterian Church and the faculty of Union Theological Seminary—Schaff increasingly identified himself with the goals and aspirations of the broad tradition of post-Civil War evangelical Protestantism in the United States, of the Broad-Church party in England and of the center party in German Protestantism, warily observing all the while the growing strength of the ultramontane party in the Roman Catholic Church. He now liked to think of himself as a "broad-churchman," whom he described as follows: "truly evangelical, Catholic, moderate, comprehensive, humble, and in hearty sympathy with all that is pure and good and Christian."[15]

It was in keeping with the character of such a "broad-churchman" that during the last decades of his life Schaff was content to reduce the task of theology, as he now saw it, to the maintenance of a minimal set of doctrinal principles and their conciliatory application, still battling polemically, however, some of those movements and forces that were outside the broad orbit of a liberal and cooperative evangelical Protestantism. More than ever, his guiding principle was the firm belief of the pietism of his youth that the spiritual reality behind the theological conceptuality is primary and alone essential. As he put it in 1884, "The piety of the heart often protests against the theology of the head, and love is better than logic."[16] Compared with the sparkling presentation of innovative ideas in the literary output of the Mercersburg years, his later theological contributions—however substantial and prominent the continuities—are indeed "tedious."[17]

A cursory comparison, for instance, of *The Principle of Protestantism* with a collection of his essays and addresses published forty years later under the title *Christ and Christianity* will confirm such an assessment. And even the volumes of the final edition of his Church History are richly but also dryly "factual": they are no longer animated by the fresh power of keen insights and suggestive ideas. This conclusion may tempt the historian to offer separate evaluations of Schaff's Mercersburg theology, that scintillating fusion of an ecumenical high-church pietism and a romantic-idealistic philosophy of history, and the theology of his New York years. The latter one might loosely characterize as follows: a sometimes superficial but always well-intentioned combination of various and at times quite disparate and even already antiquated elements which Schaff himself once characteristically described as the "liberal and progressive evangelical orthodoxy."[18] The fact is that during the last three decades of his life he would be a "doer" rather than a "thinker." He would primarily pursue, actively and energetically and in the end almost always successfully, an amazing range of scholarly and practical projects, in which all four major motifs that gave form and direction to his life's work came fully into play: the biblical, historical, ecumenical and apologetic. In 1882 his friend Julius Mann called him "the presiding genius of international theology."[19] It would be difficult to think of a more suitable designation for calling attention to what was at the heart of Schaff's professional self-understanding and gave a unique cast especially to the New York period of his career.

I can offer here no detailed evaluation but only a brief enumeration of these various "projects."[20] After he moved to New York he was for the first several years the corresponding secretary of the New York Sabbath Committee. He published a Life of Jesus (*The Person of Christ: The Perfection of His Humanity Viewed as a Proof of His Divinity* [1865]—a kind of Christology "from below," without originality but written with great apologetic fervor for the benefit of "doubters"—which turned out to be his most popular book, re-edited repeatedly and translated into many languages. The major editorial project of his career was, no doubt, the American edition of Lange's German Bible Commentary, the first comprehensive and complete English-language Bible commentary. It occupied his attention for sixteen years (1864-1880) and involved the collaboration of more than fifty scholars, representing a novel and pioneering effort at scholarship by teamwork, both international and interdenominational. But this trail-blazing effort soon proved to be no more than a minor footnote in the history of biblical scholarship, for the twenty-five volumes of this Bible commentary excelled in textual criticism (which was the greatest strength both of Schaff's biblical scholarship and of the biblical scholarship of evangelical Protestantism at that time) but consistently skirted the burning issue of the "higher" or historical-literary criticism of the Bible. Lange's Bible Commentary clung tenaciously to the precritical supernaturalistic point of view and to what today we would call a "historical literalism" in biblical interpretation.[21]

In 1880 Schaff also helped to found the Society of Biblical Literature and Exegesis. Once more he tried to transfer the harvest of German scholarship across the Atlantic Ocean when he prepared the American edition of the Herzog-Plitt-Hauck *Encyklopädie*, now known, after a further revision, as the *New Schaff-Herzog Encyclopedia of Religious Knowledge* (1908-1914). Schaff showed himself equally adept at cooperating with British scholars in the revision of the King James Version of the English Bible. Although his native tongue was not English, he was for twelve years (1872-1884) the president of the American Committee of Bible Revision, which worked alongside of the British Committee, and in the end was hailed for his signal contributions to this transatlantic effort as organizer, fund-raiser, exegete and skillful ecumenical ambassador.

He was a founder of the American branch of the Evangelical Alliance in 1867, and until his death it was this organization to which he contributed in numerous ways, for he viewed it as the chief instrument at hand in the quest for Christian unity. He was also a major force in the World Alliance of Reformed Churches since its formation in 1875. He pursued another project to adapt old creeds to nineteenth-century evangelical sensibilities in two ways, working, though in the end he was unsuccessful, toward a consensus creed in the setting of the World Alliance of Reformed Churches and toward creed revision in the Presbyterian Church in the United States.

Finally, there were his numerous contributions as a church historian. Having published the three-volume *Creeds of Christendom* in 1877 (which remained a contribution of lasting value for the next 125 years), he spent the last ten years of his life bringing out the final edition of his *History of the Christian Church*. In 1886 he began work, as coeditor, on a *Select Library of the Nicene and Post-Nicene Fathers of the Christian Church*. In 1888 he organized the American Society of Church History, and at the very last, he initiated the *American Church History Series*. His last public utterance, delivered in 1893 at the risk of his life at the World's Parliament of Religions in Chicago, was the ecumenical address "The Reunion of Christendom." It was also a telling and grand summary of his life's work.

[Concluding Remarks]

In concluding my portrayal of Schaff I can add only a few brief comments. I have tried to show that Schaff's theological program issued from the unique confluence of German and American traditions and is best characterized as a progressive orthodoxy or liberal evangelicalism that was given further distinction by the ecumenical vision of an evangelical catholicism—all of which makes his career uniquely instructive. On the strength of this program and to the best of his considerable abilities he attempted throughout his long career to mediate between conflicting and diverse forces, positions and national traditions in order to achieve or maintain an evangelical consensus and to restore the unity of the church, viewing both as means toward the ultimate goal of establishing God's kingdom on earth. A postmillenialist and ardent American he tended to conceive of the kingdom of God as a global, English-speaking Christian civilization. The key to his career is that he used scholarly and practical means for evangelical ends and his liberal evangelicalism for the accomplishment of ecumenical goals. In the nineteenth century there were few—perhaps there was none—on either side of the Atlantic who surpassed him in contributing (to use Schaff's own words) "toward the mutual understanding and appreciation of European and American divines, and toward the great cause of Christian union."[22]

But in the end it turned out that Schaff had been less successful in mediating between the past and the future. By this I mean that it is true enough that he built bridges in various fields and in several different directions, but many of them he did not cross himself (as did his students Arthur C. McGiffert [1861-1933], William Adams Brown [1865-1943] and, to a lesser extent, Charles A. Briggs [1841-1913]). Certainly, this critical appraisal holds true especially in those two fields—the biblical and historical—that were of such great interest to him and in which he did some of his major work. In his work both as a biblical scholar and a church historian there is much that we now must judge as transient, even though Lange's Bible Commentary and his Church History, both recently reissued by evangelical publishing houses, admittedly do contain a wealth of still useful materials. Most of us, however, will find their basic point of view to be dated and consequently of strictly historical interest only. In short, Schaff turned his back on most of the many new forces in church and society: Ritschl's theology; the "higher criticism"; the new orientation in historical studies for which the temporary cessation of the life of the American Society of Church History in 1896 and the name of Adolf Harnack (1851-1930) may stand; the rise of the modern university with its specialization, professionalism and liberal culture and the concomitant "Collapse of American Evangelical Academia"; and, finally, the growing industrialization with its attendant problems and tensions.[23]

156

Shortly before his death, though, Schaff publicly embraced Darwin's theory of evolution, affirming it as the counterpart in the natural sciences to his cherished notion of historical development.

More permanent, at least as an impetus, we may want to judge his work in creed and Bible revision and, perhaps above all, his ecumenical endeavors—from his contributions to liturgics and symbolics to his leading role in the Evangelical Alliance and the World Alliance of Reformed Churches—inspired, as all of these endeavors were, by his grand dual vision of an "evangelical catholicism" and the "internationalization of theology." In his quest for Christian unity and cooperation, despite the time-bound nature of the romantic-idealistic notions that shaped his ecumenical views, he was unusually insightful and truly prophetic. Indeed, his whole career may be called a nineteenth-century prelude to the ecumenical movement of our time. One should finally mention that remarkable collection of essays by members of the American Society of Church History entitled *A Century of Church History: The Legacy of Philip Schaff*, for this book offers abundant proof that the versatile Schaff's pioneering work has helped to stimulate the scholarship and research of later generations in a great variety of ways and fields.[24]

I would like to close by quoting Schleiermacher's definition of what he called "the idea of a prince of the Church": "If one could imagine both a religious interest and a scientific spirit conjoined to the highest degree and with the finest balance for the purpose of theoretical and practical activity alike, that would be the idea of a 'prince of the Church.'"[25] I will take leave, therefore, of Philip Schaff, the founder and first president of the American Society of Church History, by saluting him as "the presiding genius of international theology," as a biblical scholar, church historian, apologist of Christianity and fervent advocate of the reunion of Christendom, who in his long and distinguished career truly was such a "prince of the Church."

Abbreviations

Almost all of the unpublished Schaff Papers are available at the following two locations (some additional papers are in the Philip Schaff Library of Lancaster Theological Seminary, Lancaster, Pa.):

ERHS, Lancaster   Archives of the Evangelical and Reformed Historical Society,   Lancaster, Pa.

UTS, NY   Burke Library, Union Theological Seminary, New York City.

AR   "Autobiographical Reminiscences," unpaginated ms., Schaff Papers, ERHS, Lancaster. Schaff wrote this ms. intermittently from 1871 to 1890. A paginated copy was prepared for Schaff by Carl M. Adler in 1882 (also at ERHS, Lancaster). All citations are from the Adler copy, unless otherwise indicated.

DKF   *Der deutsche Kirchenfreund.* Schaff was the founder and editor of this journal (1848-1853), the first German language theological journal in America.

Life of Schaff   David S. Schaff, *The Life of Philip Schaff, in Part Autobiographical.* New York: Charles Scribner's, 1897.

Schaff, *Germany*   *Germany. Its Universities, Theology, and Religion. With sketches of Neander, Tholuck, Olshausen, Hengstenberg, Twesten, Müller, Ullmann, Rothe, Dorner, Lange, Ebrard, Wichern, and other distinguished German divines of the age.* Philadelphia: Lindsay & Blakiston, 1857.

Schaff, *Princip*   *Das Princip des Protestantismus.* Chambersburg: Druckerei der Hochdeutsch-Reformirten Kirche, 1845.

Schaff, *Principle*   *The Principle of Protestantism*, trans. John W. Nevin (1845), Lancaster Series on the Mercersburg Theology, ed. Bard Thomon and George H. Bricker, vol. 1. Philadelphia: United Church Press, 1964.

TRE   *Theologische Realenzyklopädie* . Berlin – New York: Walter de Gruyter, 1977ff.

Notes

Preface

1. Letter of A. Schopenhauer to F. A. Brockhaus, March 28, 1818, in *Arthur Schopenhauers Briefwechsel und andere Dokumente*, ed. Max Brahn (Leipzig: Insel-Verlag, 1911), 61.
2. Schaff, *America*, ed. Perry Miller (Cambridge, Mass.: Harvard University Press, 1961), xxxv.
3. *Life of Schaff*, 484

1. Childhood at Chur (1819-1834)

1. The name of this Swiss canton is derived from a military alliance formed in 1395, which was known as the *Graubund* (Gray League), so called because of the homespun gray cloth worn by the men. Gray in German is *grau*, in French *gris*. – For recent literature about the history of the Canton and its churches see Gäbler, n. 2.
2. Only since the thorough research of Ulrich Gäbler of the University of Basel are we well informed about Schaff's birth and childhood: "Philip Schaff in Chur, 1819-1834," *Zwingliana* 18 (1989):143-65. A shorter English version is "Philip Schaff at Chur, 1819-1834," in *Probing the Reformed Tradition: Historical Studies in Honor of Edward A. Dowey*, ed. Elsie Anne McKee and Brian G. Armstrong (Louisville, Ky.: Westminster/John Knox Press, 1989), 408-23.
3. *AR*, following p. 25.
4. Professor Gäbler first presented the story of Schaff's birth and childhood in 1988 at the Centennial Meeting of the American Society of Church History, of which Schaff was the founder and first president. His paper, needless to say, caused quite a sensation.
5. See *TRE*, art. "Basel, Christentumsgesellschaft," 5:276-78, and, for the manifold connections with Württemberg, Heinrich Hermelink, *Geschichte der Evangelischen Kirche in Württemberg von der Reformation bis zur Gegenwart* (Stuttgart and Tübingen: Rainer Wunderlich Verlag, 1949), 353-62.
6 *AR*, 20.
7. *AR*, 27.
8. *AR*, 34 and 35.
9. "Die Freundschaft," Schaff Papers, ERHS, Lancaster.
10. Gäbler, "Philip Schaff at Chur, 1819-1834," 419.

2. Kornthal and Stuttgart (1834-1837): The Württemberg Awakening

1. The standard work of the history of Pietism is *Geschichte des Pietismus*, 3 vols. (Göttingen: Vandenhoeck and Ruprecht, 1992-2000--a final volume is projected). For our purposes important is vol. 3, ed. Ulrich Gäbler, *Der Pietsmus im neunzehnten und zwanzigsten Jahrhundert*. For a brief survey of the story of German pietism and the relevant literature, see TRE, art. "Pietism," 26:606-631. That there is no scholarly consensus about the meaning of "pietism," has recently again been pointed out by Jonathan Strom, "Problems and Promises of Pietism Research," *Church History* 71, 3 (September 2002):536-54. – For Württemberg, see especially the relevant chapters in Hermelink, *Geschichte der evangelischen Kirche in Württemberg*, and Hartmut Lehmann, *Pietismus und weltliche Ordnung in Württemberg vom 17. bis 20. Jahrhundert* (Stuttgart: Kohlhammer, 1969).
2. Sixtus Carl Kapff, *Die Württembergischen Brüdergemeinden Kornthal und Wilmhelmsdorf, ihre Geschichte, Einrichtung und Erziehungsanstalten* (Kornthal: C. G. Liesching, 1839), 10.
3. For Kornthal, in addition to Kapff (n. 2), see TRE, art. "Kornthal", 19:640-644, and Walter Roth, *Die Evangelische Brüdergemeinde Kornthal* (Neuhausen – Stuttgart: Häusler, 1994).
4. See below chap. 3, n. 4 for the relevant literature. Especially important for Württemberg is Karl Müller, *Die religiöse Erweckung in Württemberg am Anfang des 19. Jahrhunderts* (Tübingen: J. C. Mohr, 1925).
5. A biography of Kapff, written in the spirit of filial piety but still informative, is Carl Kapff, *Lebensbild von Sixt Carl v. Kapff* (Stuttgart: Chr. Belser'sche Verlags-handlung, 1881).
6. Kapff, *Die Württembergischen Brüdergemeinden*, 119.
7. *AR*, 58
8. Ibid., 56f.
9. Ibid., 55.
10. *DKF*, "Das Heimweh des Christens," 4 (1851):189.
11. Tagebuch (diary) 1836, May 12, Schaff Papers, ERHS, Lancaster.
12. *AR*, 55.
13. *Life of Schaff*, 26.
14. Kapff, *Die Württembergischen Brüdergemeinden*, 167.
15. Tagebuch 1836, May 15.
16. *AR*, 10.
17. Quoted by Müller, *Die religiöse Erweckung in Württemberg*, 29.
18. Kapff, *Die Württembergischen Brüdergemeinden*, 120.
19. Cf., for instance, *A Commentary on the Holy Scriptures by Johann Peter Lange*, ed. Philip Schaff, 25 vols. (New York: Charles Scribner, 1868-80), vol. 8 of the New Testament, V.
20. Kapff, *Die Württembergischen Brüdergemeinden*, 178.
21. Quoted by Hermelink, *Geschichte der evangelischen Kirche in Württemberg*, 407.
22. Schaff, *Germany*, 158.
23. Sixtus Carl Kapff, *Die Wiederkunft des Herrn. Belehrungen aus Matthäi 24. und 25. verglichen mit den Zeichen der Zeit* (Stuttgart: J. B. Müller, 1836), 76.
24. Ibid., 44-63.
25. The translation is from the 6th German edition. No translator or editor is mentioned. Since the publisher, Schäfer and Koradi in Philadelphia, was also Schaff's publisher at that time, (e.g., *Der deutsche Kirchenfreund, Germany*), one is tempted to speculate that Schaff had a hand in the American edition.
26. Quoted by Peter Gay, *Freud for Historians* (New York: Oxford University Press paperback, 1986), 158.
27. See Gay, *Freud for Historians*, especially chapters 3-6. I have more to say on this biographically interesting and important point in "The Private Life of Philip Schaff" (The Burke Library, Union Theological Seminary, Occasional Publication, No. 3 [1995]), 6f.

28. For Passavant's role in Schaff's life, see Hans R. Guggisberg, "Ein transatlantischer 'Brückenbauer.' Der Kirchenhistoriker Philip Schaff (1819-1893), sein Amerikabild und seine Beziehungen zu Basel," *Basler Zeitschrift für Geschichte und Altertumskunde* 91 (1991):262, and Ulrich Gäbler, "Philip Schaff in Chur, 1819-1834," n. 129.

29. Adolph Späth, *D. Wilhelm Julius Mann* (Reading, Pa.: Pilger Buchhandlung, 1895), discusses at length the friendship between Schaff and Mann. His extensive excerpts from Mann's letters to his distinguished friend are the more welcome since these letters, available at the Lutheran Seminary in Philadelphia, are nearly illegible.

30. See Meta Heusser-Schweizer's autobiographical reminiscences *Hauschronik*, ed. Karl Fehr (Kilchberg: Verlag Mirio Romano, 1980).

31. *AR*, 37-47.

32. *Alpine Lyrics. A Selection from the Poems of Meta Heusser-Schweizer*, transl. H. L. L. [Jane Borthwick] (London: T. Nelson and Sons, 1875).

33. *AR*, 10.

34. Wilhelm Dilthey, "Ferdinand Christian Baur," *Gesammelte Schriften*, vol. 4, 3rd ed. (Stuttgart: B.G. Teubner – Göttingen: Vandenhoek & Ruprecht, 1963), 419.

35. *AR*, 50.

36. Heusser-Schweizer, *Hauschronik*, 125 and 127, respectively.

3. German Theology in the 1830s: Schleiermacher's and Hegel's Long Shadow

1. Friedrich Meinecke, *Die Entstehung des Historismus*, vol. 3 of *Werke*, ed. Carl Hinrichs (Munich: R. Oldenbourg Verlag, 1965), 2.

2. Ernst Troeltsch, "Der deutsche Idealismus," *Gesammelte Schriften*, 4 vols. (Tübingen: J. C. B. Mohr [Paul Siebeck], 1912-25), 4:535. - Three older monumental works offer comprehensive surveys of the history of German culture in the first half of the nineteenth century: Franz Schnabel, *Deutsche Geschichte im neunzehnten Jahrhundert*, 4 vols. (latest editions, Freiburg: Verlag Herder, 1949-55), especially vol. 4: *Die religiösen Kräfte*; Hermann August Korff, *Geist der Goethezeit*, 5 vols. (Leipzig: Koehler & Amelag, 1966 edition; Wilhelm Lütgert, *Die Religion des deutschen Idealismus und ihr Ende*, 4 vols., (Gütersloh: C. Bertelsmann, 1922-30).

3. Friedrich Meinecke, *Die Idee der Staatsräson*, vol. 1 of *Werke*, ed. Walther Hofer (1960), 425. Translation is that of Steven Lukes, "The Meanings of Individualism," *Journal of the History of Ideas* 32 (1971):56.

4. For a survey and the literature of the *Erweckungsbewegung*, see *TRE*, art. "Erweckung/Erweckungsbewegungen," 10:205-227, especially the historical section, 205-220. From the available literature one should single out Erich Beyreuther, *Die Erweckungsbewegung*, 2d ed., in *Die Kirche in ihrer Geschichte*, vol. 4, R 1 (Göttingen: Vandenhoeck & Ruprecht, 1977), and Ulrich Gäbler, ed. *Der Pietismus im neunzehnten und zwanzigsten Jahrhundert*, vol.3 of *Geschichte des Pietismus*.

5. Horst Stephan, *Geschichte der deutschen evangelischen Theologie seit dem deutschen Idealismus*, 2d ed. rev. and ed. by Martin Schmidt (Berlin: A Töpelmann, 1960), 110.

6. See *TRE*, art. "Schleiermacher," 30:143-189, with its exhaustive list of the vast and still growing literature (181-189). – The reader should note that my presentation of Schleiermacher is intended to be no more than a sketch somewhat schematically drawn to highlight those features of his theology that stood out most prominently for his contemporaries and thus for Schaff, and in this way to describe and to illuminate more fully the intellectually exciting and challenging context in which Schaff's own theological position

was formed. These remarks apply equally to my presentation of Hegel's complex system of philosophy.

7. Novalis (Friedrich von Hardenberg), *Die Christenheit oder Europa. Ein Fragment* (1799), ed. Otto Heuschele (Stuttgart: Reclam, 1961), 43.
8. *Theologische Studien und Kritiken* 7 (1834):50.
9. Immanuel Kant, *Religion within the Limits of Reason Alone*, trans. Theodore M. Greene and Hoyt H. Hudson (New York: Harper Torchbooks, 1960), 79.
10. Ludwig Jonas and Wilhelm Dilthey, ed., *Aus Schleiermachers Leben in Briefen*, 4 vols. (Berlin: G. Reimer, 1858-63) 1:309.
11. Friedrich Schleiermacher, *Der christliche Glaube nach den Grundsätzen der evangelischen Kirche im Zusammenhange dargestellt*, 7th ed. based on the 2d ed. (1830-31), ed. Martin Redeker, 2 vols. (Berlin: Walter de Gruyter, 1960). English translation by H. R. Mackintosh and J. S. Stewart, *The Christian Faith* (Edinburgh: T. & T. Clark, 1928).
12. Schleiermacher, *Two Letters on the Glaubenslehre to Dr. Lücke* (1829), trans. James Dukeand Francis Fiorenza, American Academy of Religion Texts and Translations Series, no. 3 (Chico, CA: Scholars Press, 1981), 60.
13. Ibid., 61.
14. Ibid., 64.
15. Schleiermacher's defined a "prince of the Church" as follows: "If one could imagine   both a religious interest and a scientific spirit conjoined to the highest degree and with the finest balance for the purpose of theoretical and practical activity alike, that would be the idea of a 'prince of the Church.' " (*Brief Outline on the Study of Theology*, trans. Terence N. Tice [Richmond, Va.: John Knox Press, 1966], 21, par. 9).
16. Brian Gerrish, *A Prince of the Church: Schleiermacher and the Beginnings of Modern Theology* (Philadelphia: Fortress Press, 1984), 44 (the assessment of Schleiermacher's significance is that of Alexander Schweizer [[1808-88]).
17. For Hegel, see *TRE*, art. "Hegel/Hegelianismus," 14:530-560 (sources and literature, 548-550). A stimulating introduction to Hegel is Walter Kaufmann, *Hegel. Reinterpretation, Texts, and Commentary* (Garden City, NY: Doubleday & Co., 1965)
18. Kaufmann, *Hegel*, 435.
19. Georg Friedrich Wilhelm Hegel, *Phänemonologie des Geistes*, vol. 2 of *Sämmtliche Werke* (3d ed. of *Jubiläumsausgabe*, 20 vols.), ed. Hermann Glockner (Stuttgart: F. Frommann [G. Holzboog], 1951), 24.
20. According to Karl Barth, the secret force behind Hegel's philosophy was the self-confidence of the idealistic thinker that "his thinking and the things which are thought by him are equivalent, i.e., that his thinking is completely present in the things thought by him, and that the things thought by him are completely present in his thinking." Karl Barth, *Protestant Theology in the Nineteenth Century. Its Background and History*, several translators (Valley Forge: Judson Press, 1973), 391.
21. Hegel, *Sämmtliche Werke* 1:56 (*Aufsätze aus dem kritischen Journal der Philosophie und andere Schriften aus der Jenenser Zeit*).
22. Quoted by Kaufmann, *Hegel*, 314 and 166, respectively.
23. Quoted ibid., 316.
24. Hegel, *Sämmtliche Werke* 2:54.
25. Ibid., 16:355 (*Vorlesungen über die Philosophie der Religion*, vol. 2).
26. Ibid., 15:37 (*Vorlesungen über die Philosophie der Religion*, vol. 1).
27. Karl Kupisch, *Zwischen Idealismus und Massendemokratie* (Berlin: Lettner-Verlag, 1955), 46.
28. Hegel, *Sämmtliche Werke* 16:207.
29. Ibid., 15:145.
30. Ibid., 16:191.
31. Ibid., 286.
32. Ibid., 2:410.

33. Werner Elert, *Der Kampf um das Christentum. Geschichte der Beziehungen zwischen dem evangelischen Christentum in Deutschland und dem allgemeinen Denken seit Schleiermacher und Hegel* (Munich: C. H. Beck, 1921), 34.

34. Novalis, *Die Christenheit oder Europa*, 39.

35. Friedrich Wilhelm Joseph Schelling, *Sämmtliche Werke*, ed. Karl Friedrich August Schelling (Stuttgart and Augsburg: J. G. Cotta, 1856-61), sec. 2, 4:320.

36. According to the editor of the *Democratic Review*, it is "our manifest destiny to overspread the continent allotted by Providence for the free development of our yearly multiplying millions," as quoted by the *Oxford English Dictionary* (2d ed., 1989) 9:315.

37. Friedrich Nippold, *Handbuch der neuesten Kirchengeschichte*, 3d rev. ed. (Berlin: Wiegandt & Schotte, 1890), vol. 3, sec. 1, 5.

38. Elert, *Der Kampf um das Christentum*, 93.

39. Quoted by Karl Löwith, *From Hegel to Nietzsche*, trans. David E. Green (New York: Holt, Rinehart & Winston, 1964), 67.

40. University of Berlin, *Akten* (unpublished records).

41. From Karl Marx and Friedrich Engels, *Die deutsche Ideologie* (1845-46), as quoted by Löwith, *From Hegel to Nietzsche*, 100.

42. David Friedrich Strauss, *Das Leben Jesu kritisch bearbeitet*, 2 vols. (Tübingen: C. F. Osiander, 1835-36). English trans. by George Eliot (Marian Evans) from the 4th German ed. of 1840, 3 vols. (London: Chapman, Brothers, 1846).

43. Hegel, *Sämmtliche Werke* 15:210.

44. Ibid., 10: 454 (*System der Philosophie Dritter Teil. Die Philosophie des Geistes*).

45. See n. 32.

46. Kaufmann, *Hegel*, 275. Karl Barth asserts that "Hegel's living God.....is actually the living man." Thus he answers his own earlier question: "Why did Hegel not become for the Protestant world something similar to what Thomas Aquinas was for Roman Catholicism?" (*Protestant Theology in the Nineteenth Century*, 419 and 384, respectively.)

47. Ferdinand Christian Baur, *Kirchengeschichte des neunzehnten Jahrhunderts*, ed. Eduard Zeller (Tübingen: L. F. Fues, 1862), 363.

48. Baur, *Die christliche Gnosis oder die christliche Religions-Philosophie in ihrer geschichtlichen Entwicklung*, (Tübingen: C. F. Osiander, 1835), and Wilhelm Vatke, *Die biblische Theologie wissenschaftlich dargestellt. Die Religion des Alten Testaments nach den kanonischen Büchern entwickelt* (Berlin: G. Bethge, 1835).

49. David Friedrich Strauss, *Streitschriften zur Verteidigung meiner Schriften über das Leben Jesu und zur Charakteristik der gegenwärtigen Theologie*, (Tübingen: C. F. Osiander, 1837).

50. Karl Löwith, *Die Hegelsche Linke* (Stuttgart–Bad Canstatt: F. Frommann [G. Holzboog], 1962), 7-38 (Löwith's Introduction). The quotation is from the preface of Hegel's *Grundlinien der Philosophie des Rechts* (*Sämmtliche Werke* 7:33).

51. DKF, "Das deutsche Antichristentum mit seinen Vorläufern und seinen Konsequenzen," I (1848):306.

52. Schaff, *Principle*, 202 (cf. Schaff, *Princip*, 144).

53. Friedrich Nietzsche, *Ecce Homo*, trans. A. M. Ludovici, *The Complete Works of Friedrich Nietzsche*, ed. Oscar Levy (New York: Russell & Russell, re-issue 1964), 17:55. – One wonders, though, whether Schaff, perchance, might have read the review of Kierkegaard's *Concept of Irony* (1841) in the *Hallische Jahrbücher* of 1841, the first and, for a long time, the only reference to Kierkegaard's work in German publications.

54. The literature dealing with German theology in the nineteenth century is vast. The best recent surveys are offered by Emanuel Hirsch, *Geschichte der neuern evangelischen Theologie*, 5 vols., 2d ed. (Gütersloh: Gütersloher Verlagshaus Gerd Mohn, 1960); Stephan-Schmidt, *Geschichte der deutschen evangelischen Theologie* (see n. 5); and Claude Welch, *Protestant Thought in the Nineteenth Century*, 2 vols. (New Haven and London: Yale University Press, 1972, 1985). Karl Barth, *Protestant Theology in the Nineteenth Century*, should also be mentioned, as well as an older work: Otto Pfleiderer, *The Development of Theology in*

Germany since Kant and its Progress in Great Britain since 1825, trans. J. Frederick Smith (London: Swan Sonnenschein & Co. - New York: Macmillan & Co.), 1890.

4. Tübingen - Halle – Berlin (1837-1840): The Mediating Theology

1. Strauss was one of a remarkable group of *Repetenten*. In those two years, 1833-35, this group included not only Friedrich Theodor Vischer but also several who were destined to become influential evangelical churchmen and theologians: Wilhelm Hofacker, Sixtus Carl Kapff, Wilhelm Hofmann (the son of the founder of Kornthal and later court preacher in Potsdam) and Isaac August Dorner. Kapff, Hofmann and Dorner remained Schaff's lifelong friends.
2. Hermelink, *Die evangelische Kirche in Württemberg*, 380-82.
3. Carl Heinrich Stirm, *Apologie des Christentums in Briefen für gebildete Leser* (Stuttgart: C. Belser, 1836).
4. August Tholuck, *Gespräche über die vornehmsten Glaubensfragen der Zeit für nachdenkende Laien* (Halle: R. Mühlmann, 1846), III.
5. Elert, *Der Kampf um das Christentum*, 103.
6. Schaff Papers, ERHS, Lancaster.
7. Stirm, *Apologie*, 13.
8. Ibid., 15.
9. Ibid. 14.
10. *Life of Schaff*, 24.
11. Ibid., 25.
12. Stirm, *Apologie*, 5.
13. Ibid. 17.
14. Friedrich Schleiermacher, *On Religion. Speeches to its Cultured Despisers*, trans. John Oman (New York: Harper Torchbooks, 1958), 145 (from an explanatory note to the 3d ed. of 1821).
15. *DKF*, "Deutsche Literatur in Amerika," 1 (1848):15.
16. Schaff, *Germany*, 92.
17. DKF, "Gallerie der bedeutendsten jetzt lebenden Universitätstheologen Deutschlands," 5 (1852): 296. – Schaff continued this remarkable series of articles throughout much of 1852.
18. Josef Rupert Geiselmann has provided brilliant introductions and commentaries to his critical edition of two of Möhler's major works: *Die Einheit in der Kirche oder das Prinzip des Katholizismus* (1825) (Köln and Olten: Jacob Hegner, 1956), and *Symbolik oder Darstellung der dogmatishen Gegensätze der Katholiken und Protestanten nach ihren öffentlichen Bekenntnisschriften* (1832, 5th ed. 1835), vol. 1 (Köln and Olten: Jacob Hegner, 1958); vol. 2 (Darmstadt: Wissenschaftliche Buchgesellschaft, 1960). See also Josef Rupert Geiselmann, *Die Katholische Tübinger Schule; ihre theologische Eigenart* (Freiburg: Herder, 1964).
19. Ferdinand Christian Baur, *Der Gegensatz des Katholizismus und Protestantismus nach den Prinzipien und Hauptdogmen der beiden Lehrbegriffe* (Tübingen: L. F. Fues,1834; 2d ed. 1836).
20. Schaff, *History of the Apostolic Church, With a General Introduction to Church History*, trans. Edward D. Yeomans (New York: Charles Scribner, 1853), 115.
21. *AR*, 122.
22. Karl Knüpfel, *Geschichte und Beschreibung der Universität Tübingen*, (Tübingen:L. F. Fues, 1849), 378 (Baur contributed the chapter on the history of the Protestant theological faculty).
23. *AR*, 114.
24. Ibid.

25. Klaus Scholder offered an expert introduction to Baur in *TRE*, art. "Baur," 5:352-59. He also edited *Ferdinand Christian Baur: Ausgewählte Werke in Einzelausgaben*, 5 vols. (Stuttgart – Bad Cannstatt: F. Frommann [Günther Holzboog], 1963-75). Regrettably, none of Baur's major works are available in English. Important recent studies, which differ considerably in their understanding of Baur and his contemporary significance, are Wolfgang Geiger, *Spekulation und Kritik: Die Geschichtstheologie Ferdinand Christian Baurs* (Munich: Chr. Kaiser Verlag, 1964), and Peter C. Hodgson, *The Formation of Historical Theology. A Study of Ferdinand Christian Baur* (New York: Harper & Row, 1966). See also Hodgson, trans. and ed., *Ferdinand Christian Baur: On the Writing of Church History* (New York: Oxford University Press, 1968).

26. Baur, *Die Christliche Lehre von der Versöhnung in ihrer geschichtlichen Entwicklung von der ältesten Zeit bis auf die neueste* (Tübingen: C. F. Osiander, 1838), and *Die christliche Lehre von der Dreieinigkeit und Menschwerdung Gottes in ihrer geschichtlichen Entwicklung*, 3 vols. (Tübingen: C. F. Osiander, 1841-43).

27. *DKF*, "Ein Blick in die kirchlich-religiöse Weltlage," 6 (1853):105.

28. Quoted by Hodgson, *The Formation of Historical Theology*, 96 (from an academic opinion Baur submitted in 1839).

29. *DKF*, 5 (1852):301.

30. *AR*, 115.

31. Carl Friedrich Schmid, *Biblical Theology of the New Testament*, trans. from the 4th German ed. by G. H. Venable (Edinburgh: T. & T. Clark, 1870).

32. *DKF*, loc.cit.

33. Letter of Schaff to Thiersch (April 10, 1849), Archives, Bayrische Staatsbibliothek München.

34. Schaff, *History of the Apostolic Church, with a General Introduction to Church History*, 122.

35. Ibid., 122 n.3.

36. Schaff wrote a series of articles on Irvingism in *DKF* 3 (1850): 49-57, 81-88, 161-168, 223-234. For the impact of the liturgy of the Catholic Apostolic Church on Schaff, cf. James Hastings Nichols, ed., *The Mercersburg Theology*, (New York: Oxford University Press, 1966), 263.

37. Compare Thiersch's *Vorlesungen über Katholizismus und Protestantismus* (1846) and *Die Kirche im apostolischen Zeitalter und die neutestamentliche Literatur* (1852) with Schaff's *Principle of Protestantism* (1845) and *History of the Apostolic Church* (1853).

38. Cf. Hodgson, *The Formation of Historical Theology*, 28.

39. Schaff, *Germany*, 376.

40. *AR*, 121.

41. *DKF* 5 (1852):177.

42. *AR*, 116.

43. Schaff, *Germany*, 72.

44. August Tholuck, *Die Lehre von der Sünde und vom Versöhner oder die wahre Weihe des Zweiflers* (1823), 9th ed. (Gotha: F. A. Perthes, 1871).

45. *AR*, after 135 (unpaginated).

46. Quoted by Lütgert, *Die Religion des deutschen Idealismus* 3:155.

47. *Literarischer Anzeiger für die christliche Theologie und Wissenschaft* 9,1 (1840):6.

48. Johannes Hoffmeister, ed., *Briefe von und an Hegel*, 4 vols. (Hamburg: F. Meiner, 1961) 3: 225.

49. Quoted by Otto Ritschl, *Albrecht Ritschls Leben*, 2vols. (Freiburg: J. C. B. Mohr [P. Siebeck], 1892-96) 1:52.

50. *Life of Schaff*, 31.

51. Julius Müller, *Die christliche Lehre von der Sünde*, 2 vols. (Breslau: Josef Max, 1839-44).

52. Quoted in *Die Religion in Geschichte und Gegenwart*, 3d ed., art. "Berlin," 1: col. 1057.

53. Carl Schwarz, *Zur Geschichte der neuesten Theologie*, 3d ed. (Leipzig: F. A. Brockhaus, 1864), 56.

54. Adolph Hausrath, *David Friedrich Strauss und die Theologie seiner Zeit* (Heidelberg: F. Bassermann, 1876) 1:81.

55. *Life of Schaff*, 31.
56. Elizabeth L. Smith, ed., *Henry Boynton Smith. His Life and Work* (New York: A. C. Armstrong & Son, 1881), 81.
57. *DKF* 5 (1852):132.
58. Ibid., 133.
59. University of Berlin, *Akten*.
60. Schaff, *Die Sünde wider den Heiligen Geist und die daraus gezogenen dogmatischen und ethischen Folgerungen. Eine exegetisch-dogmatische Abhandlung, nebst einem historischen Anhange über das Lebensende des Francesco Spiera* (Halle: J. F. Lippert, 1841).
61. University of Berlin, *Akten*.
62. Schaff, *Die Sünde wider den Heiligen Geist*, 54-56.
63. See chap. 3, n. 71, above.
64. Schaff, *Die Sünde*, 65.
65. Ibid., 137 and 145.
66. Cf. ibid., 173.
67. University of Berlin, *Akten*.
68. In his petition for admission to the examination Schaff had written: "In ipso examine ... imprimis in theologica dogmatica et in interpretatione Novi Ti, in quas disciplinas maxime incumbebam, explorari cupio" (*Akten*).
69. Letter of Julius Mann to Schaff (October 3, 1882), quoted by Späth, *Wilhelm Julius Mann*, 73.
70. See especially Ragnar Holte, *Die Vermittlungstheologie. Ihre theologischen Grundbegriffe kritisch untersucht* (Uppsala: Almquist & Wikselss, 1965), Hirsch, *Geschichte der neuern evangelischen Theologie* 5:364-414, and Claude Welch, *Protestant Thought in the Nineteenth Century* 1:269-291. Schwarz, *Zur Geschichte der neuesten Theologie*, 337-447, offers a polemical and insightful contemporary discussion.
71. See my article, "Philip Schaff: Sechs Briefe an Carl Ullmann (1843-1849)," *Zeitschrift für Neuere Theologiegeschichte/Journal for the History of Modern Theology* 5 (1998): 81-113.
72. Quoted by Stephan-Schmidt, *Geschichte der deutschen evangelischen Theologie*, 188.
73. Cf. Julius Müller, *Die evangelische Union, ihr Wesen und ihr göttliches Recht* (Berlin: Wiegandt and Grieben, 1854).
74. Martin Kähler, *Geschichte der protestantischen Dogmatik im 19. Jahrhundert*, ed. Ernst Kähler (Munich: C. Kaiser Verlag, 1962), 118.
75. *DKF*, "Die Studien und Kritiken," 1 (1848): 82.
76. Hirsch, *Geschichte der neuern evangelischen Theologie* 5:375.
77. Ernst Troeltsch, "Rückblick auf ein halbes Jahrhundert der theologischen Wissenschaft, " *Gesammelte Schriften*, 4 vols. (Tübingen: J. C. B. Mohr [Paul Siebeck], 1912-25) 2:202.
78. Quoted by Holte, *Die Vermittlungstheologie*, 36f. – Worth noting is the casual but pointed remark of the New England Unitarian Theodore Parker (1810-60) about Ullmann and the German mediating theology in general. Reporting on his visit with Ullmann he wrote that Ullmann "is a pacificator, a *medium-iter* man. One party says 1+1=2.' another 1+1=4.'No', says Ullmann, 'my dear friends, you are both mistaken, why quarrel? Truth takes the medium-iter, 1+1=3.' There may be three parties in theology, viz. – 1. That of *mid-night*; and 2. That of *mid-day*; and 3. That of *twilight*. I think Ullmann belongs to the latter class, and stands at the *indifference-point* between day and darkness; yet he is a good man, and I like him very much" (John Weiss, *The Life and Correspondence of Theodore Parker* [New York: D. Appleton & Co., 1864] 1:242).
79. Baur, *Kirchengeschichte des neunzehnten Jahrhunderts*, 449.
80. Troeltsch, "Rückblick auf ein halbes Jahrhundert der theologischen Wissenschaft," 206.
81. Barth, *Protestant Theology in the Nineteenth Century*, 575f.
82. Stephan-Schmidt, *Geschichte der deutschen evangelischen Theologie*, 189.
83. Hirsch, *Geschichte der neueren evangelischen Theologie* 5:430.
84. Ibid., 414.
85. Carl Ullmann, "Über den unterscheidenden Charakter des Christentums, mit Beziehung auf neuere Auffassungsweisen," *Theologische Studien und Kritiken* 18 (1845): 7-61. An enlarged

version was published separately as *Das Wesen des Christentums* (Hamburg: F. Perthes, 1845, 5th ed., 1865).

86. Hirsch, *Geschichte der neuern evangelischen Theologie* 5:414.
87. John Willamson Nevin, *The Mystical Presence. A Vindication of the Reformed or Calvinistic Doctrine of the Holy Eucharist* (Philadelphia: Lippincott, 1846), 13-47.
88. Cf. John B. Payne, "Schaff and Nevin, Colleagues at Mercersburg: The Church Question," *Church History* 61(1992):169-190, and my article, n. 71 above.
89. See n. 15 above.

5. *Privatdozent* at Berlin (1842-1844): The "Church Question"

1. The quotations from Schaff's no longer extant Italian diary are, in translation, from *Life of Schaff*, 38-62.
2. Schaff, *Das Verhältnis des Jakobus, Bruder des Herrn, zu Jakobus Alphäi, auf's Neue exegetisch und historisch untersucht* (Berlin: A. Wohlgemut, 1843).
3. University of Berlin, *Akten*.
4. *AR*, 13.
5. The following lecture mss. are available, some identified by semester, among the Schaff Papers, UTS, NY: Briefe Petri, Einleitung in die katholischen Briefe, Das theologische System Schleiermachers (WS 1842-43), Historisch-kritische Einleitungen in die Schriften des N. T. (WS 1843-44), Geschichte der protestantischen Theologie (WS 1843-44).
6. Schaff, *Germany*, 43. – The miserable life of the *pivatdozent* at that time is discussed more fully by Erich J. C. Hahn, "The Junior Faculty in 'Revolt:' Reform Plans for Berlin University in 1848," *The American Historical Review* 88, 4 (October 1977): 875-95. The revolt was more specifically directed against Eichhorn, the Minister of Public Worship and Education, who heavy- handedly favored politically and religiously conservative candidates for faculty appointments in all the Prussian universities (in the theological faculties, for instance, Hengstenberg's protégés , among them Schaff).
7. Johann Eduard Erdmann, *Vorlesungen über Glauben und Wissen als Einleitung in die Dogmatik und Religionsphilosophie* (Berlin: Dunker & Humblot, 1837), 1.
8. Theodor Kliefoth, *Einleitung in die Dogmengeschichte* (Parchim and Ludwiglust: D. C. Hinstorff, 1839), 94.
9. Wilhelm Löhe, *Drei Bücher von der Kirche* (Stuttgart: S. G. Liesching, 1845), preface.
10. Hirsch, *Geschichte der neuern evangelischen Theologie* 5:145.
11. Schaff, "Ein Wort über die theologische Kritik," *Literarische Zeitung* (Berlin), May 20 and August 2, 1843, and "Über den Unterschied zwischen Katholizismus und Romanismus," ibid., October 31 and December 16, 1843. -- I have been unable to identify articles which, according to *Life of Schaff*, 68, Schaff is said to have written for Hengstenberg's *Evangelische Kirchenzeitung* and Tholuck's *Literarischer Anzeiger*.
12. Schaff, Tagebuch (diary) 1844, August 15, Schaff Papers, UTS, NY.
13. Schaff, *Principl e*, 219f.; cf. Schaff, *Princip*, 165.
14. Kant, *Die Religin innerhalb der Grenzen der blossen Vernunft* (1793).
15. Schleiermacher, *The Christian Faith*, par.170.1, p. 738.
16. Quoted by Gyula Barczay, *Ecclesia semper reformanda. Eine Untersuchung zum Kirchenbegriff des 19. Jahrhunderts* (Zürich: EVZ-Verlag, 1961), 136.
17. Lütgert, *Die Religion des deutschen Idealismus und ihr Ende* 3:133.
18. Hirsch, *Geschichte der neueren evangelischen Theologie*, "Der Streit um den Kirchenbegriff," 5:145-231.
19. This is done in Barczay's informative study , *Ecclesia semper reformanda* , after a lengthy opening chapter on Schleiermacher's contribution.

20. "Zur Eigentümlichkeit der protestantischen Ansicht von der christlichen Kirche gehört es aber wesentlich, dass wir uns diese als ein bewegliches Ganze denken, als ein Solches, das der Fortschreitung und Entwicklung fähig ist, nur mit dieser Restriktion, ohne welche das Christentum zusammenfallen würde.....dass jede Fortschreitung nichts sein kann, als ein richtigeres Verstehen und vollkommeneres Aneignen des in Christo Gesetzten." *Die christliche Sitte nach den Grundsätzen der evangelischen Kirche im Zusammenhang dargestellt*, ed. L. Jonas, in *Sämmtliche Werke*, sec. 1, vol. 12, 2d ed. (Berlin: G. Reimer,1874), 72.

21. Schleiermacher, *The Christian Faith*, par. 115.

22. Hirsch, 5:168. See Richard Rothe, *Die Anfänge der christlichen Kirche und ihrer Verfassung* (Wittenberg: Zimmermann,1837).

23. Claude Welch, ed. and trans., *God and Incarnation in Mid-Nineteenth Century German Theology* (New York: Oxford University Press, 1965), 9.

24. See Hans Jürgen Gabriel, "Im Namen des Evangeliums gegen den Fortschritt. Zur Rolle der 'Evangelischen Kirchenzeitung' unter E. W. Hengstenberg von 1830 bis 1849," 154-76, in *Beiträge zur Berliner Kirchengeschichte*, ed. Günter Wirth (Berlin: Union Verlag, 1987), 162.

25. Friedrich Julius Stahl, *Die Kirchenverfassung nach Lehre und Recht der Protestanten* (Erlangen: Theodor Bläsig, 1840). Quotation is from Hans Felix Hedderich, *Die Gedanken der Romantik über Kirche und Staat* (Gütersloh: Verlag C. Bertelsmann, 1941), 131.

26. Hirsch, 5:185.

27. See Geiselmann's edition of Möhler's, *Symbolik* (chap. 4, n. 18, above), 626-72.

28. In his thorough and insightful study, *Romanticism in American Theology: Nevin and Schaff at Mercersburg* (Chicago: The University of Chicago Press, 1961), James Hastings Nichols highlighted the importance of Schaff's last months in Berlin by heading, one-sidedly, the chapter covering his whole German education: "Evangelical Catholicity in Prussia."

29. See Walter Wendland, *Studien zur Erweckungsbewegung in Berlin (1810-1830)*, vol. 19 of *Jahrbuch für Brandenburgische Kirchengeschichte* (Berlin: n.p., 1924), and J. F. Gerhard Goeters and Rudolf Mau (eds.), *Die Geschichte der Evangelischen Kirche der Union*, vol.1, *Die Anfänge der Union unter landesherrlichem Kirchenregiment (1817-1850)* (Leipzig: Evangelische Verlagsanstalt, 1992). – For nineteenth-century Lutheran confessionalism in general, see Holsten Fagerberg, *Bekenntnis, Kirche und Amt in der deutschen konfessionellen Theologie des 19. Jahrhunderts* (Uppsala: A.-B. Lundequistska Bokhandeln and Wiesbaden: Otto Harrassowitz, 1952).

30. *DKF* 5 (1852):162 – See Peter Maser, *Hans Ernst von Kottwitz. Studien zur Erweckunsbewegung des frühen 19. Jahrhunderts in Schlesien und Berlin* (Göttingen: Vandenhoeck & Ruprecht, 1990).

31. Schaff was not scandalized, for many years later he still spoke of "the somewhat indelicate but well deserved exposure of the frivolities of Gesenius' lectures at Halle" (*Germany*, 303).

32. *Evangelische Kirchenzeitung* , 1836, Preface.

33. Quoted by Hans Joachim Schoeps, *Das andere Preussen. Konservative Gestalten und Probleme im Zeitalter Friedrich Wilhelms IV*, 2d ed. (Honnef/Rhein: Peters Verlag, 1957), 70.

34. *Evangelische Kirchenzeitung* , 1840, 25.

35. Gabriel, "Im Namen des Evangeliums," 162.

36. *Evangelische Kirchenzeitung* , 1840, 20.

37. Schoeps, *Das andere Preussen*, 220.

38. We now have available the comprehensive and detailed biography of Hans-Christof Kraus, *Ernst Ludwig von Gerlach. Politisches Denken und Handeln eines Preussischen Altkonservativen*, 2 vols. (Göttingen: Vandenhoeck & Ruprecht, 1994). Still valuable is Eugen Jedele, *Die kirchenpolitischen Anschauungen des Ernst Ludwig von Gerlach* (Ansbach: C. Brügel & Sohn, 1910). An important biographical source is *Ernst Ludwig von Gerlach: Aufzeichnungen aus seinem Leben und Wirken*, ed. Jakob von Gerlach, 2 vols. (Schwerin: Verlag von Fr. Bahn, 1903). I am especially indebted to Schoeps, *Das andere Preussen*.

169

39. The most important articles are identified and listed in Schoeps, *Das andere Preussen*, 335-57, though this list is by no means complete.
40. Schoeps, *Das andere Preussen*, 82.
41. Archibald Alexander Hodge, *The Life of Charles Hodge* (New York: Scribner's Sons, 1880), 158. Among the pictures Hodge kept on his desk to the end of his life were those of Tholuck and Ludwig von Gerlach (ibid., 331).
42. Surprisingly, Schaff hardly ever mentioned Ludwig von Gerlach by name in his writings, not even in the Berlin chapter of his "Autobiographical Reminiscences." That chapter, unfortunately, is in any case tantalizingly brief, for Schaff wrote it last, in 1890; by that time he had long shed the most distinctive views of the Hengstenberg circle of the 1840s. Only the son's brief remark in his father's biography that Ludwig von Gerlach's "views of the church had a permanent influence upon his mind" (*Life of Schaff*, 67) has alerted later students of Schaff to this Prussian aristocrat's significant contribution to the further evolution of Schaff's theology at the end of his German years of study.
43. Schaff, *Germany*, 316.
44. Quoted by William O. Shanahan, *German Protestants Face the Social Question* (Notre Dame, IN: University of Notre Dame Press, 1954), 195.
45. Ibid., 127.
46. Ibid., 110.
47. Quoted by Schoeps, *Das andere Preussen*, 77.
48. Quoted by Jedele, *Die Kirchenpoltischen Anschaungen des Ernst Ludwig von Gerlach*, 57.
49. See n. 33 above.
50. Jedele, 27.
51. Quoted by Jedele 32.
52. Ibid.
53. Schoeps, 23 (from *Evangelische Kirchenzeitung* [1836], 275).
54. Schoeps, 22.
55. Quoted by Schoeps, 19.
56. Quoted by Kurt Schmidt-Clausen, *Vorweggenommene Einheit. Die Gründung des Bistums Jerusalem im Jahre 1841* (Berlin and Hamburg: Lutherisches Verlagshaus, 1965), 206.
57. Quotations in Schoeps, 62, 67, 66, respectively.
58. Friedrich Julius Stahl, *Die lutherische Kirche und die Union* (Berlin: Verlag von Wilhelm Hertz, 1859), 466.
59. Schoeps, *Das andere Preussen*, ch. 4, "'Evangelische Katholizität'," focuses on Friedrich Julius Stahl's contributions, in addition to a briefer discussion of Ludwig von Gerlach's ecumenical views in the first chapter (69-76). How widespread the ideal of "evangelical catholicity" in Europe was in the nineteenth century is shown by Sven-Erik Brodd, *Evangelisk Katolicitet. Ett studium av innehåll och function under 1800- och 1900-talen* (Lund: LiberFörlag, 1982). – For Schaff, see my article, "Philip Schaff's Life-long Quest for 'Evangelical Catholicism'," *The New Mercersburg Review* 14 (1993):3-17.
60. Walter Bussmann, *Zwischen Preussen und Deutschland. Friedrich Wilhelm IV* (Berlin: Siedler Verlag, 1990), 126.
61. Theodor Kliefoth, "Die neuere Kirchengeschichtsschreibung in der deutsch-evangelischen Kirche," *Allgemeines Repertorium* (ed. Hermann Reuter) 49 (1845):215.
62. Ludwig von Gerlach is not so singular a figure with his ecumenical contributions, however. Nineteenth-century German Protestantism was unusually fruitful in producing various serious and significant contributions to the ecumenical discussion, proving Johann Adam Möhler's observation correct that "ever since Christianity has again been accorded greater honor and Christ has again been acknowledged in his proper dignity, the desire for unity has also everywhere been astir, and most of all among the profoundest Protestant theologians"(Geiselmann's edition of Möhler's *Die Einheit in der Kirche* [1825], 97). For literature, see Kurt Frör, *Evangelisches Denken und Katholizismus seit Schleiermacher* (Munich: Kaiser Verlag, 1932); Hans Joachim Birkner/ Heinz Liebing/Klaus Scholder, *Das konfessionelle Problem in der evangelischen Theologie des 19. Jahrhunderts* (Tübingen: J. C.

170

B. Mohr, 1966); Klaus-Martin Beckmann, *Unitas Ecclesiae. Eine systematische Studie zur Theologiegeschichte des 19. Jahrhunderts* (Gütersloh: Gerd Mohn, 1967); and Geiselmann's brilliant Introduction (which is so comprehensive and insightful as to belie its introductory character) to his edition of Möhler's *Symbolik* 1:15-148 (for Geiselmann's editions of Möhler's *Die Einheit in der Kirche* and *Symbolik,* see chap. 4 n. 18 above). For Schelling's noteworthy and unique ecumenical scheme and its significance for Schaff, see below.

63. Ludwig von Gerlach, *Aufzeichnungen* 1:205.

64. Cf. the beautiful vision of a united Christian Europe which the romantic poet Novalis (Friedrich Leopold von Hardenberg [1772-1801]) had set forth in his *Die Christenheit oder Europa. Ein Fragment* (1799).

65. Quoted by Schaff, *DKF*, "Dr. Hengstenberg," 2 (1849):235 (from *Evangelische Kirchenzeitung*, "Die Römisch-Katholische Kirche und die Revolution" [1848],762).

66. Quoted by Schoeps, 75.

67. *DKF* 5 (1852):136.

68. Quoted by Schoeps, 221 (from a presentation at the Bremen *Kirchentag*, 1852).

69. Quoted by Schoeps, 71.

70. Quoted by Schoeps, 75.

71. Ludwig von Gerlach, *Aufzeichnungen* 2:177.

72. Cf. Schmidt-Clausen, *Vorweggenommene Einheit*, chap. 4, "Ernst Ludwig von Gerlachs Ideen und ihre Bedeutung für die Bistumsgründung," 191-218.

73. Ms. in Schaff Papers, ERHS, Lancaster.

74. See Johannes Bachmann, *Ernst Wilhelm Hengstenberg. Sein Leben und Wirken*, 2 vols. (Gütersloh: C. Bertelsmann, 1876-1880), vol. 3, ed. Theodor Schmalenbach (1892); Hirsch, *Geschichte der neuern evangelischen Theologie* 5:118-30; *TRE*, art. "Hengstenberg," 15:39-42 (lit.). In the end one will agree with Hirsch's conclusion that Hengstenberg's fierce and uncompromising advocacy of the orthodox Lutheran position contributed considerably to the growing de-Christianization of the German people in the nineteenth century (ibid., 130).

75. *DKF* 5 (1852):135.

76. For contemporary discussions of Neander's work see Kurt-Victor Selge, "August Neander—ein getaufter Hamburger Jude der Emanzipations- und Restaurationszeit als erster Berliner Kirchenhistoriker (1813-1850)," in *450 Jahre Evangelischer Theologie in Berlin*, ed. Gerhard Bessier and Christof Gestrich (Göttingen: Vandenhoeck & Ruprecht, 1989), 233-76, and *TRE*, art. "Neander," 24:238-42 (lit.).

77. Ludwig von Gerlach, *Aufzeichnungen* 1:193.

78. Schaff, "Neander's Life of Christ," *Methodist Quarterly Review* 30 (April 1848):248-68.

79. *DKF*, "Erinnerungen an Neander," 4 (1851):20.

80. *Berlin 1842 – New York 1892. The Semi-Centennial of Philip Schaff* (New York: Privately printed, 1893), 5.

81. *DKF* 5 (1852):404.

82. Quoted by Maurer, "Das Prinzip des Organischen" (see n. 90, below), 275.

83. Neander, *General History of the Christian Religion and Church,* trans. J. Torrey, vol. 1 (2d ed.; Boston: Crocker and Brewster, 1851), from Preface to 1st edition.

84. [John Emerich] Lord Acton said of Baur that he "grafted Hegel on Ranke," in: "German Schools of History," *Historical Essays and Studies* (London: MacMillan & Co., 1908), 368.

85. *DKF* 4 (1851):34.

86. Karl Kupisch, "Schelling in Berlin," *Zeitschrift für Kirchengeschichte* 76, 3 and 4 (1965):258-81.

87. Ms. of Schaff's lecture notes, Schaff Papers, ERHS, Lancaster.

88. Schelling, *Studium Generale. Vorlesungen über die Methode des akademischen Studiums*, ed. Hermann Glockner (Stuttgart: Alfred Kröner Verlag, 1954). Engl. translation by E. S. Morgan, *On University Studies*, ed. and introd. by Norbert Guterman (Athens, OH: Ohio University Press. 1966). – For the claim that this book was the most influential of Schelling's writings, see Fagerberg, *Bekenntnis, Kirche und Amt*, 52 n. 4.

89. See Wilhelm Maurer, "Der Organismusgedanke bei Schelling und in der Theologie der Katholischen Tübinger Schule," *Kirche und Dogma* 8 (July 1962):202-16, and "Das Prinzip des Organischen in der evangelischen Kirchengeschichtsschreibung des 19. Jahrhunderts," ibid. 8 (October 1962):265-92.

90. Schelling, *On University Studies*, 136, 107, 95, respectively.

91. Schaff, *Princip*, 156; cf. Schaff, *Principle*, 217.

92. A reprint of the Paulus edition is F. W. J. Schelling, *Philosophie der Offenbarung (1841/42)*, ed. Manfred Frank (Frankfurt: Suhrkampf Verlag, 1977). In the Paulus edition, Schelling's ecumenical construction of the history of Christianity is presented in the 35th lecture, that is, as one lecture only.

93. Troeltsch, art. "Idealismus, deutscher," *Realencyklopädie für protestantische Theologie und Kirche* (3d. ed.) 8:632.

94. Reinhold Seeberg, *Die Kirche Deutschlands im neunzehnten Jahrhundert* (Leipzig: A. Deichert, 1903), 123. - Contemporary assessments of the philosophy of the old Schelling are more favorable: see, for instance, Paul Tillich's doctoral dissertation of 1910, *The Construction of the History of Religion in Schelling's Positive Philosophy: Its Presuppositions and Principles*, trans. Victor Nuovo (Lewisburg, PA: Bucknell University Press, 1974); Walter Kasper, *Das Absolute in der Geschichte. Philosophie und Theologie der Geschichte in der Spätphilosophie Schellings* (Mainz: Matthias-Grünewald-Verlag, 1965); and Robert Gascoigne, *Religion, Rationality, and Community. Sacred and Secular in the Thought of Hegel and His Critics* (The Hague and Boston: M. Nijhoff, 1985), chap. 4, "The Late Schelling: The Philosophy of Mythology and Revelation," 169-210. – One might be tempted to call it most appropriate that Walter Kasper, the expert on the philosophy of the old Schelling with its universal and ecumenical aspirations, is now, as Cardinal Kasper, heading the Vatican's Pontifical Council for Promoting Christian Unity.

95. Schelling, *Philosophie der Mythologie und Offenbarung*, section 2, vols. 1-4, *Sämmtliche Werke*, ed. Karl Friedrich August von Schelling (Stuttgart and Augsburg: J. G. Cotta, 14 vols., 1856-61). The concluding two lectures are in section 2, vol. 4, 294-334. – An English translation is available in my article "An Ecumenical Vision of Church History: F. W. J. Schelling," *Perkins School of Theology Journal* 17 (winter-spring 1964):3-19. The same translation also in *Lutheran Quarterly* 18, no. 4, 362-78. – It should be noted that Schelling offered his "Philosophie der Offenbarung" only once in Berlin, during his first semester 1841/42.

96. *Perkins School of Theology Journal* 17:18.

97. Ludwig von Gerlach, *Aufzeichnungen* 1:303. Neander, on the other hand, in dedicating in 1842 the 2d edition of his *General History of the Christian Religion and Church* to Schelling stated publicly "how much there was that struck in harmony with my own views" in Schelling's ecumenical vision of the history of Christianity. It should also be noted that German students, most of them poor and eager to save on expensive books, were known to take meticulously accurate and extensive lecture notes

98. Schaff, *Princip*, 156-57, footnote; cf. Schaff, *Principle*, 216-18 (the remarks about Schelling are here included in the text).

99. Schaff, *History of the Christian Church*, vol. 1 (3d ed.; New York: Charles Scribner's Sons, 1890), 517, footnote. Schaff mentioned this "interesting modification....as containing a grain of truth."

100. Schaff, *Literature and Poetry* (New York: Charles Scribner's Sons, 1890), 427, footnote.

101. Fagerberg, *Bekenntnis, Kirche und Amt*, 37-40. It is worth noting that *"Evangelisch,"* in contrast to "Lutheran" or "Reformed," in the journal's title was meant to be an endorsement of the Union.

102. Schaff, *Princip* 135f; cf. Schaff, *Principle*, 194f.

103. Ludwig von Gerlach, *Aufzeichnungen* 1:452. The text of the General Synod's creedal formulary for ordination, as well as the text of a handwritten copy of the memorandum Ludwig von Gerlach submitted to the king pointing out the several shortcomings of the proposed creedal formulary and pleading for its rejection, can be found in Joachim

Cochlovius, *Bekenntnis und Einheit der Kirche im deutschen Protestantismus 1840-1850* (Gütersloh: Verlagshaus Mohn, 1980), 255-56 and 265-69, respectively. - It would take more than a century for the Protestant churches, now not only of Germany but of Europe, to formulate and accept the first common creedal affirmation, the *Leuenberger Konkordie* of 1973!

104. Schoeps, *Das andere Preussen*, 72.
105. Schaff, *Germany*, 319.
106. Hirsch, *Geschichte der neuern evangelischen Theologie* 5:211-15. Cf. also Barczay, *Ecclesia semper reformanda.* 160-84 (the chapter on the mediating theology and related theological currents). - Surprisingly, Hirsch draws his brief discussion of Dorner's position from a major publication toward the end of Dorner's life, for, as he avers, that later publication mirrors the spirit of the 1840s: "Dorner developed those insights gained in his youth purely according to the law of the interior formation of the self and closed his mind against all outside stimulation after the middle of the century." (211) The same can be said of Schaff, for the basic principles and aims of the mediating theology of the 1840s determined indeed his theology to the end of his life. Hence the importance of a study of the formative years of Schaff's German education!
107. *AR*, unpaginated ms.

6. Called to Mercersburg Seminary in Pennsylvania

1. Cf. H. M. J. Klein, *The History of the Eastern Synod of the Reformed Church in the United States* (Lancaster, Pa.: Published by the Eastern Synod, 1943) and George Warren Richards, *History of the Theological Seminary of the Reformed Church in the United States, 1825-1934, Evangelical and Reformed Church, 1934-1952* (Lancaster, Pa.: Rudisill, 1952).
2. *Schriften betreffend die deutsche Professur in Mercersburg, Pennsylvania. Auf Befehl der Synode gedruckt* (Chambersburg, Pa.: Druckerei der Reformirten Kirche, 1843), 9. - Karl Kupisch, *Vom Pietismus zum Kommunismus* (Berlin: Lettner-Verlag, 1953), 38-46, has given some astonishing examples of Krummacher's sermonic oratory, which on occasion could present a highly emotional blend of pietism, Prussian patriotism and flattery of royalty. One cannot but wonder how Krummacher would have fared at Mercersburg! One might also mention that Krummacher played a significant role in Friedrich Engels's fateful development "from pietism to communism, " for, as Kupisch shows, Engels's "whole critique of the inherited piety was ignited by his person" (38, see also 32-33). Engels grew up in the Barmen-Elberfeld area, the Wuppertal. He arrived in Berlin a few months after Schaff had left on his Italian journey, and in Berlin came completely under the sway of the Hegelian Left.
3. Cf. Wilhelm Löhe, "Zuruf aus der Heimat an die deutsch-lutherische Kirche Nordamerikas," (1845), reprinted in Martin Schmidt, *Wort Gottes und Fremdlingschaft. Die Kirche vor dem Auswanderungsproblem des 19. Jahrhunderts* (Erlangen and Rothenburg o. Tauber: Martin Luther-Verlag, 1953), 158-159.
4. Schaff's ordination sermon was published in *Palmblätter*, ed. Friedrich Wilhelm Krummacher, 1 (1844):44-69, quotation on p. 46. Cf. the original ms. "Ordinationspredigt" (Schaff Papers, ERHS, Lancaster). An English translation appeared in *The Weekly Messenger* 9 (September 4, 1844):1869-1870.
5. Schaff, *Principle*, 54; cf. Schaff, *Princip*, 9.
6. Max Lenz, *Geschichte der königlichen Friedrich-Wilhelms-Universität zu Berlin*, 4 vols. (Halle: Verlag der Buchhandlung des Waisenhauses, 1910-18) 2, sec. 2:72-73.
7. Ibid., 113.
8. Schaff, *Principle*, 54; cf. Schaff, *Princip*, 10.

173

9. *Schriften betreffend die deutsche Professur in Mercersburg*, 12.
10. Quoted in translation in *Weekly Messenger* (February 7, 1844), 1751.
11. Schmidt, *Wort Gottes und Fremdlingschaft*, 35.
12. For Kornthal's close ties to the Basle Mission, cf. *Pietismus und Neuzeit* 7 (1981):187. In the years 1828-1915 the Basel Mission sent out 1,100 foreign missionaries, of whom 503 came from Württemberg, many of those from Kornthal, the representative center of Württemberg pietism.
13. Quoted by Schmidt, *Wort Gottes und Fremdlingschaft*, 67.
14. *DKF*, "Schlusswort an unsere Leser," 1 (1848):383.
15. *Palmblätter* 1 (1844):47 and 49, respectively.
16. Ibid., 55.
17. Ibid., 67.
18. Schaff, Tagebuch 1844, March 14 and 15, Schaff Papers, UTS, NY.
19. Tagebuch 1845, Easter, Schaff Papers, ERHS, Lancaster.
20. Cf. Adolph Haurath, *Richard Rothe und seine Freunde* (Berlin: G. Grothe, 1902) 1: 191.
21. *Life of Schaff*, dedication.
22. Cf.Schaff, *In Memoriam. Our Children in Heaven* (privately printed, 1876).
23. *Evangelische Kirchenzeitung* 28 (March 3, 1841): col. 142.
24. Friedrich Wynecke, *Die Not der deutschen Lutheraner in Nordamerika* (Erlangen: Theodor Bläsig, 1843); first published in *Zeitschrift für Protestantismus und Kirche* (February 1843).
25. Robert Baird, *Religion in America* (1843, rev. ed. 1856). - *Kirchengeschichte, kirchliche Statistik und religiöses Leben der Vereinigten Staaten von Nordamerika*, vol.1, trans. and ed. Karl Brandes (Berlin: G. Reimer, 1844).
26. Schaff, *History of the Apostolic Church, with a General Introduction to Church History*, trans. Edward D. Yeomans (New York: Charles Scribner, 1853), 124.
27. Schaff, "Impressions of England," *Mercersburg Review* 9 (April 1858):329.
28. Schaff, *America. A Sketch of Its Political, Social, and Religious Character* (1855), ed. Perry Miller(Cambridge, Mass.: Harvard University Press, 1961), 104 n.
29. *Life of Schaff*, 76 (translated from Schaff's diary, December 31, 1843).
30. Ibid.., 87.
31. Ibid., 84.
32. *Evangelische Kirchenzeitung* 28 (May 5, 1841): col. 286.
33. Ludwig von Gerlach, *Aufzeichnungen aus seinem Leben und Wirken* 1:368.
34. *Life of Schaff*, 88- 90.
35. Schaff, *Principle*, 158; cf. Schaff, *Princip* 102.
36. *Life of Schaff*, 90.
37. The original German ms., Schaff Papers, UTS, NY.

Conclusion

1. Johann Peter Eckermann, *Gespräche mit Goethe*, ed. Ludwig Geiger (Leipzig: Max Hesse's Verlag, 1902), 239.
2. Quoted by Adolf Hausrath, *Richard Rothe und seine Freunde* (vol. 1 (Berlin: G. Grote, 1902), 168.
3. *Palmblätter* (ed. Friedrich Wilhelm Krummacher) 4 (1847):84.
4. See my article, "Philip Schaff: Sechs Briefe an Carl Ullmann (1843-1849)," *Zeitschrift für Neuere Theologiegeschichte/Journal for the History of Modern Theology* 5 (1998):89. – The journal *Palmblätter* (1844-49), growing out of the Rhineland Awakening, was especially interested in the German-language churches of North America and published several contributions by and about Schaff.

5. Schaff, *Princip*, 10; cf. Schaff, *Principle*, 54.
6. Letter of Arthur Schopenhauer to. F. A. Brockhaus (March 28, 1818), in *Arthur Schopenhauers Briefwechsel und andere Dokumente*, ed. Max Brahn (Leipzig: Insel-Verlag, 1911), 61.
7. Schaff, *America*, ed. Perry Miller (Cambridge, Mass.: Harvard University Press, 1961), xxx.
8. A valuable beginning is made by Stephen R. Graham, *Cosmos in the Chaos: Philip Schaff's Interpretation of Nineteenth-Century American Religion* (Grand Rapids, Mich.: William B. Eerdmans, 1995). See also my introduction to Chapter 4 "Religion in America" in my edition of *Philip Schaff. Historian and Ambassador of the Universal Church. Selected Writings* (Macon, GA: Mercer University Press, 1991), 151-58.

Epilogue: Schaff's American Career—An Appraisal

[biographical sources are again cited in full]

1. Schaff, *Das Princip des Protestantismus* (Chambersburg, Pa.: Druckerei der Hochdeutsch-Reformierten Kirche, 1845), 10; cf. *The Principle of Protestantism*, trans. John W. Nevin (1845), Lancaster Series on the Mercersburg Theology, vol. 1 (Philadelphia: United Church Press, 1964), 54.
2. Friedrich Meinecke, *Die Entstehung des Historismus*, vol. 3 of *Werke*, ed. C. Hinrichs (Munich: R. Oldenbourg Verlag, 1965), 2; Ernst Troeltsch, "Der deutsche Idealismus," in *Gesammelte Schriften*, vol. 4 (Tübingen: Mohr, 1925), 535.
3. Schaff, *America*, ed. Perry Miller (Cambridge, Mass.: Harvard University Press, 1961), xx.
4. We owe a masterful interpretation of the Mercersburg Theology to James H. Nichols's *Romanticism in American Theology: Nevin and Schaff at Mercersburg* (Chicago: University of Chicago Press, 1961), and, as editor, *The Mercersburg Theology* (New York: Oxford University Press, 1966). For a discussion of significant aspects of Schaff's Mercersburg program, see my article "The Reformation Goes West: The Notion of Historical Development in the Thought of Philip Schaff," *Journal of Religion* 62 (July 1982):219-241, and John B. Payne, "Schaff and Nevin, Colleagues at Mercersburg: The Church Question," *Church History* 61 (June 1992):169-190.
5. Miller (ed.), *America* , xxxv.
6. See Owen Chadwick, *From Bossuet to Newman: The Idea of Doctrinal Development* (Cambridge: Cambridge University Press, 1957), x.
7. John Henry Newman, *An Essay on the Development of Christian Doctrine*, 6th ed. (London and New York: Longman, Green, 1890), 8. For a fuller discussion of Schaff's position as a church historian, see David W. Lotz, "Philip Schaff and the Idea of Church History," in *A Century of Church History: The Legacy of Philip Schaff*, ed. Henry W. Bowden (Carbondale and Edwardsville, Ill.: Southern Illinois University Press, 1988), 1-35, and my own essay, "Church History in Context: The Case of Philip Schaff," in *Our Common History as Christians*, eds. John Deschner/Leroy Howe/Klaus Penzel (New York: Oxford University Press), 217-260.
8. Schaff, "Reisebilder für den Kirchenfreund: Trient," *Der deutsche Kirchenfreund* 8 (1855):327.
9. See Hans Joachim Schoeps, *Das andere Preussen*, 2d. (Honef/Rhein: Peters Verlag), 72.
10. Schaff, *What is Church History?*, trans. John W. Nevin (Philadelphia: J. B. Lippincott, 1846), 118.
11. Nichols, *Romanticism in American Theology*, 310.
12. Schaff, *Das Princip des Protestantismus*, 101; cf. *The Principle of Protestantism*, 155.

13. Schaff, "The Reunion of Christendom," *Evangelical Alliance Document* 33 (1893):8.
14. See Winthrop S. Hudson, *American Protestantism* (Chicago: University of Chicago Press, 1961), 37, and Sidney E. Mead, "Prospects for the Church in America," in *The Future of the American Church*, ed. Philip J. Hefner (Philadelphia: Fortress Press, 1968), 17. – It is characteristic of Schaff's eclecticism that he never reflected systematically on these ecumenical options, nor was he apparently aware of a shift in his ecumenical thought. A comparison with his contemporary Richard Rothe, who offered the most carefully reasoned combination of these ecumenical positions (*Theologische Ethik*, 3 vols. [Wittenberg: Zimmermann, 1845-48], pars. 998, 1186) is therefore instructive. Rothe held the idealistic dialectics to be applicable only to the Roman Catholic-Protestant relationship, while he employed Schleiermacher's romantic principle of individuality as a means only for comprehending the denominational diversity of Protestantism. However, for the modern period, Rothe believed, Christians of all churches should more and more embrace a third ecumenical alternative, that of an *ethical union* only of all those individuals who are working for the final, world-encompassing triumph of the kingdom of God. This was an ecumenical orientation that such liberal theologians as Albrecht Ritschl (1822-89) and Adolf Harnack (1851-1930)—and in the end also Schaff himself—would find congenial.
15. David S. Schaff, *Life of Schaff in Part Autobiographical* (New York: Charles Scribner's Sons, 1897), 323.
16. Schaff, *Christ and Christianity* (New York: Charles Scribner's Sons, 1885), 308.
17. "Tedious" is how Karl Barth characterized the theological productions of one typical mediating theologian, Alexander Schweizer (1808-88), in *Protestant Theology in the Nineteenth Century. Its Background and History*, several translators (Valley Forge: Judson Press, 1973), 575.
18. Schaff, *Theological Propaedeutic*, (New York: Charles Scribner's Sons, 1894), 228.
19. Letter of Mann to Schaff, 3 October 1882, quoted by A. Späth, *D. Wilhelm Julius Mann* (Reading Pa.: Pilger Buchhandlung, 1895), 73.
20. More detailed evaluations can be found in my introductions in *Philip Schaff. Historian and Ambassador of the Universal Church: Selected Writings*, ed. Klaus Penzel (Macon, Ga.: Mercer University Press, 1991).
21. Typical of Schaff's (and the whole Commentary's) precritical, supernaturalistic point of view, which, moreover, perceived no literary problem with the biblical texts since they are all to be taken at face value as faithfully and accurately representing what actually happened, was his discussion of the resurrection of Lazarus (John 11). He rejected all theories that deny the miracle, for they all "owe their origin to a disbelief in the supernatural." Then, confronting the remaining alternative of "historic truth or dishonest fiction," he averred that the "historic truth is abundantly attested by the simplicity, vivacity and circumstantiality of the narrative, the four days in the tomb (vers. 39), and the good sense and moral honesty—to say the very least—of Lazarus and his sisters, the Evangelist, and Christ Himself" (*Lange's Commentary on the Holy Scriptures*, ed. Philip Schaff, 25 vols. [New York: Charles Scribner, 1864-1880], vol. 3 of the New Testament [*John*], 339). This is what Herbert Hovenkamp recently called the "essentially positivistic stance" that evangelical biblical scholars in the United States at that time maintained. For them, "nothing existed between historical and non-historical—no myths, symbols, epics, or poetic expressions." "American orthodoxy," he concluded in words that apply to Schaff's exegesis and Lange's Commentary as well, "was a long way from seeing the need to be rescued from its facts" (*Science and Religion in America, 1800-1860* [Philadelphia: University of Pennsylvania Press, 1978], 73 and 78.
22. Schaff, "Autobiographical Reminiscences," 15, Schaff Papers, ERHS, Lancaster.
23. See George Marsden's informative essay "The Collapse of Evangelical Academia," in *Faith and Rationality: Reason and Belief in God*, eds. Alvin Plantinga and Nicholas Woltersdorff (Notre Dame: University of Notre Dame Press, 1983), 219-264.
24. See n. 7 above.
25. Friedrich Schleiermacher, *Brief Outline on the Study of Theology*, trans. Terrence N. Tice (Richmond, Va.: John Knox Press, 1966), 21 (par.9).

176

BIBLIOGRAPHY

Literature until the 1850s

Baird, Robert. *Kirchengeschichte, kirchliche Statistik und religiöses Leben der Vereinigten Staaten von Nordamerika*, vol.1. Translated and edited by Karl Brandes. Berlin: G. Reimer, 1844. Originally published in Scotland as *Religion in America* (1843).

Ferdinand Christian Baur: On the Writing of Church History (*Die Epochen der kirchlichen Geschichtsschreibung*, 1852). Translated and edited by Peter C. Hodgson. New York: Oxford University Press, 1968.
_____. *Der Gegensatz des Katholizismus und Protestantismus nach den Prinzipien und Hauptdogmen der beiden Lehrbegriffe*. Tübingen: L. F. Fues, 1834; 2d ed. 1836.
_____. *Kirchengeschichte des neunzehnten Jahrhunderts*. Edited by Eduard Zeller. Tübingen: L. F. Fues, 1862.

Erdmann, Johann Eduard. *Vorlesungen über Glauben und Wissen als Einleitung in die Dogmatik und Religionsphilosophie*. Berlin: Dunker & Humblot, 1837.

Gerlach, Ernst Ludwig von. *Aufzeichnungen aus seinem Leben und Wirken*. 2 vols. Edited by Jakob von Gerlach. Schwerin: Verlag Fr. Bahn, 1903.

Hegel, Georg Friedrich Wilhelm. *Sämmtliche Werke: Jubiläumsausgabe,* 20 vols., 3d ed. Edited by Hermann Glockner. Stuttgart: F. Frommann [G. Holzboog], 1951.
_____. *Lectures on the Philosophy of History*. Translated from the 3d German ed. by John Sibree. New York: Dover Publications, 1956.
_____. *Lectures on the Philosophy of Religion*. 3 vols. Several translators. Edited by Peter C. Hodgson. Berkeley and Los Angeles: University of California Press, 1984-87.
_____. *G. W. F. Hegel: Theologian of the Spirit*. Edited by Peter C. Hodgson. Minneapolis: Fortress Press, 1997.

Heusser-Schweizer, Meta. *Hauschronik*. Edited by Karl Fehr. Kilchberg: Verlag Mirio Romano, 1980.

Kant, Immanuel. *Religion within the Limits of Reason Alone* (1793). Translated by Theodore M. Greene and Hoyt H. Hudson. New York: Harper Torchbooks, 1960.

Kapff, Sixtus Carl. *Admonitions of a Friend of Youth, against the most dangerous enemy of youth; or instructions in regard to secret sins; their consequences, cure, and prevention. Commended to the affectionate consideration of the young and their teachers* (translated from the 6th German ed.). Philadelphia: Schäfer and Koradi, 1858.
_____. *Die Wiederkunft des Herrn. Belehrungen aus Matthäi 24. und 25. verglichen mit den Zeichen der Zeit.* Stuttgart: J. B. Müller, 1836.
_____. *Die Württembergischen Brüdergemeinden Kornthal und Wilhelmsdorf, ihre Geschichte, Einrichtungen und Erziehungsanstalten.* Kornthal: C. G. Liesching, 1839.

Kliefoth, Theodor. *Einleitung in die Dogmengeschichte.* Parchim and Ludwigslust: D. C. Hinsorff, 1839.
_____. "Die neuere Kirchengeschichtsschreibung in der deutsch-evangelischen Kirche." *Allgemeines Repertorium* (ed. H. Reuter) 48 (1845): 105-118; 49 (1846): 18-29, 106-113, 207-215; 50 (1847): 18-24.

Knüpfel, Karl. *Geschichte und Beschreibung der Universität Tübingen.* Tübingen: L. F. Fues, 1849.

Löhe, Wilhelm. *Three Books about the Church* (1845). Translated and edited by James Schaaf. Philadelphia: Fortress Press, 1969.

Möhler, Johann Adam. *Die Einheit in der Kirche oder das Prinzip des Katholizismus* (1825). Edited, with Introduction, by Josef Rupert Geiselmann. Köln and Olten: Jacob Hegner, 1956.
_____. *Symbolik oder Darstellung der dogmatischen Gegensätze der Katholiken und Protestanten nach ihren öffentlichen Bekenntnisschriften* (1832; 5th ed. 1835). Edited, with Introduction, by Josef Rupert Geiselmann. Vol. 1. Köln and Olten: Jacob Hegner, 1958. Vol. 2. Darmstadt: Wissenschaftliche Buchgesellschaft, 1960.

Müller, Julius. *Die evangelische Union, ihr Wesen und ihr göttliches Recht.* Berlin: Wiegandt and Grieben, 1854.
_____. *Die christliche Lehre von der Sünde.* 2 vols. Breslau: Josef Max, 1839-44.

Neander, August. *Allgemeine Geschichte der christlichen Religion und Kirche,* 10 sections. Hamburg: F. Perthes, 1825-45. Translated by J. Torry. *General History of the Christian Religion and Church.* 8 vols. Edinburgh: T. & T. Clark, 1847-52.

Nevin, John Williamson. *The Mystical Presence. A Vindication of the Reformed or Calvinistic Doctrine of the Holy Eucharist.* Philadelphia: Lippincott, 1846.

Novalis [Friedrich von Hardenberg]. *Die Christenheit oder Europa. Ein Fragment* (1799). Edited by O. Heuschele. Stuttgart: P. Reclam, 1961.

Rothe, Richard. *Die Anfänge der christlichen Kirche und ihrer Verfassung.* Wittenberg: Zimmermann, 1837.

Schaff, Philip. "Ein Wort über die Theologische Kritik." *Literarische Zeitung* (Berlin), May 20 and August 2, 1843.
_____. "Über den Unterschied zwischen Katholizismus und Romanismus." *Literarische Zeitung* (Berlin), October 31 and December 16, 1843.
_____. *Die Sünde wider den heiligen Geist und die daraus gezogenen dogmatischen und ethischen Folgerungen. Eine exegetisch-dogmatische Abhandlung, nebst einem historischen Anhange über das Lebensende des Francesco Spiera.* Halle: J. F. Lippert, 1841.
_____. *Das Verhältnis des Jakobus, Bruder des Herrn, zu Jakobus Alphäi, auf's Neue exegetisch und historisch untersucht.* Berlin: A. Wohlgemut, 1843.
_____. *Das Princip des Protestantismus.* Chambersburg: Druckerei der Hochdeutsch-Reformirten Kirche, 1845. Translated by John W. Nevin. *The Principle of Protestantism* (1845). Reprint in *Lancaster Series on the Mercersburg Theology.* Edited by Bard Thompson and George H. Bricker, vol. 1. Philadelphia: United Church Press, 1964.
_____. *What is Church History? A Vindication of the Idea of Historical Developmen.* Translated from the German. Philadelphia: J. B. Lippincott and Co., 1846. Reprint in *Reformed and Catholic: Selected Historical and Theological Writings of Philip Schaff.* Edited by Charles Yrigoyen , Jr. and George M. Bricker. Pittsburgh, Pa.: Pickwick Press, 1979.
_____. *History of the Apostolic Church, with a General Introduction to Church History.* Translated by Edward D. Yeomans. New York: Charles Scribner, 1853
_____, ed. *Der deutsche Kirchenfreund.* 6 vols., 1848-53.
_____. *Amerika. Die politischen, socialen und kirchlich-religiösen Zustände der Vereinigten Staaten von Nord-Amerika mit besonderer Rücksicht auf die Deutschen, aus eigener Anschauung dargestellt,* Berlin: Wiegandt and Grieben, 1854; 2d enlarged ed., 1858 Translated from the German, *America: A Sketch of the Political, Social, and Religious Character of the United States of North America.* New York: C. Scribner, 1855. New edition by Perry Miller. Cambridge: The Belknap Press of Harvard University Press, 1961.
_____. *Germany: Its Universities, Theology, and Religion. With sketches of Neander, Tholuck, Olshausen, Hengstenberg, Twesten, Müller, Ullmann,*

Rothe, Dorner, Lange, Ebrard, Wichern, and other distinguished German divines of the age. Philadelphia: Lindsay &Blakiston, 1857.
_____. "Autobiographical Reminiscences." Unpaginated manuscript, 1871-90. Paginated copy by Carl M. Adler, 1882. Schaff Papers. Archives of the Evangelical and Reformed Historical Society, Lancaster, Pa..
_____, ed. *Berlin 1842 – New York 1892: The Semi-Centennial of Philip Schaff.* New York: privately printed, 1893.

Schaff Papers. Archives of the Evangelical and Reformed Historical Society, Lancaster, Pa..
_____. Burke Library, Union Theological Seminary, New York City.

Schelling, Friedrich Wilhelm Joseph. *Philosophie der Mythologie und Offenbarung,* section 2, vols.1-4. *Sämmtliche Werke.* 14 vols. Edited by Karl Friedrich August von Schelling. Stuttgart and Augsburg: J. G. Cotta, 1856-61.
_____. *Philosophie der Offenbarung (1841/42).* The Paulus edition, edited by Manfred Frank. Frankfurt: Suhrkampf Verlag, 1977.
_____. *Vorlesungen über die Methode des akademischen Studiums* (1803). Edited by Hermann Glockner. Stuttgart: Alfred Kröner Verlag, 1954. Translated by E. S. Morgan, *On University Studies,* and edited by Norbert Guterman. Athens, Ohio: Ohio University Press, 1966.

Schleiermacher, Friedrich. *Der christliche Glaube nach den Grundsätzen der evangelischen Kirche im Zusammenhang dargestellt* , 7th ed. based on the 2d ed. (1830-31). 2 vols. Edited by Martin Redecker. Berlin: Walter de Gruyter, 1960. English translation of the 2d German ed., *The Christian Faith.* Edited by H. R. Mackintosh and J. S. Stewart. Edinburgh: T. and T. Clark, 1928.
_____. *Brief Outline on the Study of Theology.* Translated by Terrence N. Tice. Richmond, Va.: John Knox Press, 1966.
_____. *On the Glaubenslehre: Two Letters to Dr. Lücke* (German 1829). Translated by James Duke and Francis Fiorenza. American Academy of Religion Texts and Translations Series, no. 3. Chico, Calif.: Scholars Press, 1981.
_____. *On Religion: Speeches to its Cultured Despisers.* Translated (from the 3d German ed.) by John Oman. 1894. Reprint, Louisville, Ky.: Westminster/John Knox Press, 1994.

Schmid, Carl Friedrich. *Biblical Theology of the New Testament.* Translated (from the 4th German ed.) by G. H. Venable. Edinburgh: T. & T. Clark, 1870.

Schriften betreffend die deutsche Professur in Mercersburg, Pennsylvanien. Chambersburg, Pa.: Druckerei der Reformirten Kirche, 1843.

Schwarz, Carl., *Zur Geschichte der neuesten Theologie*, 3d ed. Leipzig: F. A. Brockhaus, 1864.

Stahl, Friedrich Julius. *Die Kirchenverfassung nach Lehre und Recht der Protestanten.* Erlangen: Theodor Bläsig, 1840.
_____. *Die lutherische Kirche und die Union.* Berlin: Hertz, 1859.

Stirm, Carl Heinrich. *Apologie des Christentums in Briefen für gebildete Leser.* Stuttgart: C. Belser,1836.

Strauss, David Friedrich. *Das Leben Jesu kritisch bearbeitet.* 2 vols. Tübingen: C. F. Osiander, 1835-36. *The Life of Jesus Critically Examined.* English translation by George Eliot (Marian Evans) from the 4ᵗʰ German ed., 1840. 3 vols. London: Chapman, Brothers, 1846. New edition by Peter C. Hodgson. Lives of Jesus Series. Philadelphia: Fortress Press, 1972.
_____. *Streitschriften zur Verteidigung meiner Schriften über das Leben Jesu und zur Charakteristik der gegenwärtigen Theologie.* Tübingen: C. F. Osiander, 1837.

Tholuck, *Die Lehre von der Sünde und vom Versöhner oder die wahre Weihe des Zweiflers* (1823), 9ᵗʰ ed. Gotha: F. A. Perthes, 1871.
_____. *Gespräche über die vornehmsten Glaubensfragen der Zeit nach-denkende Laien.* Halle: R. Mühlmann, 1843.

Ullmann, Carl. *Das Wesen des Christentums.* Hamburg: F. Perthes, 1845; 5ᵗʰ ed. 1865.

Wynecke, Friedrich. *Die Not der deutschen Lutheraner in Nordamerika.* Erlangen: Theodor Bläsig, 1843.

Secondary Literature

Bachmann, Johannes. *Ernst Wilhelm Hengstenberg: Sein Leben und Wirken.* 2 vols. Gütersloh: C. Bertelsmann, 1876-80; vol. 3, edited by Theodor Schmalenbach, 1892.

Barczay, Gyula. *Ecclesia semper reformanda: Eine Untersuchung zum Kirchenbegriff des 19. Jahrhunderts.* Zürich: EVZ-Verlag, 1961.

Barth, Karl. *Protestant Theology in the Nineteenth Century: Its Background and History.* Several translators. Valley Forge: Judson Press, 1973.

Beckmann, Klaus-Martin. *Unitas Ecclesiae: Eine systematische Studie zur Theologiegeschichte des 19. Jahrhunderts.* Gütersloh: Gerd Mohn, 1967.

Beyreuther, Erich. *Die Erweckungsbewegung,* 2d ed. Vol.4, R1 of *Die Kirche in ihrer Geschichte.* Göttingen: Vandenhoeck & Ruprecht, 1977.

Bigler, Robert M. *The Politics of German Protestantism: The Rise of the Protestant Church Elite in Prussia, 1815-1848.* Berkeley: University of California Press, 1972.

Birkner, Joachim, Heinz Liebing, and Klaus Scholder. *Das konfessionelle Problem in der evangelischen Theologie des 19. Jahrhunderts.* Tübingen: J. C. B. Mohr, 1966.

Bowden, Henry W., ed. *A Century of Church History: The Legacy of Philip Schaff.* Carbondale and Edwardsville, Ill.: Southern Illinois University Press, 1988.

Brodd, Sven-Erik. *Evangelisk Katolicitet. Ett studium av innehåll och function under 1800- och 1900-talen.* Lund: LiberFörlag, 1982.

Brown, Colin. *Jesus in European Protestant Thought, 1778-1860.* Grand Rapids, Mich.: Baker Book House, 1985.

Bussmann, Walter. *Zwischen Preussen und Deutschland. Friedrich Wilhelm IV.* Berlin: Siedler Verlag, 1990.

Cochlovius, Joachim. *Bekenntnis und Einheit der Kirche im deutschen Protestantismus 1840-1850.* Gütersloh: Verlagshaus Mohn, 1980.

Conser, Walter H., Jr. *Church and Confession. Conservative Theologians in Germany, England, and America, 1815-1866.* Macon, Ga.: Mercer University Press, 1984.

Elert, Werner. *Der Kampf um das Christentum. Geschichte der Beziehungen zwischen dem evangelischen Christentum in Deutschland und dem allgemeinen Denken seit Schleiermacher und Hegel.* Munich: C. H. Beck, 1921.

Fagerberg, Holsten. *Bekenntnis, Kirche und Amt in der deutschen konfessionellen Theologie des 19. Jahrhunderts.* Uppsala: A.-B. Lundequistska Bokhandeln ; Wiesbaden: Otto Harrassowitz, 1952.

Frör, Kurt. *Evangelisches Denken und Katholizismus seit Schleiermacher.* Munich: Kaiser Verlag, 1932.

Gabriel, Hans Jürgen. "Im Namen des Evangeliums gegen den Fortschritt. Zur Rolle der 'Evangelischen Kirchenzeitung' unter E. W. Hengstenberg von 1830 bis 1849," 154-76. In *Beiträge zur Berliner Kirchengeschichte,* edited by Günter Wirth. Berlin: Union Verlag, 1987.

Gäbler, Ulrich. "Philip Schaff in Chur, 1819-1834." *Zwingliana* 18 (1989): 143-65. English translation (shortened) in *Probing the Reformed Tradition: Historical Studies in Honor of Edward A. Downey.* Edited by Elsie Anne Mckee and Brian G. Armstrong. Louisville, Ky.: Westminster/John Knox Press, 1989, 408-23.
_____, ed. *Der Pietismus im neunzehnten und zwanzigsten Jahrhundert.* Vol. 3 of *Geschichte des Pietismus.* Göttingen: Vandenhoeck and Ruprecht, 2000.

Gascoigne, Robert. *Religion, Rationality, and Community. Sacred and Secular in the Thought of Hegel and His Critics.* The Hague and Boston: M. Nijhoff, 1985.

Gay, Peter. *Freud for Historians.* New York: Oxford University Press paperback, 1986.

Geiger, Wolfgang. *Spekulation und Kritik: Die Geschichtstheologie Ferdinand Christian Baurs.* Munich: Chr. Kaiser Verlag, 1964.

Geiselmann, Josef Rupert. *Die katholische Tübinger Schule.* Freiburg: Herder, 1964.

Gerrish, Brian. *A Prince of the Church: Schleiermacher and the Beginnings of Modern Theology.* Philadelphia: Fortress Press, 1984.

Goeters, J. F. and Rudolf Mau, eds. *Die Anfänge der Union unter landesherrlichem Kirchenregiment (1817-1850).* Vol. 1 of *Die Geschichte der Evangelischen Union.* Leipzig: Evangelische Verlagsanstalt, 1992.

Graham, Stephen R.. *Cosmos in the Chaos: Philip Schaff's Interpretation of Nineteenth-Century American Religion.* Grand Rapids, Mich.: William B. Eerdmans, 1995.

Guggisberg, Hans R. "Ein transatlantischer 'Brückenbauer.' Der Kirchenhistoriker Philip Schaff (1819-1893), sein Amerikabild und seine

Beziehungen zu Basel." *Basler Zeitschrift für Geschichte und Altertumskunde* 91 (1991): 251-70.

Hahn, Erich J. C. "The Junior Faculty in 'Revolt:' Reform Plans for Berlin University in 1848." *The American Historical Review* 88, 4 (October 1977): 875-95.

Hausrath, Adolph. *Richard Rothe und seine Freunde*. 2 vols. Berlin: G. Grothe, 1902-06.

_____. *David Friedrich Strauss und die Theologie seiner Zeit*. 2 vols. Heidelberg: F. Bassermann, 1876-78.

Hermelink, Heinrich. *Geschichte der evangelischen Kirche in Württemberg von der Reformation bis zur Gegenwart*. Stuttgart and Tübingen: Rainer Wunderlich Verlag H. Leins, 1949.

Hirsch, Emmanuel. *Geschichte der neuern evangelischen Theologie*. 5 vols. , 2d ed. Gütersloh: C. Bertelsmann, 1960.

Hodgson, Peter C. *The Formation of Historical Theology: A Study of Ferdinand Christian Baur*. New York: Harper & Row, 1966.

Holte, Ragnar. *Die Vermittlungstheologie: Ihre theologischen Grundbegriffe kritisch untersucht*. Uppsala: Almquist & Wiksells, 1965.

Iggers, Georg G. *The German Conception of History: The National Tradition of Historical Thought from Herder to the Present*. Middletown, CT.: Wesleyan University Press, 1968.

Jedele, Eugen. *Die kirchenpolitischen Anschauungen des Ernst Ludwig von Gerlach*. Ansbach: C. Brügel & Sohn, 1910.

Kähler, Martin. *Geschichte der protestantischen Dogmatik im 19. Jahrhundert*. Edited by Ernst Kähler. Munich: C. Kaiser Verlag, 1962.

Kapff, Carl. *Lebensbild von Sixt Carl v. Kapff*. Stuttgart: Chr. Belser'sche Verlagshandlung, 1881.

Kasper, Walter. *Das Absolute in der Geschichte: Philosophie und Theologie der Geschichte in der Spätphilosophie Schellings*. Mainz: Matthias-Grünewald-Verlag, 1965.

Kaufmann, Walter. *Hegel: Reinterpretation, Texts, and Commentary*. Garden City, NY: Doubleday & Co., 1965.

Klein, J. M. J. *The History of the Eastern Synod of the Reformed Church in the United States*. Lancaster, Pa.: Eastern Synod of the Reformed Church in the United States, 1943.

Kloeden, Gesine von. *Evangelische Katholizität: Philip Schaffs Beitrag zur Oekumene—eine reformirte Perspektive*. Münster: LIT Verlag, 1998.

Korff, Hermann August. *Geist der Goethezeit*. 4 vols. Leipzig: Koehler & Amelag, 1966 edition.

Kraus, Hans-Christof. *Ernst Ludwig von Gerlach: Politisches Denken und Handeln eines Preussischen Altkonservativen*. 2 vols. Göttingen: Vandenhoeck & Ruprecht, 1994.

Kupisch, Karl. *Vom Pietismus zum Kommunismus*. Berlin: Lettner-Verlag, 1953.
_____. "Schelling in Berlin." *Zeitschrift für Kirchengeschichte* 76, 3 and 4 (1965): 258-81.
_____. *Zwischen Idealismus und Massendemokratie*. Berlin: Lettner-Verlag, 1955.

Lehmann, Hartmut. *Pietismus und weltliche Ordnung in Württemberg vom 17. bis 20. Jahrhundert*. Stuttgart: Kohlhammer, 1969.

Lenz, Max. *Geschichte der königlichen Friedrich-Wilhelms-Universität zu Berlin*. 4 vols. Halle: Verlag der Buchhandlung des Waisenhauses, 1910-18.

Löwith, Karl. *Die Hegelsche Linke*. Stuttgart-Bad Canstatt: F. Frommann (G. Holzboog), 1962.
_____. *From Hegel to Nietzsche*. Translated by David E. Green. New York: Holt, Rinehart and Winston, 1964.

Lütgert, Wilhelm. *Die Religion des deutschen Idealismus und ihr Ende*. 4 vols. Gütersloh: C. Bertelsmann, 1922-30.

Maser, Peter. *Hans Ernst von Kottwitz: Studien zur Erweckunsbewegung des frühen 19. Jahrhunderts in Schlesien und Berlin*. Göttingen: Vandenhoeck & Ruprecht, 1990.

Maurer, Wilhelm. "Der Organismusgedanke bei Schelling und in der Theologie der Katholischen Tübinger Schule." *Kirche und Dogma* 8 (July 1962): 202-16.
_____. "Das Prinzip des Organischen in der evangelischen Kirchengeschichtsschreibung des 19. Jahrhunderts." *Kirche und Dogma* 8 (October 1962): 265-92.

185

Meinecke, Friedrich. *Die Entstehung des Historismus*. Vol. 3 of *Werke*, edited by Carl Hinrichs. Munich: R. Oldenbourg Verlag, 1965.

Müller, Karl. *Die religiöse Erweckung in Württemberg am Anfang des 19. Jahrhunderts*. Tübingen: J. C. Mohr, 1925.

Nichols, James Hastings. *Romanticism in American Theology: Nevin and Schaff at Mercersburg*. Chicago: University of Chicago Press, 1961.
_____, ed. *The Mercersburg Theology*. New York: Oxford University Press, 1966.

Payne, John B. " Schaff and Nevin, Colleagues at Mercersburg: The Church Question." *Church History* 61 (1992): 169-90.

Penzel, Klaus. "An Ecumenical Vision of Church History: F. W. J. Schelling." *Perkins School of Theology Journal* 17 (winter-spring 1964): 3-19.
_____. "Will the Real Ferdinand Christian Baur Please Stand Up?" *Journal of Religion* 48 (July 1968):310-23.
_____. "Church History in Context: The Case of Philip Schaff," 217-60. In *Our Common History as Christians*, edited by John Deschner, Leroy Howe, and Klaus Penzel. New York: Oxford University Press, 1974.
_____. "The Reformation Goes West: The Notion of Historical Development in the Thought of Philip Schaff." *Journal of Religion* 62 (July 1982): 219-41.
_____. "Philip Schaff – A Centennial Appraisal." *Church History* 59 (June 1990): 207-21.
_____, ed. *Philip Schaff: Historian and Ambassador of the Universal Church. Selected Writings*. Macon, Ga.: Mercer University Press, 1991.
_____. "Philip Schaff's Lifelong Quest for 'Evangelical Catholicism.'" *The New Mercersburg Review* 24 (autumn 1993): 3-14.
_____. "The Private Life of Philip Schaff." Union Theological Seminary, New York: The Burke Library Occasional Publication, No. 3, 1995.
_____. "Philip Schaff: Sechs Briefe an Carl Ullmann." *Zeitschrift für Neuere Theologiegeschichte/Journal for the History of Modern Theology* 5 (1998): 81-113.
_____. Art. "Schaff, Philip." *Theologische Realenzyklopädie* 30 (1998):62-65.

Pfleiderer, Otto. *The Development of Theology in Germany since Kant and its Progress in Great Britain since 1825*. Translated by J. Frederick Smith. London: Swan Sonnenschein & Co.; New York: Macmillan & Co., 1890.

Pranger, Gary K. *Philip Schaff (1819-1893): Portrait of an Immigrant Theologian*. New York: Peter Lang, 1997.

Richards, George Warren. *History of the Theological Seminary of the Reformed Church in the United States, 1825-1934, Evangelical and Reformed Church, 1934-1952.* Lancaster, Pa.: Rudisill, 1952.

Roth, Walter. *Die Evangelische Brüdergemeinde Kornthal* . Neuhausen-Stuttgart: Häusler, 1994.

Schaff, David S. *The Life of Philip Schaff, in Part Autobiographical.* New York: Charles Scribner's Sons, 1897.

Schmidt, Martin. *Wort Gottes und Fremdlingsschaft: Die Kirche vor dem Auswanderungsproblem des 19. Jahrhunderts.* Erlangen and Rothenburg o. Tauber: Martin Luther-Verlag, 1953.

Schmidt-Clausen, Kurt. *Vorweggenommene Einheit: Die Gründung des Bistums Jerusalem im Jahre 1841.* Berlin and Hamburg: Lutherisches Verlagshaus, 1965.

Schnabel, Franz. *Die religiösen Kräfte.* Vol. 4 of *Deutsche Geschichte im neunzehnten Jahrhundert*, 4 vols. Freiburg: Verlag Herder, 1949-55.

Schoeps, Hans Joachim. *Das andere Preussen: Konservative Gestalten und Probleme im Zeitalter Friedrich Wilhelms IV*, 2d ed. Honnef/Rhein: Peters Verlag. 1957.

Seeberg, Reinhold. *Die Kirche Deutschlands im neunzehnten Jahrhundert.* Leipzig: A. Deichert, 1903.

Selge, Kurt Victor. "August Neander--ein getaufter Hamburger Jude der Emanzipations- und Restaurationszeit als erster Berliner Kirchenhistoriker (1813-1850)," 233-76. In *450 Jahre Evangelischer Theologie in Berlin*, edited by Gerhard Bessier and Christof Gestrich. Göttingen: Vandenhoeck & Ruprecht, 1989.

Shanahan, William O. *German Protestants Face the Social Question.* Notre Dame: University of Notre Dame Press, 1954.

Shriver, George H. *Philip Schaff: Christian Scholar and Ecumenical Prophet.* Macon, Ga.: Mercer University Press, 1987.
_____, ed. *American Religious Heretics: Formal and Informal Trials in American Protestantism.* Nashville: Abingdon, 1966.

Späth, Adolph. *D. Wilhelm Julius Mann.* Reading, Pa.: Pilger Buchhandlung, 1895.

Stephan, Horst. *Geschichte der deutschen evangelischen Theologie seit dem deutschen Idealismus*. 2d ed. revised by Martin Schmidt. Berlin: Alfred Töpelmann, 1960.

Strom, Jonathan. "Problems and Promises of Pietism Research." *Church History* 71, 3 (September 2002): 536-545.

Tillich, Paul. *The Construction of the History of Religion in Schelling's Positive Philosophy: Its Presuppositions and Principles*, translated by Victor Nuovo. Lewisburg, Pa.: Bucknell University Press, 1974.

Troeltsch, Ernst. *Aufsätze zur Geistesgeschichte und Religionssoziologie*. Vol.4 of *Gesammelte Schriften*. 4 vols. Tübingen: J. C. B. Mohr [Paul Siebeck], 1912-25.

Welch, Claude. *Protestant Thought in the Nineteenth Century*. 2 vols. New Haven and London: Yale University Press, 1972-85.
_____, ed. *God and Incarnation in Mid-Nineteenth Century German Theology*. New York: Oxford University Press, 1965.

Wellek, René. *Confrontations: Studies in the Intellectual and Literary Relations between Germany, England, and the United States during the Nineteenth Century*. Princeton, N.J.: Princeton University Press, 1965.

Wendland, Walter. *Studien zur Erweckungsbewegung in Berlin (1810-1830)*. Vol. 19 of *Jahrbuch für Brandenburgische Kirchengeschichte*. Berlin: n. p., 1924.

Witte, Leopold. *Friedrich August Gotttreu Tholuck*. 2 vols. Bielefeld and Leipzig: Velhagen & Klasing, 1884-86.

Index

Achilles, 28

Acton, Lord, 149

Age of Reason, 41, 43, 48, 49, 50. *See also* Enlightenment

America (PS), 145, 148

American Christianity, denominational diversity of: 97, 150, 152; free church tradition of, 151; German knowledge of, 135-36; millenianism, messianism, racism of, 150; post-civil war evangelical Protestantism, 152

American Committee of Bible Revision, 154

American Society of Church History, 1, 147, 157, 160n.4; PS founder and first president of, 1, 155

Americanization, 4; of PS, 123, 145, 47, 149-50, 152

Anti-Christ, 20, 111

apostolic doctrinal types, 65-66

Augsburg Confession, 27

Augustine, 108, 138

"Autobiographical Reminiscences" (PS), 5, 13, 26, 65, 124

Awakening, 33, 38-40, 42, 44, 48, 56, 58-59, 68, 70, 71-72, 74, 95, 96, 106, 110, 114-16, 148; dominant force in German Protestantism, 2-3, 21, 38, 49-50, 54, 80, 93; fraternity spirit of, 142; missionary and ecumenical impulses of, 130-31. *See also* Berlin, Lower Rhine, Württemberg Awakening

Baird, Robert, 135

Bakunin, Mikhail, 117

Barth, Karl, 84, 163n.20, 164n.46, 176n.17

Basel, 12, 13, 32, 117; Mission 131, 174n.12

Bauer, Bruno, 53

Baur, Ferdinand Christian, 33, 53, 62, 63-64, 68; and mediating theology, 83; and Möhler, 61-62; PS reaction to, criticism of, 64-65, 92, 144; taught PS concept of dialectical development, 67, 115. *See also* Tübingen School

Beethoven, Ludwig van, 37

Bengel, Johann Albrecht, 19-20, 29

Berg, Joseph, 140

Berlin, 2, 5, 40, 68, 89, 90, 93, 102, 105, 117, 118, 124, 128, 129, 141; University of, 3, 14, 48, 51, 72-75, 78-79, 85, 90, 103, 105, 113, 114

Berlin Awakening, 3, 38, 103-4. *See also Evangelische Kirchenzeitung*; Prussian High Orthodoxy

Bismarck, Otto von, 108, 112

Böhme, Jacob, 19

Briggs, Charles A., 156

Brown, Williams Adam, 156

Burckhardt, Jacob, 50, 72, 117

Calvin, John, 25, 42

Catholic Apostolic Church. *See* Irvingism

Chlebus, Wilhelm Rudolf, 129

Christ, as absolute truth: 98, Body of (church), 94, 101, 107, 110, 113, 132, 151-52; experience of, 59; head of church, 94, 107; incarnation of, 48, 94; as object of faith, 99; OT pointing to, 113; return of, 19, 29

194

TORONTO STUDIES IN THEOLOGY

31. Robert B. Sheard, **Interreligious Dialogue in the Catholic Church Since Vatican II: An Historical and Theological Study**

32. Paul Merkley, **The Greek and Hebrew Origins of Our Idea of History**

33. Ruth Coates (ed.), **The Emancipation of Russian Christianity**, with an Introduction by Natalia Pecherskaya and Ruth Coates

34. Joyce A. Little, **Toward a Thomist Methodology**

35. Dan Cohn-Sherbok, **Jewish Petitionary Prayer: A Theological Exploration**

36. C. Don Keyes, **Foundations For an Ethic of Dignity: A Study in the Degradation of the Good**

37. Paul Tillich, **The Encounter of Religions and Quasi-Religions: A Dialogue and Lectures,** Terence Thomas (ed.)

38. Arnold A. van Ruler, **Calvinist Trinitarianism and Theocentric Politics: Essays Toward a Public Theology,** John Bolt (trans.)

39. Julian Casserley, **Evil and Evolutionary Eschatology: Two Essays,** C. Don Keyes (ed.)

40. J. M. B. Crawford and J. F. Quinn , **The Christian Foundations of Criminal Responsibility: A Philosophical Study of Legal Reasoning**

41. William C. Marceau, **Optimism in the Works of St. Francis De Sales**

42. A. James Reimer, **The Emanuel Hirsch and Paul Tillich Debate: A Study in the Political Ramifications of Theology**

43. George Grant, *et al., Two Theological Languages* by George Grant and Other Essays in Honour of His Work, Wayne Whillier (ed.)

44. William C. Marceau, **Stoicism and St. Francis De Sales**

45. Lise van der Molen, **A Complete Bibliography of the Writings of Eugen Rosenstock-Huessy**

46. Franklin H. Littell (ed.), **A Half Century of Religious Dialogue, 1939-1989: Making the Circles Larger**

47. Douglas J. Davies, **Frank Byron Jevons, 1858-1936: An Evolutionary Realist**

48. John P. Tiemstra (ed.), **Reforming Economics: Calvinist Studies on Methods and Institutions**

49. Max A. Myers and Michael R. LaChat (eds.), **Studies in the Theological Ethics of Ernst Troeltsch**

50. Franz G. M. Feige, **The Varieties of Protestantism in Nazi Germany: Five Theopolitical Positions**

51. John W. Welch, **A Biblical Law Bibliography: Arranged by Subject and by Author**

52. Albert W. J. Harper, **The Theodicy of Suffering**

53. Bryce A. Gayhart, **The Ethics of Ernst Troeltsch: A Commitment to Relevancy**

54. David L. Mueller, **Foundation of Karl Barth's Doctrine of Reconciliation: Jesus Christ Crucified and Risen**

55. Henry O. Thompson (ed.), **The Contribution of Carl Michalson to Modern Theology: Studies in Interpretation and Application**

56. David G. Schultenover (ed.), **Theology Toward the Third Millennium**: **Theological Issues for the Twenty-first Century**

57. Louis J. Shein, **The Philosophy of Lev Shestov (1866-1938)**

58. Hans Schwartz, **Method and Context as Problems for Contemporary Theology**

59. William C. Marceau, **The Eucharist in Théodore de Bèze and St. Francis de Sales**

60. Russell F. Aldwinckle, **The Logic of the Believing Mind**

61. John Musson, **Evil - Is it Real?: A Theological Analysis**

62. Kenneth Cauthen, **Theological Biology: The Case for a New Modernism**